THE COMPLETE BREAD MACHINE

FOR BEGINNERS COOKBOOK

500

Fuss-Free Recipes for Making delicious Homemade Bread with Any Bread Maker

AMANDA COOK

Copyright

Table of Contents

INTRODUCTION

The Complete Bread Machine Cookbook will be the only book and guide you need to help you easily bake the most mouthwatering loaves of bread every time, regardless if you are a beginner or seasoned baker.

The Complete Bread Machine Cookbook: The Best, Easy, Gluten-Free, and Foolproof recipes for your Bread Machine.

There is nothing better than the exquisite and delicious aroma of freshly baked bread that fills the kitchen. However, baking bread from scratch is a slow, challenging, and complicated process.

Having to knead, taste, and bake the dough can take hours, and creating the perfect rise and crispy increase can take years to master.

When it comes to baking bread at home from scratch, things can get tricky. Thankfully, that's where The Complete Bread Machine Cookbook for Beginners comes in!

Everyone loves the taste and smell of the fresh bread, but not the time it takes to bake it.

Making bread should be simple... and now it is. The Bread machine is now the hot item in the kitchen because it takes the work out of making homemade bread. Even better, The Complete Bread Machine Cookbook takes the mystery out of the bread machine and brings you easy-to-use recipes.

The Complete Bread Machine Cookbook is an assortment of techniques, tips, tricks, and near and dear recipes that were collected throughout the years and wishes to share with you now.

With more than 500 recipes that use easy-to-find ingredients and require minimal work, this Complete Bread Machine Cookbook will set you up for baking success.

Put down the dough and pick up this book. The Complete Bread Machine Cookbook is the first and only collection of easy, hassle-free recipes that give you delicious homemade loaves of bread every time.

The best sweet bread machine recipes in this Complete bread machine recipe cookbook allow you to create healthy breads with a conventional kitchen appliance.

I test each bread machine recipe in this bread machine cookbook, and all the tips for improving bread are taken from my own experience.

There's nothing than the taste and smell of homemade bread!

Enjoy The Complete Bread Machine Cookbook!

Enjoy the Homemade Bread recipes!

Basic Bread

Classic White Bread I

PREP: 10 MINUTES/ MAKES 1 LOAF/16 SLICE BREAD (2pounds)

Ingredients

1½ cups lukewarm water
1 tablespoon + 1 teaspoon olive oil
1½ teaspoons sugar
1 teaspoon table salt
¼ teaspoon baking soda
2½ cups all-purpose flour
1 cup white bread flour
2½ teaspoons bread machine yeast

Directions

1. **Preparing the Ingredients.**
   Choose the size of loaf you would like to make and measure your ingredients.
   Add the ingredients to the bread pan in the order listed above.
   Place the pan in the bread machine and close the lid.

2. **Select the Bake cycle**
   Turn on the bread maker. Select the White/Basic setting, then the loaf size, and finally the crust color. Start the cycle.
   When the cycle is finished and the bread is baked, carefully remove the pan from the machine. Use a potholder as the handle will be very hot. Let rest for a few minutes.
   Remove the bread from the pan and allow to cool on a wire rack for at least 10 minutes before slicing.

Everyday White Bread

PREP: 10 MINUTES/ MAKES 8 – 16 SLICES/8 SLICE BREAD (1pound)

Ingredients

¾ cup water, at 80°F to 90°F
1 tablespoon melted butter, cooled
1 tablespoon sugar
¾ teaspoon salt
2 tablespoons skim milk powder
2 cups white bread flour
¾ teaspoon bread machine or instant yeast

Directions

1. **Preparing the Ingredients.**
   Place the ingredients in your bread machine as recommended by the manufacturer.
   Program the machine for Basic/White bread, select light or medium crust, and press Start.
   When the loaf is done, remove the bucket from the machine.
   Let the loaf cool for 5 minutes.
   Gently shake the bucket to remove the loaf, and turn it out onto a rack to cool.

2. **Select the Bake cycle**
   Powdered milk is usually made from skim milk. This is because the fat particles in regular milk could go rancid, shortening the shelf life of powdered milk, despite the fact that all the water has been removed. Whenever possible, smell the powdered milk, and if there is any odor at all, do not buy it.

Classic White Bread II

PREP: 10 MINUTES/MAKES 1 LOAF/16 SLICE BREAD (2 pounds)

Ingredients

1 ½ cups water, lukewarm between 80 and 90°F
3 tablespoons unsalted butter, melted
1 tablespoon sugar
2 teaspoons salt
3 tablespoons dry milk powder
4 cup white bread flour
1 ¼ teaspoons bread machine yeast
1 ½ teaspoons bread machine yeast

Directions

1. Preparing the Ingredients.

Choose the size of loaf you would like to make and measure your ingredients.

Add the ingredients to the bread pan in the order listed above.

Place the pan in the bread machine and close the lid Gently shake the bucket to remove the loaf, and turn it out onto a rack to cool.

2. Select the Bake cycle

Turn on the bread maker. Select the White/Basic setting, then the loaf size, and finally the crust color. Start the cycle. When the cycle is finished and the bread is baked, carefully remove the pan from the machine. Use a potholder as the handle will be very hot. Let rest for a few minutes. Remove the bread from the pan and allow to cool on a wire rack for at least 10 minutes before slicing.

Whole-Wheat Bread

PREP: 10 MINUTES / MAKES 1 LOAF

Ingredients

Water - ¾ cup
Melted butter - 1½ tbsp., cooled
Honey - 1½ tbsp.
Salt - ¾ tsp.
Whole-wheat bread flour - 2 cups
Bread machine or instant yeast - 1 tsp.

Directions

1. Preparing the Ingredients.

Choose the size of loaf you would like to make and measure your ingredients.

Add the ingredients in the machine according to the manufacturer's instructions.

2. Select the Bake cycle

Press Whole-Wheat/Whole-Grain bread, choose Light or Medium crust, and press Start.

When done, remove the bread from the machine and cool.

Slice and serve.

Honey Whole-Wheat Bread

PREP: 10 MINUTES OR LESS/MAKES 1 LOAF/12 SLICE BREAD (1½ pound)

Ingredients

1⅛ cups water, at 80°F to 90°F

2 tablespoons honey

1½ tablespoons melted butter, cooled

¾ teaspoon salt

2½ cups whole-wheat flour

¾ cup white bread flour

1 ¼teaspoons bread machine yeast

1½ teaspoons bread machine or instant yeast

1 teaspoon bread machine or instant yeast

Directions

1. **Preparing the Ingredients.**

   Place the ingredients in your bread machine as recommended by the manufacturer. Program the machine for Basic/White bread, select light or medium crust, and press Start.

2. **Select the Bake cycle**

   When the loaf is done, remove the bucket from the machine. Let the loaf cool for 5 minutes. Gently shake the bucket to remove the loaf, and turn it out onto a rack to cool.

French Bread

PREP: 10 MINUTES OR LESS/MAKES 1 LOAF

Ingredients

Water - ⅔ cup

Olive oil - 2 tsp.

Sugar - 1 tbsp.

Salt - ⅔ tsp.

White bread flour - 2 cups

Bread machine or instant yeast - 1 tsp.

Directions

1. **Preparing the Ingredients.**

   Place everything in the bread machine according to machine recommendation.

2. **Select the Bake cycle**

   Press French bread and Light or Medium crust. Press Start. Remove the loaf from the machine and cool. Slice and serve.

Classic White Sandwich Bread

PREP: 10 MINUTES OR LESS/ MAKES 1 LOAF/12 SLICE BREAD (1½ pound)

Ingredients

¾ cup water, lukewarm between 80 and 90°F

1 ½tablespoons unsalted butter, melted

1 tablespoon melted butter, cooled

1 ½ ounces sugar

2 egg whites or 1 egg, beaten

2 ¼ cups white bread flour

1 ⅛ teaspoons bread machine yeast

Directions

1. **Preparing the Ingredients.**

   Choose the size of loaf you would like to make and measure your ingredients. Add the ingredients to the bread pan in the order listed above. Place the pan in the bread machine and close the lid.

2. **Select the Bake cycle**

   Turn on the bread maker. Select the White/Basic setting, then the loaf size, and finally the crust color. Start the cycle. When the cycle is finished and the bread is baked, carefully remove the pan from the machine. Use a potholder as the handle will be very hot. Let rest for a few minutes. Remove the bread from the pan and allow to cool on a wire rack for at least 10 minutes before slicing

Gluten-Free White Bread
PREP: 10 MINUTES OR LESS/ MAKES 1 LOAF

Ingredients
2 eggs
1⅓ cups milk
6 Tbsp oil
1 tsp vinegar
3⅝ cups white bread flour
1 tsp salt
2 Tbsp sugar
2 tsp dove farm quick yeast

Directions
1. **Preparing the Ingredients.** Add each ingredient to the bread machine in the order and at the temperature recommended by your bread machine manufacturer.
2. **Select the Bake cycle.** Close the lid and start the machine on the gluten free bread program, if available. Alternatively use the basic or rapid setting with a dark crust option. When the bread machine has finished baking, remove the bread and put it on a cooling rack.

Oat Bran Molasses Bread
PREP: 10 MINUTES / MAKES 1 LOAF

Ingredients
Water - ½ cup
Melted butter - 1½ tbsp., cooled
Blackstrap molasses - 2 tbsp.
Salt - ¼ tsp.
Ground nutmeg - ⅛ tsp.
Oat bran - ½ cup
Whole-wheat bread flour - 1½ cups
Bread machine or instant yeast - 1⅛ tsp.

Directions
1. **Preparing the Ingredients**
   Place the ingredients in the bread machine according to instructions.
2. **Select the Bake cycle**
   Choose Whole-Wheat/Whole-Grain bread, and Light or Medium crust. Press Start. Remove when done and cool. Slice and serve.

Molasses Wheat Bread
PREP: 10 MINUTES OR LESS/MAKES 1 LOAF/12 SLICE BREAD (1½ pound)

Ingredients
¾ cup water, at 80°F to 90°F
⅓ cup milk, at 80°F
1 tablespoon melted butter, cooled
3¾ tablespoons honey
2 tablespoons molasses
2 teaspoons sugar
2 tablespoons skim milk powder
¾ teaspoon salt
2 teaspoons unsweetened cocoa powder
1¾ cups whole-wheat flour
1¼ cups white bread flour
1⅛ teaspoons bread machine yeast or instant yeast

Directions
1. **Preparing the Ingredients.** Place the ingredients in your bread machine as recommended by the manufacturer.
   Select the Bake cycle
   Program the machine for Basic/White bread, select light or medium crust, and press Start. When the loaf is done, remove the bucket from the machine.
   Let the loaf cool for 5 minutes. Gently shake the bucket to remove the loaf, and turn it out onto a rack to cool

Baguette Style French Bread
PREP: 10 MINUTES OR LESS/MAKES 1 LOAF/8 SLICE BREAD (1pound)

Ingredients
2 baguettes of 1-pound each
1 ⅔ cups water, lukewarm between 80 and 90°F
1 teaspoon table salt 4 ⅔ cups white bread flour
2 ⅔ teaspoons bread machine yeast or rapid rise yeast
2 baguettes of ¾-pound each
12 slice bread (1½ pound)
¾ cup water, at 80°F to 90°F
1 ¼ cups water, lukewarm between 80 and 90°F
¾ teaspoon table salt
3 ½ cups white bread flour
2 teaspoons bread machine yeast or rapid rise yeast

Directions
1. **Preparing the Ingredients.**
   Choose the size of crusty bread you would like to make and measure your ingredients. Add the ingredients for the bread machine to the bread pan in the order listed above. Place the pan in the bread machine and close the lid. Turn on the bread maker.
2. **Select the Bake cycle**
   Select the dough/manual setting. When the dough cycle is completed, remove the pan and lay the dough on a floured working surface. Knead the dough a few times and add flour if needed so the dough is not too sticky to handle. Cut the dough in half and form a ball with each half. Grease a baking sheet with olive oil. Dust lightly with cornmeal. Preheat the oven to 375° and place the oven rack in the middle position. With a rolling pin dusted with flour, roll one of the dough balls into a 12-inch by 9-inch rectangle for the 2 pounds bread size or a 10-inch by 8-inch rectangle for the 1 ½ pound bread size. Starting on the longer side, roll the dough tightly. Pinch the ends and the seam with your fingers to seal. Roll the dough in a back in forth movement to make it into a nice French baguette shape. Repeat the process with the second dough ball. Place loaves of bread onto the baking sheet with the seams down and brush with some olive oil with enough space in between them to rise. Dust top of both loaves with a little bit of cornmeal. Cover with a clean kitchen towel and place in a warm area with any air draught. Let rise for 10 to 15 minutes, or until loaves doubled in size. Mix the egg white and 1 tablespoon of water and lightly brush over both loaves of bread. Place in the oven and bake for 20 minutes. Remove from oven and brush with remaining egg wash on top of both loaves of bread. Place back into the oven taking care of turning around the baking sheet. Bake for another 5 to 10 minutes or until the baguettes are golden brown. Let rest on a wired rack for 5-10 minutes before serving.

Italian Bread
PREP: 10 MINUTES OR LESS/MAKES 1 LOAF

Ingredients
Water - ⅔ cup
Olive oil - 1 tbsp.
Sugar - 1 tbsp.
Salt - ¾ tsp.
White bread flour - 2 cups
Bread machine or instant yeast - 1 tsp.

Directions
1. **Preparing the Ingredients**
   Add everything in the bread machine according to instructions.
2. **Select the Bake cycle**
   Select Basic/White bread and Light or Medium crust. Press Start.
   When done, remove the bread. Cool, slice, and serve.

100 Percent Whole-Wheat Bread
PREP: 10 MINUTES OR LESS/MAKES 1 LOAF/12 SLICE BREAD (1½ pounds)

Ingredients

    1⅛ cups water, at 80°F to 90°F
    2¼ tablespoons melted butter, cooled
    2¼ tablespoons honey
    1⅛ teaspoons salt
    3 cups whole-wheat bread flour
    2 teaspoons sugar
    2 tablespoons skim milk powder
    ¾ teaspoon salt
    1½ teaspoons bread machine or instant yeast

Directions

1. **Preparing the Ingredients.**

   Place the ingredients in your bread machine as recommended by the manufacturer. Program the machine for Whole-Wheat/Whole-Grain bread, select light or medium crust, and press Start. When the loaf is done, remove the bucket from the machine.

2. **Select the Bake cycle**

   Let the loaf cool for 5 minutes. Gently shake the bucket to remove the loaf, and turn it out onto a rack to cool.

Bread Machine Bread
PREP: 10 MINUTES /MAKES 1 LOAF

Ingredients

Flour – 2 cups, sifted
Warm water – ¾ cup
Sugar – 1 tsp.
Active dry yeast – 1.25 tsp.
Salt – 1 tsp.
Oil – 1 tsp.

Directions

1. **Preparing the Ingredients**

   Add ingredients according to bread machine recommendation.

2. **Select the Bake cycle**

   Select the Basic setting and press Start. Remove the loaf once it is baked. Cool and slice.

100% Whole Wheat Bread
PREP: 10 MINUTES /MAKES 1 LOAF/16 SLICE BREAD (2 pounds)

Ingredients

    1¼ cups lukewarm water
    2 tablespoons vegetable oil or olive oil
    ¼ cup honey or maple syrup
    1½ teaspoons table salt
    3½ cups whole wheat flour
    ¼ cup sesame, sunflower, or flax seeds (optional)
    1½ teaspoons bread machine yeast

Directions

1. **Preparing the Ingredients.**

   Choose the size of loaf you would like to make and measure your ingredients. Add the ingredients to the bread pan in the order listed above. Place the pan in the bread machine and close the lid.

2. **Select the Bake cycle**

   Turn on the bread maker. Select the Whole Wheat/Wholegrain setting, then the loaf size, and finally the crust color. Start the cycle. When the cycle is finished, and the bread is baked, carefully remove the pan from the machine. Use a potholder as the handle will be very hot. Let rest for a few minutes. Remove the bread from the pan and allow to cool on a wire rack for at least 10 minutes before slicing.

Banana Bread

Ingredients

Eggs – 2
Butter – ⅓ cup
Milk – ⅛ cup
Bananas – 2, mashed
Bread flour – 1 ⅓ cups
Sugar – ⅔ cup
Baking powder – 1 ¼ tsp.
Baking soda – ½ tsp.
Salt – ½ tsp.
Chopped nuts – ½ cup, lightly toasted

Directions

1. **Preparing the Ingredients**
   Add the butter, eggs, milk, and bananas to the bread pan and set aside. Combine the remaining dry ingredients in a bowl and add the bread pan.
2. **Select the Bake cycle**
   Use Quick Bread setting to bake the bread. Remove the bread when done. Slice and serve.

Crusty French Bread
PREP: 10 MINUTES /MAKES 1 LOAF/12 SLICE BREAD (1½ pounds)

Ingredients

1 cup water, at 80°F to 90°F
1¼ tablespoons olive oil
2 tablespoons sugar
1¼ teaspoons salt
3 cups white bread flour
1¼ teaspoons bread machine or instant yeast, or flax seeds (optional)

Directions

1. **Preparing the Ingredients.**
   Place the ingredients in your bread machine as recommended by the manufacturer.
2. **Select the Bake cycle**
   Program the machine for French bread, select light or medium crust, and press Start.
   When the loaf is done, remove the bucket from the machine. Let the loaf cool for 5 minutes.
   Gently shake the bucket to remove the loaf, and turn it out onto a rack to cool.

Onion Bread
PREP: 10 MINUTES /MAKES 1 LOAF

Ingredients

Water – 1 ½ cup
Butter – 2 tbsp. plus 2 tsp.
Salt – 1 tsp.
Sugar – 1 tbsp. plus 1 ½ tsp.
Bread flour – 4 cups
Nonfat dry milk – 2 tbsp. plus 2 tsp.
Active dry yeast – 2 tsp.
Dry onion soup mix – 4 tbsp.

Directions

1. **Preparing the Ingredients.**
   Place ingredients in the bread pan in the order listed, except the soup.
2. **Select the Bake cycle**
   Select Basic cycle. Add the onion soup mix at the fruit and nut signal.
   When done, remove and cool. Slice and serve.

Buttermilk Bread

PREP: 10 MINUTES /MAKES 1 LOAF/16 SLICE BREAD (2 pounds)

Ingredients

1¼ cups lukewarm buttermilk
1½ tablespoons unsalted butter, melted
1½ tablespoons sugar
1⅛ teaspoons table salt
⅓ teaspoon baking powder
2⅔ cups white bread flour
1⅔ teaspoons bread machine yeast

Directions

1. **Preparing the Ingredients.**
   Choose the size of loaf you would like to make and measure your ingredients. Add the ingredients to the bread pan in the order listed above.
   Place the pan in the bread machine and close the lid.
2. **Select the Bake cycle**
   Turn on the bread maker. Select the White/Basic setting, then the loaf size, and finally the crust color. Start the cycle. When the cycle is finished and the bread is baked, carefully remove the pan from the machine. Use a potholder as the handle will be very hot. Let rest for a few minutes.
   Remove the bread from the pan and allow to cool on a wire rack for at least 10 minutes before slicing.

Pumpernickel Bread

PREP: 10 MINUTES /MAKES 1 LOAF /8 SLICE BREAD (1 pound)

Ingredients

½ cup water, at 80°F to 90°F
¼ cup brewed coffee, at 80°F to 90°F
2 tablespoons dark molasses
5 teaspoons sugar
4 teaspoons melted butter, cooled
1 tablespoon powdered skim milk
1 teaspoon salt
⅔ cup dark rye flour
½ cup whole-wheat bread flour
1 teaspoon caraway seeds
1 cup white bread flour
1½ teaspoons bread machine or active dry yeast

Directions

1. **Preparing the Ingredients.**
   Place the ingredients in your bread machine as recommended by the manufacturer.
2. **Select the Bake cycle**
   Program the machine for Basic/White bread, select light or medium crust, and press Start.
   When the loaf is done, remove the bucket from the machine. Let the loaf cool for 5 minutes.
   Gently shake the bucket to remove the loaf, and turn it out onto a rack to cool.

Oat Molasses Bread
PREP: 10 MINUTES /MAKES 1 LOAF /12 SLICE BREAD (1½ pounds)

Ingredients

1 cup boiling water
⅓ cup brewed coffee, at 80°F to 90°F
2 tablespoons butter
1 large egg, lightly beaten
3 cups white bread flour
1½ teaspoons table salt
3 tablespoons honey
1 tablespoon dark molasses
3 cups white bread flour
2 teaspoons bread machine yeast

Directions

1. **Preparing the Ingredients.**
   Add the boiling water and oats to a mixing bowl. Allow the oats to soak well and cool down completely. Do not drain the water. Choose the size of loaf you would like to make and measure your ingredients Add the soaked oats, along with any remaining water, to the bread pan. Add the remaining ingredients to the bread pan in the order listed above.

2. **Select the Bake cycle**
   Place the pan in the bread machine and close the lid.
   Turn on the bread maker. Select the White/Basic setting, then the loaf size, and finally the crust color. Start the cycle.
   When the cycle is finished and the bread is baked, carefully remove the pan from the machine. Use a potholder as the handle will be very hot. Let rest for a few minutes.
   Remove the bread from the pan and allow to cool on a wire rack for at least 10 minutes before slicing.

Fat-Free Whole Wheat Bread
PREP: 10 MINUTES /MAKES 1 LOAF

Ingredients

Water – 1 ⅞ cup
White whole wheat flour – 4 ⅔ cups
Vital wheat gluten – 4 tbsp.
Sugar – 2 tbsp.
Salt – 1 ½ tsp.
Rapid rise yeast – 2 ½ tsp.

Directions

1. **Preparing the Ingredients.**
   Add the water in the bread machine pan. mAdd the remaining ingredients according to bread machine recommendation.

2. **Select the Bake cycle**
   Choose Quick-Bake Whole Wheat cycle and press Start. Remove the bread when complete. Cool, slice, and serve.

Peanut Butter Bread
PREP: 10 MINUTES /MAKES 1 LOAF

Ingredients

Water – 1 cup, plus 1 tbsp.
Peanut butter – ½ cup
Bread flour – 3 cups
Brown sugar – 3 tbsp.
Salt – 1 tsp.
Bread machine yeast – 2 tsp.

Directions

1. **Preparing the Ingredients**
   Place every ingredient in the bread machine according to the manufacturer's recommendation.

2. **Select the Bake cycle**
   Select Basic/White or Sweet and choose Medium or Light crust. Press Start. Remove the bread when finished.
   Cool, slice, and serve.

Whole Wheat Corn Bread

PREP: 10 MINUTES /MAKES 1 LOAF/16 SLICE BREAD (2 pounds)

Ingredients

1⅓ cups lukewarm water
2 tablespoons light brown sugar
1 large egg, beaten
2 tablespoons unsalted butter, melted
1½ teaspoons table salt
¾ cup whole wheat flour
¾ cup cornmeal
3 cups whole-wheat bread flour
2¾ cups white bread flour
2½ teaspoons bread machine yeast

Directions

1. **Preparing the Ingredients.**
   Choose the size of loaf you would like to make and measure your ingredients. Add the ingredients to the bread pan in the order listed above
   Place the pan in the bread machine and close the lid   .
2. **Select the Bake cycle**
   Turn on the bread maker. Select the White/Basic setting, then the loaf size, and finally the crust color. Start the cycle. When the cycle is finished and the bread is baked, carefully remove the pan from the machine. Use a potholder as the handle will be very hot. Let rest for a few minutes.
   Remove the bread from the pan and allow to cool on a wire rack for at least 10 minutes before slicing.

Multigrain Bread

PREP: 10 MINUTES /MAKES 1 LOAF

Ingredients

Water – 1 ¼ cups
Butter – 2 tbsp. softened
Bread flour – 1 ⅓cups
Whole wheat flour – 1 ⅓cups
Seven grain or multigrain cereal – 1 cup
Brown sugar – 3 tbsp.
Salt – 1 ¼ tsp.
Bread machine yeast – 2 ½ tsp.

Directions

1. **Preparing the Ingredients.**
   Place everything in the bread machine pan according to bread machine recommendation.
2. **Select the Bake cycle**
   Select Basic/White or Whole Wheat cycle and Medium or Light crust. Press Start.
   Remove the bread when done. Cool, slice, and serve.

Whole-Wheat Buttermilk Bread
PREP: 10 MINUTES /MAKES 1 LOAF/12 SLICE BREAD (1½ pounds)

Ingredients
¾ cup plus 3 tablespoons buttermilk, at 80°F to 90°F

1½ tablespoons melted butter, cooled

1½ tablespoons honey

¾ teaspoon salt

1⅛ cups whole-wheat flour

1¾ cups plus

1 tablespoon white bread flour

1⅔ teaspoons bread machine or instant yeast

Directions
1. **Preparing the Ingredients.**
    Place the ingredients in your bread machine as recommended by the manufacturer.
    Program the machine for Basic/White bread, select light or medium crust, and press Start.

2. **Select the Bake cycle**
    When the loaf is done, remove the bucket from the machine.
    Let the loaf cool for 5 minutes. Gently shake the bucket to remove the loaf, and turn it out onto a rack to cool

Quinoa Oatmeal Bread
PREP: 10 MINUTES /MAKES 1 LOAF

Ingredients
Quinoa flakes – ½ cup

Buttermilk – 1 cup

Salt – 1 tsp.

Sugar – 1 tbsp.

Honey – 1 tbsp.

Unsalted butter – 4 tbsp.

Quick-cooking oats – ½ cup

Whole wheat flour – ½ cup

Bread flour – 1 ½ cups

Yeast – 1 ½ tsp.

Directions
1. **Preparing the Ingredients.**
    Add everything according to the bread machine instructions.

2. **Select the Bake cycle**
    Select Whole Grain and bake. Remove the bread when done. Cool, slice, and serve.

Wheat Bran Bread

PREP: 10 MINUTES /MAKES 1 LOAF/16 SLICE BREAD (2 pounds)

Ingredients

1½ cups lukewarm milk

3 tablespoons unsalted butter, melted

2 teaspoons table salt

½ cup wheat bran

3½ cups white bread flour

1½ cups whole-wheat bread flour

1 cup oat bran

3 cups whole-wheat bread flour

2 teaspoons bread machine yeast

Directions

1. **Preparing the Ingredients.**

   Choose the size of loaf you would like to make and measure your ingredients. Add the ingredients to the bread pan in the order listed above.

   Place the pan in the bread machine and close the lid.

2. **Select the Bake cycle**

   Turn on the bread maker. Select the White/Basic setting, then the loaf size, and finally the crust color. Start the cycle. When the cycle is finished and the bread is baked, carefully remove the pan from the machine. Use a potholder as the handle will be very hot. Let rest for a few minutes. Remove the bread from the pan and allow to cool on a wire rack for at least 10 minutes before slicing.

Soft Egg Bread

PREP: 10 MINUTES /MAKES 1 LOAF/16 SLICE BREAD (2 pounds)

Ingredients

1 cup milk, at 80°F to 90°F

5 tablespoons melted butter, cooled

3 eggs, at room temperature

⅓ cup sugar

2 teaspoons salt

4 cups white bread flour

1 cup oat bran

3 cups whole-wheat bread flour

1½ teaspoons bread machine or instant yeast

Directions

1. **Preparing the Ingredients.**

   Place the ingredients in your bread machine as recommended by the manufacturer.

   Program the machine for Basic/White bread, select light or medium crust, and press Start.

2. **Select the Bake cycle**

   When the loaf is done, remove the bucket from the machine.

   Let the loaf cool for 5 minutes. Gently shake the bucket to remove the loaf, and turn it out onto a rack to cool

Date and Nut Bread
PREP: 10 MINUTES /MAKES 1 LOAF

Ingredients
Water – 1 cup
Oil – 1 ½ tbsp.
Honey – 2 tbsp.
Salt – ½ tsp.
Rolled oats – ¾ cup
Whole wheat flour – ¾ cup
Bread flour – 1 ½ cups
Active dry yeast – 1 ½ tsp.
Dates – ½ cups, pitted and chopped
Chopped almonds – ½ cup

Directions
1.   **Preparing the Ingredients**
     Place everything into the bread pan according to the bread machine recommendation.
2.   **Select the Bake cycle**
     Select Fruit bread/Basic cycle and press Start. You can add the dates and nuts after the beep or at the very beginning.

Rye Bread
PREP: 10 MINUTES /MAKES 1 LOAF/16 SLICE BREAD (2 pounds)

Ingredients
1⅔ cups lukewarm water
¼ cup + 4 teaspoons Dijon mustard
2 tablespoons unsalted butter, melted
4 teaspoons sugar
1 teaspoon table salt
2 cups rye flour
2⅔ cups white bread flour
1½ teaspoons bread machine yeast

Directions
1.   **Preparing the Ingredients.**
     Choose the size of loaf you would like to make and measure your ingredients.   Add the ingredients to the bread pan in the order listed above. Place the pan in the bread machine and close the lid.
2.   **Select the Bake cycle**
     Turn on the bread maker. Select the White/Basic setting, then the loaf size, and finally the crust color. Start the cycle. When the cycle is finished and the bread is baked, carefully remove the pan from the machine. Use a potholder as the handle will be very hot. Let rest for a few minutes. Remove the bread from the pan and allow to cool on a wire rack for at least 10 minutes before slicing.

Multi-Seed Bread
PREP: 10 MINUTES /MAKES 1 LOAF

Ingredients
Tepid water – 1 cup
Salt – 1 tsp.
Olive oil – 2 tbsp.
Whole wheat bread flour – 1 cup
White bread flour – 2 cups
Dried yeast – 1 ½ tsp.
Mixed seeds – ⅓ cup sesame, pumpkin, sunflower, poppy

Directions
1.   **Preparing the Ingredients.**
     Add the ingredients according to bread machine recommendation.
2.   **Select the Bake cycle**
     Select White bread/Basic cycle and press Start. Remove the bread when done. Cool, slice, and serve.

Healthy Bran Bread
PREP: 10 MINUTES /MAKES 1 LOAF/12 SLICE BREAD (1½ pounds)

Ingredients
1⅛ cups milk, at 80°F to 90°F
2¼ tablespoons melted butter, cooled
1½ tablespoons unsalted butter, melted
3 tablespoons sugar
1½ teaspoons salt
½ cup wheat bran
2⅔ cups white bread flour
1½ teaspoon bread machine or instant yeast

Directions
1. **Preparing the Ingredients.**
   Place the ingredients in your bread machine as recommended by the manufacturer.
   Program the machine for Basic/White bread, select light or medium crust, and press Start.

2. **Select the Bake cycle**
   When the loaf is done, remove the bucket from the machine.
   Let the loaf cool for 5 minutes.
   Gently shake the bucket to remove the loaf, and turn it out onto a rack to cool.

Sunflower and Flax Seed Bread
PREP: 10 MINUTES /MAKES 1 LOAF

Ingredients
Water – 1 ⅓cups
Butter – 2 tbsp., softened
Honey – 3 tbsp.
Bread flour – 1 ½ cups
Whole wheat bread flour – 1 ⅓cups
Salt – 1 tsp.
Active dry yeast – 1 tsp.
Flax seeds – ½ cup
Sunflower seeds – ½ cup

Directions
1. **Preparing the Ingredients**
   Place everything (except sunflower seeds) in the bread machine according to machine recommendation.

2. **Select the Bake cycle**
   Select Basic White cycle and press Start. Add the seeds after the alert sounds.
   Cool, slice, and serve.

Classic Whole Wheat Bread

PREP: 10 MINUTES /MAKES 1 LOAF/12 SLICE BREAD (1½ pounds)

Ingredients

1⅛ cups milk, at 80°F to 90°F
2¼ tablespoons melted butter, cooled
1½ tablespoons unsalted butter, melted
3 tablespoons sugar
1½ teaspoons salt
½ cup wheat bran
¾ cup lukewarm water
⅓ cup unsalted butter, melted
2 eggs, at room temperature
1½ teaspoons table salt
3 tablespoons sugar
1 cup whole-wheat flour
2 cups white bread flour
1⅔ teaspoons bread machine yeast

Directions

1. **Preparing the Ingredients.**
    Choose the size of loaf you would like to make and measure your ingredients. Add the ingredients to the bread pan in the order listed above. Place the pan in the bread machine and close the lid.
2. **Select the Bake cycle**
    Turn on the bread maker. Select the Whole Wheat/ Wholegrain or White/Basic setting, wither one will work well for this recipe. Then select the loaf size, and finally the crust color. Start the cycle.
    When the cycle is finished and the bread is baked, carefully remove the pan from the machine. Use a potholder as the handle will be very hot. Let rest for a few minutes.
    Remove the bread from the pan and allow to cool on a wire rack for at least 10 minutes before slicing.

Coffee Rye Bread

PREP: 10 MINUTES /MAKES 1 LOAF

Ingredients

Lukewarm water – ½ cup
Brewed coffee – ¼ cup, 80ºF
Dark molasses – 2 tbsp.
Brown sugar – 5 tsp.
Unsalted butter – 4 tsp., softened
Powdered skim milk – 1 tbsp.
Kosher salt – 1 tsp.
Unsweetened cocoa powder – 4 tsp.
Dark rye flour – ⅔cup
Whole-wheat bread machine flour – ½ cup
Caraway seeds – 1 tsp.
White bread machine flour – 1 cup
Bread machine yeast – 1 ½ tsp

Directions

1. **Preparing the Ingredients**
    Place everything in the bread machine pan according to the bread machine recommendation.
2. **Select the Bake cycle**
    Select Basic and Light crust. Press Start. Remove the bread. Cool, slice, and serve.

Dark Rye Bread

PREP: 10 MINUTES /MAKES 1 LOAF/12 SLICE BREAD (1½ pounds)

Ingredients

1 cup water, at 80°F to 90°F

1½ tablespoons melted butter, cooled

1½ tablespoons unsalted butter, melted

⅓ cup molasses

⅓ teaspoon salt

1½ tablespoons unsweetened cocoa powder

Pinch ground nutmeg

¾ cup rye flour

2 cups white bread flour

1⅔ teaspoons bread machine or instant yeast

Directions

1. **Preparing the Ingredients.**

   Place the ingredients in your bread machine as recommended by the manufacturer.

   Program the machine for Basic/White bread, select light or medium crust, and press Start.

2. **Select the Bake cycle**

   When the loaf is done, remove the bucket from the machine.

   Let the loaf cool for 5 minutes. Gently shake the bucket to remove the loaf, and turn it out onto a rack to cool.

Honey Nut Bread

PREP: 10 MINUTES /MAKES 1 LOAF

Ingredients

Eggs – 2

Cottage cheese – ⅔cup

Milk – ½ cup

Butter – ¼ cup

Honey – 2 tbsp.

All-purpose flour – 4 cups

Instant yeast – 1 tbsp.

Salt – 1 tsp.

Candied nuts – ¾ cups, chopped

Directions

1. **Preparing the Ingredients**

   Add everything, except nuts to your bread machine according to manufacturer recommendation.

2. **Select the Bake cycle**

   Select Basic and choose Light crust type. Press Start. Add the nuts when the machine beeps.

   Remove the bread when ready. Cool, slice, and serve.

Oat Bran Nutmeg Bread

PREP: 10 MINUTES /MAKES 1 LOAF/16 SLICE BREAD (2 pounds)

Ingredients

1 cup lukewarm water

3 tablespoons unsalted butter, melted

¼ cup blackstrap molasses

½ teaspoon table salt

3 cups whole-wheat bread flour

¼ teaspoon ground nutmeg

1 cup oat bran

3 cups whole-wheat bread flour

2¼ teaspoons bread machine yeast

Directions

1. **Preparing the Ingredients.**
   Choose the size of loaf you would like to make and measure your ingredients.   Add the ingredients to the bread pan in the order listed above. Place the pan in the bread machine and close the lid.

2. **Select the Bake cycle**
   Turn on the bread maker. Select the White/Basic setting, then the loaf size, and finally the crust color. Start the cycle. When the cycle is finished and the bread is baked, carefully remove the pan from the machine. Use a potholder as the handle will be very hot. Let rest for a few minutes. Remove the bread from the pan and allow to cool on a wire rack for at least 10 minutes before slicing.

Three-Seed Bread

PREP: 10 MINUTES /MAKES 1 LOAF

Ingredients

Water – ⅔cup plus 2 tsp.

Butter – 1 tbsp., softened

Honey – 1 tbsp.

Sunflower seeds – 2 tbsp.

Sesame seeds – 2 tbsp.

Poppy seeds – 2 tbsp.

Salt – ¾ tsp.

Whole wheat flour – 1 cup

Bread flour - 1 cup

Nonfat dry milk powder – 3 tbsp.

Active dry yeast – 2 tsp.

Directions

1. **Preparing the Ingredients**
   Put all ingredients in the bread machine pan according to its order.

2. **Select the Bake cycle**
   Select Basic bread and press Start. Remove the bread when done.
   Cool, slice, and serve.

Peasant Bread
PREP: 10 MINUTES /MAKES 12 SLICES

Ingredients
2 tablespoons full rounded yeast
2 cups white bread flour
1 ½tablespoons sugar
1 tablespoon salt
⅞ cup water
For the topping:
Olive oil
Poppy seeds

Directions
1. **Preparing the Ingredients**
   Add water first, then add the dry ingredients to the bread machine, reserving yeast.
   Make a well in the center of the dry ingredients and add the yeast.
2. **Select the Bake cycle**
   Choose French cycle, light crust color, and push Start.
   When bread is finished, coat the top of loaf with a little olive oil and lightly sprinkle with poppy seeds.
   Allow to cool slightly and serve warm with extra olive oil for dipping.

Golden Raisin Bread
PREP: 10 MINUTES /MAKES 1 LOAF/8 SLICE BREAD (1 pound)

Ingredients
¾ cup milk, at 80°F to 90°F

1 tablespoon melted butter, cooled

¼ cup molasses

1 tablespoon sugar

¾ teaspoon salt

2 cups white bread flour

1 teaspoon bread machine or instant yeast

½ cup golden raisins

12 slice bread (1½ pounds)

1⅛ cups milk, at 80°F to 90°F

1½ tablespoons melted butter, cooled

Directions
1. **Preparing the Ingredients.**
   Place the ingredients, except the raisins, in your bread machine as recommended by the manufacturer.
2. **Select the Bake cycle**
   Program the machine for Basic/White or Sweet bread, select light or medium crust, and press Start. Add the raisins at the raisin/nut signal. When the loaf is done, remove the bucket from the machine.
   Let the loaf cool for 5 minutes. Gently shake the bucket to remove the loaf, and turn it out onto a rack to cool.

Multigrain Honey Bread
PREP: 10 MINUTES /MAKES 1 LOAF/12 SLICE BREAD (1½ pounds)

Ingredients
1⅛ cups lukewarm milk

2¼ tablespoons unsalted butter, melted

3 tablespoons sugar

1½ teaspoons table salt

⅓ cup wheat bran

1½ tablespoons honey

1⅛ cups multigrain flour

2 cups white bread flour

1⅛ cups lukewarm water

2 tablespoons unsalted butter, melted

Directions
1. **Preparing the Ingredients.**
   Choose the size of loaf you would like to make and measure your ingredients. Add the ingredients to the bread pan in the order listed above. Place the pan in the bread machine and close the lid.
2. **Select the Bake cycle**
   Turn on the bread maker. Select the White/Basic setting, then the loaf size, and finally the crust color. Start the cycle. When the cycle is finished and the bread is baked, carefully remove the pan from the machine. Use a potholder as the handle will be very hot. Let rest for a few minutes.
   Remove the bread from the pan and allow to cool on a wire rack for at least 10 minutes before slicing.

Golden Corn Bread

PREP: 10 MINUTES /MAKES 1 LOAF/12 SLICE BREAD (1½ pounds)

Ingredients

1 cup buttermilk, at 80°F to 90°F
¼ cup melted butter, cooled
2 eggs, at room temperature
1⅓ cups all-purpose flour
1 cup cornmeal
¼ cup sugar
2¼ cups whole-wheat bread flour
1½ teaspoons bread machine yeast

Directions

1. **Preparing the Ingredients.**

   Place the buttermilk, butter, and eggs in your in your bread machine as recommended by the manufacturer. Program the machine for Quick/Rapid bread and press Start. While the wet ingredients are mixing, stir together the flour, cornmeal, sugar, baking powder, and salt in a small bowl.

2. **Select the Bake cycle**

   After the first fast mixing is done and the machine signals, add the dry ingredients. When the loaf is done, remove the bucket from the machine. Let the loaf cool for 5 minutes. Gently shake the bucket to remove the loaf, and turn it out onto a rack to cool.

Classic Dark Bread

PREP: 10 MINUTES /MAKES 1 LOAF/12 SLICE BREAD (1½ pounds)

Ingredients

1 cup lukewarm water
1½ tablespoons unsalted butter, melted
⅓ cup molasses
⅓ teaspoon table salt
¾ cup rye flour
2 cups white bread flour
2¼ cups whole-wheat bread flour
1½ tablespoons unsweetened cocoa powder
Pinch ground nutmeg
1⅔ teaspoons bread machine yeast

Directions

1. **Preparing the Ingredients.**

   Choose the size of loaf you would like to make and measure your ingredients.   Add the ingredients to the bread pan in the order listed above. Place the pan in the bread machine and close the lid.

2. **Select the Bake cycle**

   Turn on the bread maker. Select the White/Basic setting, then the loaf size, and finally the crust color. Start the cycle. When the cycle is finished and the bread is baked, carefully remove the pan from the machine. Use a potholder as the handle will be very hot. Let rest for a few minutes.

   Remove the bread from the pan and allow to cool on a wire rack for at least 10 minutes before slicing.

English muffin Bread

Ingredients

1¼ cups buttermilk, at 80°F to 90°F

1½ tablespoons melted butter, cooled

1½ tablespoons sugar

1⅛ teaspoons salt

⅓ teaspoon baking powder

2⅔ cups white bread flour

1⅔ teaspoons bread machine or instant yeast

Directions

1.   **Preparing the Ingredients.**
     Place the ingredients in your bread machine as recommended by the manufacturer

2.   **Select the Bake cycle**
     Program the machine for Basic/White bread, select light or medium crust, and press Start.
     When the loaf is done, remove the bucket from the machine. Let the loaf cool for 5 minutes. Gently shake the bucket to remove the loaf, and turn it out onto a rack to cool.

Classic Corn Bread

PREP: 10 MINUTES /MAKES 1 LOAF/12 SLICE BREAD (1½ pounds)

Ingredients

1 cup lukewarm buttermilk

¼ cup unsalted butter, melted

2 eggs, at room temperature

¼ cup sugar

1 teaspoon table salt

1⅓ cups all-purpose flour

1 cup cornmeal

1 tablespoon baking powder

Directions

1.   **Preparing the Ingredients.**
     Choose the size of loaf you would like to make and measure your ingredients.   Add the ingredients to the bread pan in the order listed above. Place the pan in the bread machine and close the lid.

2.   **Select the Bake cycle**
     Turn on the bread maker. Select the White/Basic setting, then the loaf size, and finally the crust color. Start the cycle.
     When the cycle is finished and the bread is baked, carefully remove the pan from the machine. Use a potholder as the handle will be very hot. Let rest for a few minutes.
     Remove the bread from the pan and allow to cool on a wire rack for at least 10 minutes before slicing.

Traditional Italian Bread

PREP: 10 MINUTES /MAKES 1 LOAF/12 SLICE BREAD (1½ pounds)

Ingredients

1 cup water, at 80°F to 90°F

1½ tablespoons olive oil

1½ tablespoons sugar

1⅛ teaspoons salt

3 cups white bread flour

2⅔ cups white bread flour

1½ teaspoons bread machine or instant yeast

Directions

1. **Preparing the Ingredients.**

   Place the ingredients in your bread machine as recommended by the manufacturer

   Program the machine for Basic/White bread, select light or medium crust, and press Start.

2. **Select the Bake cycle**

   When the loaf is done, remove the bucket from the machine.

   Let the loaf cool for 5 minutes. Gently shake the bucket to remove the loaf, and turn it out onto a rack to cool.

Basic Seed Bread

PREP: 10 MINUTES /MAKES 1 LOAF/12 SLICE BREAD (1½ pounds)

Ingredients

1⅛ cups lukewarm water

1½ tablespoons unsalted butter, melted

1½ tablespoons sugar

1⅛ teaspoons table salt

2½ cups white bread flour

¾ cup ground chia seeds

2 tablespoons sesame seeds

1½ teaspoons bread machine yeast

Directions

1. **Preparing the Ingredients.**

   Choose the size of loaf you would like to make and measure your ingredients. Add the ingredients to the bread pan in the order listed above. Place the pan in the bread machine and close the lid.

2. **Select the Bake cycle**

   Turn on the bread maker. Select the White/Basic setting, then the loaf size, and finally the crust color. Start the cycle. When the cycle is finished and the bread is baked, carefully remove the pan from the machine. Use a potholder as the handle will be very hot. Let rest for a few minutes.

   Remove the bread from the pan and allow to cool on a wire rack for at least 10 minutes before slicing.

Double-Chocolate Zucchini Bread

PREP: 10 MINUTES /MAKES 1 LOAF

Ingredients

225 grams grated zucchini

125 grams All-Purpose Flour Blend

50 grams all-natural unsweetened cocoa powder (not Dutch-process)

1 teaspoon xanthan gum

¾ teaspoon baking soda

¼ teaspoon baking powder

¼ teaspoon salt

½ teaspoon ground espresso

135 grams chocolate chips or nondairy alternative

100 grams cane sugar or granulated sugar

2 large eggs

¼ cup avocado oil or canola oil

60 grams vanilla Greek yogurt or nondairy alternative

1 teaspoon vanilla extract

Directions

1. **Preparing the Ingredients.**
   Choose the size of loaf you would like to make and measure your ingredients. Add the ingredients to the bread pan in the order listed above. Place the pan in the bread machine and close the lid.

2. **Select the Bake cycle**
   Turn on the bread maker. Select the White/Basic setting, then the loaf size, and finally the crust color. Start the cycle. When the cycle is finished and the bread is baked, carefully remove the pan from the machine. Use a potholder as the handle will be very hot. Let rest for a few minutes. Let the bread cool in the pan for at least 15 minutes. Gently remove from the pan and transfer the bread to a wire rack to cool completely. Store leftovers in an airtight container at room temperature for up to 5 days, or freeze to enjoy a slice whenever you desire. Let each slice thaw naturally

Basic Bulgur Bread

PREP: 10 MINUTES /MAKES 1 LOAF/16 SLICE BREAD (2 pounds)

Ingredients

½ cup lukewarm water

½ cup bulgur wheat

1⅓ cups lukewarm milk

1⅓ tablespoons unsalted butter, melted

1⅓ tablespoons sugar

1 teaspoon table salt

4 cups bread flour

3 cups whole-wheat bread flour

2 teaspoons bread machine yeast

Directions

1. **Preparing the Ingredients.**
   Choose the size of loaf you would like to make and measure your ingredients. Add the water and bulgur wheat to the bread pan and set aside for 25–30 minutes for the bulgur wheat to soften.
   Add the other ingredients to the bread pan in the order listed above.

2. **Select the Bake cycle**
   Place the pan in the bread machine and close the lid.
   Turn on the bread maker. Select the White/Basic setting, then the loaf size, and finally the crust color. Start the cycle. When the cycle is finished and the bread is baked, carefully remove the pan from the machine. Use a potholder as the handle will be very hot. Let rest for a few minutes. Remove the bread from the pan and allow to cool on a wire rack for at least 10 minutes before slicing.

Oat Quinoa Bread

PREP: 10 MINUTES /MAKES 1 LOAF/12 SLICE BREAD (1½ pounds)

Ingredients

1 cup lukewarm milk
⅔ cup cooked quinoa, cooled
¼ cup unsalted butter, melted
1 tablespoon sugar
1 teaspoon table salt
1½ cups white bread flour
¼ cup quick oats
¾ cup whole-wheat flour
1½ teaspoons bread machine yeast

Directions

1. **Preparing the Ingredients.**
   Choose the size of loaf you would like to make and measure your ingredients. Add the ingredients to the bread pan in the order listed above. Place the pan in the bread machine and close the lid.
2. **Select the Bake cycle**
   Turn on the bread maker. Select the White/Basic setting, then the loaf size, and finally the crust color. Start the cycle. When the cycle is finished and the bread is baked, carefully remove the pan from the machine. Use a potholder as the handle will be very hot. Let rest for a few minutes.
   Remove the bread from the pan and allow to cool on a wire rack for at least 10 minutes before slicing.

Whole Wheat Sunflower Bread

PREP: 10 MINUTES /MAKES 1 LOAF/12 SLICE BREAD (1½ pounds)

Ingredients

1 cup lukewarm water
1½ tablespoons honey
1½ tablespoons unsalted butter, melted
¾ teaspoon table salt
2½ cups whole-wheat flour
¾ cup white bread flour
1 tablespoon sesame seeds
3 tablespoons raw sunflower seeds
1½ teaspoons bread machine yeast

Directions

1. **Preparing the Ingredients.**
   Choose the size of loaf you would like to make and measure your ingredients. Add the ingredients to the bread pan in the order listed above. Place the pan in the bread machine and close the lid.
2. **Select the Bake cycle**
   Turn on the bread maker. Select the White/Basic setting, then the loaf size, and finally the crust color. Start the cycle. When the cycle is finished and the bread is baked, carefully remove the pan from the machine. Use a potholder as the handle will be very hot. Let rest for a few minutes.
   Remove the bread from the pan and allow to cool on a wire rack for at least 10 minutes before slicing.

Chocolate Chip Banana Bread
PREP: 10 MINUTES /MAKES 1 LOAF

Ingredients
Shortening or gluten-free cooking spray, for preparing the pan
250 grams All-Purpose Flour Blend
1 teaspoon ground cinnamon
1 teaspoon xanthan gum
1 teaspoon baking powder
½ teaspoon baking soda
¼ teaspoon salt
2 large eggs
1 teaspoon vanilla extract
90 grams mini semisweet chocolate chips or nondairy alternative
80 grams plain Greek yogurt or nondairy alternative
450 grams mashed bananas (about 4 large bananas)
8 tablespoons (1 stick) butter or nondairy alternative
150 grams light brown sugar

Directions
1. **Preparing the Ingredients.**
    Choose the size of loaf you would like to make and measure your ingredients.   Add the ingredients to the bread pan in the order listed above. Place the pan in the bread machine and close the lid.
2. **Select the Bake cycle**
    Turn on the bread maker. Select the White/Basic setting, then the loaf size, and finally the crust color. Start the cycle. When the cycle is finished and the bread is baked, carefully remove the pan from the machine. Use a potholder as the handle will be very hot. Let rest for a few minutes.
    Let the bread cool in the pan for at least 20 minutes, then gently transfer it to a wire rack to cool completely

Honey Sunflower Bread
PREP: 10 MINUTES /MAKES 1 LOAF/12 SLICE BREAD (1½ pounds)

Ingredients
1 cup lukewarm water
1 egg, at room temperature
3 tablespoons unsalted butter, melted
3 tablespoons skim milk powder
1½ tablespoons honey
1½ teaspoons table salt
3 cups white bread flour
1 teaspoon bread machine yeast
¾ cup raw sunflower seeds

Directions
1. **Preparing the Ingredients.**
    Choose the size of loaf you would like to make and measure your ingredients. Add the ingredients to the bread pan in the order listed above. Place the pan in the bread machine and close the lid.
2. **Select the Bake cycle**
    Turn on the bread maker. Select the White/Basic setting, then the loaf size, and finally the crust color. Start the cycle. When the cycle is finished and the bread is baked, carefully remove the pan from the machine. Use a potholder as the handle will be very hot. Let rest for a few minutes.
    Remove the bread from the pan and allow to cool on a wire rack for at least 10 minutes before slicing.

Flaxseed Milk Bread

PREP: 10 MINUTES /MAKES 1 LOAF/16 SLICE BREAD (2 pounds)

Ingredients
1½ cups lukewarm milk
2 tablespoons unsalted butter, melted
2 tablespoons honey
2 teaspoons table salt
4 cups white bread flour
½ cup flaxseed
1½ teaspoons bread machine yeast

Directions
1. **Preparing the Ingredients.**
Choose the size of loaf you would like to make and measure your ingredients. Add the ingredients to the bread pan in the order listed above. Place the pan in the bread machine and close the lid.

2. **Select the Bake cycle**
Turn on the bread maker. Select the White/Basic setting, then the loaf size, and finally the crust color. Start the cycle. When the cycle is finished and the bread is baked, carefully remove the pan from the machine. Use a potholder as the handle will be very hot. Let rest for a few minutes.
Remove the bread from the pan and allow to cool on a wire rack for at least 10 minutes before slicing.

Honey Wheat Bread

PREP: 10 MINUTES /MAKES 1 LOAF/16 SLICE BREAD (2 pounds)

Ingredients
1⅔ cups boiling water
¼ cup + 4 teaspoons cracked wheat
¼ cup unsalted butter, melted
3 tablespoons honey
1½ teaspoons table salt
1 cup whole-wheat flour
2 cups white bread flour
2 teaspoons bread machine yeast

Directions
1. **Preparing the Ingredients.**
Choose the size of loaf you would like to make and measure your ingredients. Add the ingredients to the bread pan in the order listed above. Add the boiling water and cracked wheat to the bread pan; set aside for 25–30 minutes for the wheat to soften. Place the pan in the bread machine and close the lid.

2. **Select the Bake cycle**
Turn on the bread maker. Select the White/Basic setting, then the loaf size, and finally the crust color. Start the cycle. When the cycle is finished and the bread is baked, carefully remove the pan from the machine. Use a potholder as the handle will be very hot. Let rest for a few minutes.
Remove the bread from the pan and allow to cool on a wire rack for at least 10 minutes before slicing.

Toasted Almond Whole Wheat Bread
PREP: 10 MINUTES /MAKES 1 LOAF

Ingredients
1 cup, plus 2 tablespoons water
3 tablespoons agave nectar
2 tablespoons butter, unsalted
1 ½cups bread flour
1 ½cups whole wheat flour
¼ cup slivered almonds, toasted
1 teaspoon salt
1 ½teaspoons quick active dry yeast

Directions
1. **Preparing the Ingredients**
   Add all of the ingredients in bread machine pan in the order they appear above, reserving yeast.
   Make a well in the center of the dry ingredients and add the yeast.

2. **Select the Bake cycle**
   Select the Basic cycle, light or medium crust color, and press Start.
   Remove baked bread from pan and cool on a rack before slicing.

Bagels
PREP: 10 MINUTES /MAKES 9

Ingredients
1 cup warm water
1 ½teaspoons salt
2 tablespoons sugar
3 cups bread flour
2 ¼teaspoons active dry yeast
3 quarts boiling water
3 tablespoons white sugar
1 tablespoon cornmeal
1 egg white
Flour, for surface

Directions
1. **Preparing the Ingredients**
   Place in the bread machine pan in the following order: warm water, salt, sugar, and flour.
   Make a well in the center of the dry ingredients and add the yeast.
2. **Select the Bake cycle**
   Select Dough cycle and press Start.
   When Dough cycle is complete, remove pan and let dough rest on a lightly floured surface. Stir 3 tablespoons of sugar into the boiling water.
   Cut dough into 9 equal pieces and roll each piece into a small ball. Flatten each ball with the palm of your hand. Poke a hole in the middle of each using your thumb. Twirl the dough on your finger to make the hole bigger, while evening out the dough around the hole.   Sprinkle an ungreased baking sheet with 1 teaspoon cornmeal. Place the bagel on the baking sheet and repeat until all bagels are formed.
   Cover the shaped bagels with a clean kitchen towel and let rise for 10 minutes.
   Preheat an oven to 375°F.
   Carefully transfer the bagels, one by one, to the boiling water. Boil for 1 minute, turning halfway.   Drain on a clean towel.
   Arrange boiled bagels on the baking sheet. Glaze the tops with egg white and sprinkle any toppings you desire.
   Bake for 20 to 25 minutes or until golden brown.   Let cool on a wire rack before serving.

Cracked Wheat Bread
PREP: 10 MINUTES / MAKES 10 SLICES

Ingredients
1¼cup plus 1 tablespoon water
2 tablespoons vegetable oil
3 cups bread flour
¾ cup cracked wheat
1½ teaspoons salt
2 tablespoons sugar
2¼teaspoons active dry yeast

Directions
1. **Preparing the Ingredients**
   Bring water to a boil.
   Place cracked wheat in small mixing bowl, pour water over it and stir.   Cool to 80°F.   Place cracked wheat mixture into pan, followed by all ingredients (except yeast) in the order listed.   Make a well in the center of the dry ingredients and add the yeast.
2. **Select the Bake cycle**
   Select the Basic Bread cycle, medium color crust, and press Start.
   Check dough consistency after 5 minutes of kneading. The dough should be a soft, tacky ball. If it is dry and stiff, add water one ½tablespoon at a time until sticky. If it's too wet and sticky, add 1 tablespoon of flour at a time.
   Remove bread when cycle is finished and allow to cool before serving.

SOURDOUGH BREADS

Simple Sourdough Starter
PREP: 10 MINUTES PLUS FERMENTING TIME
MAKES 2 CUPS (32 SERVINGS)

Ingredients
2½ teaspoons active dry yeast
2 cups water, at 100°F to 110°F
2 cups all-purpose flour

Directions
1. **Preparing the Ingredients.**
   In a large nonmetallic bowl, stir together the yeast, water, and flour. Cover the bowl loosely and place it in a warm place to ferment for 4 to 8 days, stirring several times per day.
2. **Select the Bake cycle**
   When the starter is bubbly and has a pleasant sour smell, it is ready to use.
   Store the starter covered in the refrigerator until you wish to use it.

Classic White Bread
PREP: 10 MINUTES /MAKES 1 LOAF/12 SLICE BREAD (1½ pounds)

Ingredients
1¼ cup lukewarm water
3 tablespoons canola oil
¾ teaspoon apple cider vinegar
2 eggs, room temperature, slightly beaten
1½ cups white rice flour
⅔ cup tapioca flour
½ cup nonfat dry milk powder
½ cup potato starch
⅓ cup cornstarch
2 tablespoon sugar
⅔ tablespoon xanthan gum
⅔ teaspoon table salt
1¼ teaspoons bread machine yeast

Directions
1. **Preparing the Ingredients.**
   Choose the size of loaf you would like to make and measure your ingredients.   Add the ingredients to the bread pan in the order listed above. Place the pan in the bread machine and close the lid.
2. **Select the Bake cycle**
   Turn on the bread maker. Select the White/Basic setting, then the loaf size, and finally the crust color. Start the cycle. When the cycle is finished and the bread is baked, carefully remove the pan from the machine. Use a potholder as the handle will be very hot. Let rest for a few minutes.
   Remove the bread from the pan and allow to cool on a wire rack for at least 10 minutes before slicing.

No-Yeast Sourdough Starter
PREP: 10 MINUTES PLUS FERMENTING TIME
MAKES 4 CUPS

Ingredients

2 cups all-purpose flour

2 cups chlorine-free bottled water, at room temperature

Directions

1. **Preparing the Ingredients.**

   Stir together the flour and water in a large glass bowl with a wooden spoon. Loosely cover the bowl with plastic wrap and place it in a warm area for 3 to 4 days, stirring at least twice a day, or until bubbly.

2. **Select the Bake cycle**

   Store the starter in the refrigerator in a covered glass jar, and stir it before using.

   Replenish your starter by adding back the same amount you removed, in equal parts flour and water.

Potica
PREP: 20 MINUTES/ MAKES 10 SERVINGS

Ingredients

Bread dough

½ cup milk

¼ cup cold butter, cut into small pieces

1 egg

2 cups bread flour

¼ cup sugar

¼ teaspoon salt

1 teaspoon bread machine yeast or fast-acting dry yeast filling

2 cups finely chopped or ground walnuts (about 7 oz)

⅓ cup honey

⅓ cup milk

3 tablespoons sugar

1 egg white, beaten

Directions

1. **Preparing the Ingredients.**

   Measure carefully, placing all bread dough ingredients in bread machine pan in the order recommended by the manufacturer.

2. **Select the Bake cycle**

   Select Dough/Manual cycle. Do not use delay cycle. Remove dough from pan, using lightly floured hands. Cover and let rest 10 minutes on lightly floured surface. In small saucepan, combine all filling ingredients except egg white. Bring to a boil over medium heat, stirring frequently. Reduce heat; simmer uncovered 5 minutes, stirring occasionally. Spread in shallow dish; cover and refrigerate until chilled.

   Grease large cookie sheet with shortening. Roll dough into 16×12-inch rectangle on lightly floured surface. Spread filling over dough to within ½ inch of edges. Starting with 16-inch side, roll up tightly; pinch seam to seal. Stretch and shape roll until even. Coil roll of dough to form a snail shape. Place on cookie sheet. Cover and let rise in warm place 30 to 60 minutes or until doubled in size. Dough is ready if indentation remains when touched.

   Heat oven to 325°F. Brush egg white over dough. Bake 45 to 55 minutes or until golden brown. Remove from cookie sheet to cooling rack.

Pecan Apple Spice Bread
PREP: 10 MINUTES /MAKES 1 LOAF/12 SLICE BREAD (1½ pounds)

Ingredients
⅓ cup lukewarm water
2¼ tablespoons canola oil
¾ teaspoon apple cider vinegar
2¼ tablespoons light brown sugar, packed
¾ cup Granny Smith apples, grated
2 eggs, room temperature, slightly beaten
½ cup nonfat dry milk powder
½ cup brown rice flour
½ cup tapioca flour
½ cup millet flour
⅓ cup corn starch
1½ tablespoons apple pie spice
¾ tablespoon xanthan gum
¾ teaspoon table salt
1¼ teaspoons bread machine yeast
⅓ cup pecans, chopped

Directions
1. **Preparing the Ingredients.**
    Choose the size of loaf you would like to make and measure your ingredients.   Add the ingredients to the bread pan in the order listed above. Place the pan in the bread machine and close the lid.
2. **Select the Bake cycle**
    Turn on the bread maker. Select the White/Basic setting, then the loaf size, and finally the crust color. Start the cycle. When the cycle is finished and the bread is baked, carefully remove the pan from the machine. Use a potholder as the handle will be very hot. Let rest for a few minutes.
    When the machine signals to add ingredients, add the chopped pecans. Remove the bread from the pan and allow to cool on a wire rack for at least 10 minutes before slicing

No-Yeast Whole-Wheat Sourdough Starter
PREP: 10 MINUTES PLUS FERMENTING TIME
MAKES 2 CUPS (32 SERVINGS)

Ingredients
1 cup whole-wheat flour, divided
½ teaspoon honey
1 cup chlorine-free bottled water, at room temperature, divided

Directions
1. **Preparing the Ingredients.**
    Stir together ½ cup of flour, ½ cup of water, and the honey in a large glass bowl with a wooden spoon. Loosely cover the bowl with plastic wrap and place it in a warm area for 5 days, stirring at least twice a day. After 5 days, stir in the remaining ½ cup of flour and ½ cup of water.
2. **Select the Bake cycle**
    Cover the bowl loosely again with plastic wrap and place it in a warm area.
    When the starter has bubbles and foam on top, it is ready to use.
    Store the starter in the refrigerator in a covered glass jar, and stir it before using. If you use half, replenish the starter with ½ cup flour and ½ cup water

Pumpkin Jalapeno Bread

PREP: 10 MINUTES /MAKES 1 LOAF/12 SLICE BREAD (1½ pounds)

Ingredients

½ cup lukewarm water

2 medium eggs, beaten

⅓ cup pumpkin puree

2¼ tablespoons honey

1½ tablespoons vegetable oil

¾ teaspoon apple cider vinegar

1½ teaspoons sugar

¾ teaspoon table salt

½ cup brown rice flour

½ cup tapioca flour

⅓ cup corn starch

⅓ cup yellow cornmeal

¾ tablespoon xanthan gum

1 small jalapeno pepper, seeded and deveined

1½ teaspoons crushed red pepper flakes

1¼ teaspoons bread machine yeast

Directions

1. **Preparing the Ingredients.**

    Choose the size of loaf you would like to make and measure your ingredients.   Add the ingredients to the bread pan in the order listed above. Place the pan in the bread machine and close the lid.

2. **Select the Bake cycle**

    Turn on the bread maker. Select the White/Basic setting, then the loaf size, and finally the crust color. Start the cycle. When the cycle is finished and the bread is baked, carefully remove the pan from the machine. Use a potholder as the handle will be very hot. Let rest for a few minutes.

    When the machine signals to add ingredients, add the chopped pecans. Remove the bread from the pan and allow to cool on a wire rack for at least 10 minutes before slicing.

Basic Sourdough Bread

PREP: 10 MINUTES /MAKES 1 LOAF/12 SLICE BREAD (1½ pounds)

Ingredients

2 cups Simple Sourdough Starter (here), fed, active, and at room temperature

2 tablespoons water, at 80°F to 90°F

¾ teaspoon apple cider vinegar

1⅓ teaspoons sugar

1 teaspoon salt

1⅔ cups white bread flour

½ cup nonfat dry milk powder

1 teaspoon bread machine or instant yeast

Directions

1. **Preparing the Ingredients.**

    Place the ingredients in your bread machine as recommended by the manufacturer. Program the machine for Basic/White bread, select light or medium crust, and press Start.

2. **Select the Bake cycle**

    When the loaf is done, remove the bucket from the machine.

    Let the loaf cool for 5 minutes.

    When the machine signals to add ingredients, add the chopped pecans. Gently shake the bucket to remove the loaf, and turn it out onto a rack to cool.

Walnut Banana Bread

PREP: 10 MINUTES /MAKES 1 LOAF/12 SLICE BREAD (1½ pounds)

Ingredients

⅓ cup lukewarm water

2 tablespoons canola oil

¾ teaspoon apple cider vinegar

2 eggs, beaten

1½ small bananas, mashed

¾ teaspoon table salt

½ cup brown rice flour

½ cup white rice flour

½ cup amaranth flour

⅓ cup corn starch

¾ tablespoon xanthan gum

¾ teaspoon cinnamon

⅓ teaspoon nutmeg

1½ teaspoons bread machine yeast

¾ cup walnuts, chopped

Directions

1. **Preparing the Ingredients.**
   Choose the size of loaf you would like to make and measure your ingredients.   Add the ingredients to the bread pan in the order listed above. Place the pan in the bread machine and close the lid.

2. **Select the Bake cycle**
   Turn on the bread maker. Select the Quick/Rapid setting, then the loaf size, and finally the crust color. Start the cycle. When the cycle is finished and the bread is baked, carefully remove the pan from the machine. Use a potholder as the handle will be very hot. Let rest for a few minutes.
   Remove the bread from the pan and allow to cool on a wire rack for at least 10 minutes before slicing.

Whole-Wheat Sourdough Bread

PREP: 10 MINUTES /MAKES 1 LOAF/12 SLICE BREAD (1½ pounds)

Ingredients

¾ cup plus 2 tablespoons water, at 80°F to 90°F

¾ cup plus 2 tablespoons No-Yeast Whole-Wheat Sourdough Starter, fed, active, and at room temperature

2 tablespoons melted butter, cooled

2 eggs, beaten

1 tablespoon sugar

1 teaspoon salt

½ cup brown rice flour

1½ teaspoons bread machine yeast

¾ cup walnuts, chopped

Directions

1. **Preparing the Ingredients.**
   Place the ingredients in your bread machine as recommended by the manufacturer. Program the machine for Whole-Wheat/Whole-Grain bread, select light or medium crust, and press Start.

2. **Select the Bake cycle**
   When the loaf is done, remove the bucket from the machine.
   Let the loaf cool for 5 minutes. Gently shake the bucket to remove the loaf, and turn it out onto a rack to cool.

Basic Honey Bread

PREP: 10 MINUTES /MAKES 1 LOAF/12 SLICE BREAD (1½ pounds)

Ingredients

1½ cups warm milk

¼ cup unsalted butter, melted

2 eggs, beaten

1 teaspoon apple cider vinegar

½ cup honey

1 teaspoon table salt

3 cups gluten-free flour(s) of your choice

1½ teaspoons xanthan gum

1¾ teaspoons bread machine yeast

Directions

1. Preparing the Ingredients.

Choose the size of loaf you would like to make and measure your ingredients. Add the ingredients to the bread pan in the order listed above. Place the pan in the bread machine and close the lid.

2. Select the Bake cycle

Turn on the bread maker. Select the White/Basic or Gluten-Free (if your machine has this setting) setting, then the loaf size, and finally the crust color. Start the cycle.

When the cycle is finished and the bread is baked, carefully remove the pan from the machine. Use a potholder as the handle will be very hot. Let rest for a few minutes.

Remove the bread from the pan and allow to cool on a wire rack for at least 10 minutes before slicing.

Multigrain Sourdough Bread

PREP: 10 MINUTES /MAKES 1 LOAF/8 SLICE BREAD (1 pound)

Ingredients

⅓ cup plus 1 tablespoon water, at 80°F to 90°F

½ cup Simple Sourdough Starter, fed, active, and at room temperature

4 teaspoons melted butter, cooled

1⅔ tablespoons sugar

½ teaspoon salt

1½ cup multigrain cereal

1¾ cups white bread flour

1 teaspoon bread machine or instant yeast

Directions

1. Preparing the Ingredients.

Place the ingredients in your bread machine as recommended by the manufacturer. Program the machine for Whole-Wheat/Whole-Grain bread, select light or medium crust, and press Start.

2. Select the Bake cycle

When the loaf is done, remove the bucket from the machine. Let the loaf cool for 5 minutes.

Gently shake the bucket to remove the loaf, and turn it out onto a rack to cool.

Onion Buttermilk Bread

PREP: 10 MINUTES /MAKES 1 LOAF/12 SLICE BREAD (1½ pounds)

Ingredients

1 cup lukewarm water
3 tablespoons unsalted butter, melted
¾ teaspoon apple cider vinegar
3 tablespoons dry buttermilk powder
3 medium eggs, beaten
3 tablespoons sugar
1 teaspoon table salt
⅓ cup potato flour
⅓ cup tapioca flour
1½ cups white rice flour
¾ tablespoon dill, chopped
3 tablespoons green onion, chopped
2⅔ teaspoons xanthan gum
1½ teaspoons bread machine yeast

Directions

1. **Preparing the Ingredients.**
   Choose the size of loaf you would like to make and measure your ingredients.   Add the ingredients to the bread pan in the order listed above. Place the pan in the bread machine and close the lid.

2. **Select the Bake cycle**
   Turn on the bread maker. Select the White/Basic or Gluten-Free (if your machine has this setting) setting, then the loaf size, and finally the crust color. Start the cycle.
   When the cycle is finished and the bread is baked, carefully remove the pan from the machine. Use a potholder as the handle will be very hot. Let rest for a few minutes.
   Remove the bread from the pan and allow to cool on a wire rack for at least 10 minutes before slicing.

Faux Sourdough Bread

PREP: 10 MINUTES /MAKES 1 LOAF/12 SLICE BREAD (1½ pounds)

Ingredients

¾ cup plus 1 tablespoon water, at 80°F to 90°F
⅓ cup sour cream, at room temperature
2¼ tablespoons melted butter, cooled
1½ tablespoons apple cider vinegar
¾ tablespoon sugar
¾ teaspoon salt
3 cups white bread flour
1 teaspoon bread machine or instant yeast

Directions

1. **Preparing the Ingredients.**
   Place the ingredients in your bread machine as recommended by the manufacturer.
2. **Select the Bake cycle**
   Program the machine for Whole-Wheat/Whole-Grain bread, select light or medium crust, and press Start. When the loaf is done, remove the bucket from the machine. Let the loaf cool for 5 minutes.
   Gently shake the bucket to remove the loaf, and turn it out onto a rack to cool.

Pecan Cranberry Bread
PREP: 10 MINUTES /MAKES 1 LOAF/12 SLICE BREAD (1½ pounds)

Ingredients

1⅛ cups lukewarm water
3 tablespoons canola oil
¾ tablespoon orange zest
¾ teaspoon apple cider vinegar
2 eggs, slightly beaten
2¼ tablespoons sugar
¾ teaspoon table salt
1½ cups white rice flour
½ cup nonfat dry milk powder
⅓ cup tapioca flour
⅓ cup potato starch
¼ cup corn starch
¾ tablespoon xanthan gum
1½ teaspoons bread machine yeast
½ cup dried cranberries
½ cup pecan pieces

Directions

1.   **Preparing the Ingredients.**
      Choose the size of loaf you would like to make and measure your ingredients.   Add all of the ingredients except for the pecans and cranberries to the bread pan in the order listed above. Place the pan in the bread machine and close the lid.

2.   **Select the Bake cycle**
      Turn on the bread maker. Select the Gluten Free or Fruit/Nut (if your machine has this setting) setting, then the loaf size, and finally the crust color. Start the cycle. (If you don't have either of the above settings, use Basic/White.). When the machine signals to add ingredients, add the pecans and cranberries. (Some machines have a fruit/nut hopper where you can add the pecans and cranberries when you start the machine. The machine will automatically add them to the dough during the baking process.).
      When the cycle is finished and the bread is baked, carefully remove the pan from the machine. Use a potholder as the handle will be very hot. Let rest for a few minutes.
      Remove the bread from the pan and allow to cool on a wire rack for at least 10 minutes before slicing.

Sourdough Milk Bread
PREP: 10 MINUTES /MAKES 1 LOAF/12 SLICE BREAD (1½ pounds)

Ingredients

1½ cups Simple Sourdough Starter or No-Yeast Sourdough Starter, fed, active, and at room temperature
⅓ cup milk, at 80°F to 90°F
3 tablespoons olive oil
1½ tablespoons honey
1 teaspoon salt
3 cups white bread flour
1 teaspoon bread machine or instant yeast

Directions

1.   **Preparing the Ingredients.**
      Place the ingredients in your bread machine as recommended by the manufacturer. Program the machine for Whole-Wheat/Whole-Grain bread, select light or medium crust, and press Start.

2.   **Select the Bake cycle**
      When the loaf is done, remove the bucket from the machine.
      Let the loaf cool for 5 minutes.
      Gently shake the bucket to remove the loaf, and turn it out onto a rack to cool.

Cheese Potato Bread
PREP: 10 MINUTES /MAKES 1 LOAF/12 SLICE BREAD (1½ pounds)

Ingredients
1 cup lukewarm water
2¼ tablespoons vegetable oil
2 large eggs, beaten
⅓ cup dry skim milk powder
3 tablespoons sugar
¾ teaspoon apple cider vinegar
1⅛ teaspoons table salt
⅓ cup cornstarch
½ cup cottage cheese
3 tablespoons snipped chives
⅓ cup instant potato buds
⅓ cup potato starch
⅓ cup tapioca flour
1½ cups white rice flour
1½ teaspoons bread machine yeast

Directions
1. **Preparing the Ingredients.**
   Choose the size of loaf you would like to make and measure your ingredients.
   Add the ingredients to the bread pan in the order listed above.
   Place the pan in the bread machine and close the lid.
2. **Select the Bake cycle**
   Turn on the bread maker. Select the White/Basic or Gluten-Free (if your machine has this setting) setting, then the loaf size, and finally the crust color. Start the cycle.
   When the cycle is finished and the bread is baked, carefully remove the pan from the machine. Use a potholder as the handle will be very hot. Let rest for a few minutes.
   Remove the bread from the pan and allow to cool on a wire rack for at least 10 minutes before slicing.

Lemon Sourdough Bread
PREP: 10 MINUTES /MAKES 1 LOAF/12 SLICE BREAD (1½ pounds)

Ingredients
¾ cup Simple Sourdough Starter or No-Yeast Sourdough Starter, fed, active, and at room temperature
¾ cup water, at 80°F to 90°F
1 egg, at room temperature
3 tablespoons butter, melted and cooled
⅓ cup honey
1½ teaspoons salt
2 teaspoons lemon zest
1½ teaspoons lime zest
⅓ cup wheat germ
3 cups white bread flour
1¾ teaspoons bread machine or instant yeast

Directions
1. **Preparing the Ingredients.**
   Place the ingredients in your bread machine as recommended by the manufacturer
2. **Select the Bake cycle**.
   Program the machine for Whole-Wheat/Whole-Grain bread, select light or medium crust, and press Start.
   When the loaf is done, remove the bucket from the machine.
   Let the loaf cool for 5 minutes. Gently shake the bucket to remove the loaf, and turn it out onto a rack to cool.

Instant Cocoa Bread

PREP: 10 MINUTES /MAKES 1 LOAF/12 SLICE BREAD (1½ pounds)

Ingredients

1⅛ cups lukewarm water
2 large eggs, beaten
2¼ tablespoons molasses
1½ tablespoons canola oil
¾ teaspoon apple cider vinegar
2¼ tablespoons light brown sugar
1⅛ teaspoons table salt
1½ cups white rice flour
½ cup potato starch
¼ cup tapioca flour
1½ teaspoons xanthan gum
1½ teaspoons cocoa powder
1½ teaspoons instant coffee granules
2 teaspoons bread machine yeast

Directions

1. **Preparing the Ingredients.**
    Choose the size of loaf you would like to make and measure your ingredients.
2. Add the ingredients to the bread pan in the order listed above. Place the pan in the bread machine and close the lid.
    Select the Bake cycle
    Turn on the bread maker. Select the White/Basic or Gluten-Free (if your machine has this setting) setting, then the loaf size, and finally the crust color. Start the cycle.
    When the cycle is finished and the bread is baked, carefully remove the pan from the machine. Use a potholder as the handle will be very hot. Let rest for a few minutes.
    Remove the bread from the pan and allow to cool on a wire rack for at least 10 minutes before slicing.

San Francisco Sourdough Bread

PREP: 10 MINUTES /MAKES 1 LOAF/12 SLICE BREAD (1½ pounds)

Ingredients

1 cup plus 2 tablespoons Simple Sourdough Starter or No-Yeast Sourdough Starter, fed, active, and at room temperature
½ cup plus 1 tablespoon water, at 80°F to 90°F
2¼ tablespoons olive oil
1½ teaspoons salt
2 tablespoons sugar
1½ tablespoons skim milk powder
⅓ cup whole-wheat flour
2⅔ cups white bread flour
1⅔ teaspoons bread machine or instant yeast

Directions

1. **Preparing the Ingredients.**
    Place the ingredients in your bread machine as recommended by the manufacturer. Program the machine for Whole-Wheat/Whole-Grain bread, select light or medium crust, and press Start.
2. **Select the Bake cycle**
    When the loaf is done, remove the bucket from the machine.
    Let the loaf cool for 5 minutes. Gently shake the bucket to remove the loaf, and turn it out onto a rack to cool.

Mix Seed Bread

PREP: 10 MINUTES /MAKES 1 LOAF/12 SLICE BREAD (1½ pounds)

Ingredients
2 cups lukewarm milk
6 tablespoons cooking oil
1 teaspoon vinegar
2 eggs, slightly beaten
1 tablespoon sugar
1 teaspoon table salt
2⅔ cups gluten-free flour(s) of your choice
2 tablespoons poppy seeds
2 tablespoons pumpkin seeds
2 tablespoons sunflower seeds
2 teaspoons bread machine yeast

Directions
1. **Preparing the Ingredients.**
   Choose the size of loaf you would like to make and measure your ingredients.
   Add the ingredients to the bread pan in the order listed above.
   Place the pan in the bread machine and close the lid.
2. **Select the Bake cycle**
   Turn on the bread maker. Select the White/Basic or Gluten-Free (if your machine has this setting) setting, then the loaf size, and finally the crust color. Start the cycle.
   When the cycle is finished and the bread is baked, carefully remove the pan from the machine. Use a potholder as the handle will be very hot. Let rest for a few minutes.
   Remove the bread from the pan and allow to cool on a wire rack for at least 10 minutes before slicing.

Sourdough Beer Bread

PREP: 10 MINUTES /MAKES 1 LOAF/8 SLICE BREAD (1 pound)

Ingredients
⅔ cup Simple Sourdough Starter or No-Yeast Sourdough Starter, fed, active, and at room temperature
⅓ cup dark beer, at 80°F to 90°F
1 tablespoon melted butter, cooled
1½ teaspoons sugar
¾ teaspoon salt
1¾ cups white bread flour
¾ teaspoon bread machine or instant yeast

Directions
1. **Preparing the Ingredients.**
   Place the ingredients in your bread machine as recommended by the manufacturer. Program the machine for Whole-Wheat/Whole-Grain bread, select light or medium crust, and press Start.
2. **Select the Bake cycle**
   When the loaf is done, remove the bucket from the machine.
   Let the loaf cool for 5 minutes. Gently shake the bucket to remove the loaf, and turn it out onto a rack to cool.

Garlic Parsley Bread

PREP: 10 MINUTES /MAKES 1 LOAF/12 SLICE BREAD (1½ pounds)

Ingredients

1¼ cups almond or coconut milk
3 tablespoons flax meal
½ cup + 1 tablespoon warm water
3 tablespoons butter
2¼ tablespoons maple syrup
2¼ teaspoons apple cider vinegar
3 tablespoons parsley, loosely chopped
8–9 cloves garlic, minced
¾ teaspoon table salt
6 tablespoons + 2 teaspoons brown rice flour
⅓ cup corn starch
3 tablespoons potato starch
2 teaspoons xanthan gum
1½ tablespoons garlic powder
1½ tablespoons onion powder
1½ teaspoons bread machine yeast

Directions

1. **Preparing the Ingredients.**
   Combine the water and flax meal in a bowl; set aside for 5–10 minutes to mix well.
   Choose the size of loaf you would like to make and measure your ingredients.
   Add the ingredients to the bread pan in the order listed above, including the flax meal. Place the pan in the bread machine and close the lid.
2. **Select the Bake cycle**
   Turn on the bread maker. Select the White/Basic or Gluten-Free (if your machine has this setting) setting, then the loaf size, and finally the crust color. Start the cycle.
   When the cycle is finished and the bread is baked, carefully remove the pan from the machine. Use a potholder as the handle will be very hot. Let rest for a few minutes.
   Remove the bread from the pan and allow to cool on a wire rack for at least 10 minutes before slicing.

Crusty Sourdough Bread

PREP: 10 MINUTES /MAKES 1 LOAF/12 SLICE BREAD (1½ pounds)

Ingredients

1 cup Simple Sourdough Starter, fed, active, and at room temperature
½ cup water, at 80°F to 90°F
2 tablespoons honey
1½ teaspoons salt
3 cups white bread flour
1 teaspoon bread machine or instant yeast

Directions

1. **Preparing the Ingredients.**
   Place the ingredients in your bread machine as recommended by the manufacturer. Program the machine for Whole-Wheat/Whole-Grain bread, select light or medium crust, and press Start.
2. **Select the Bake cycle**
   When the loaf is done, remove the bucket from the machine.
   Let the loaf cool for 5 minutes.
   Gently shake the bucket to remove the loaf, and turn it out onto a rack to cool.

Italian Herb Bread

PREP: 10 MINUTES /MAKES 1 LOAF/12 SLICE BREAD (1½ pounds)

Ingredients

1½ cups lukewarm water
3 eggs, beaten
¼ cup vegetable oil
1½ teaspoons table salt
3 tablespoons sugar
1 cup white bean flour
1 tablespoon mixed Italian herbs, dried
1 cup white rice flour
1 cup potato starch
½ cup tapioca flour
1 tablespoon xanthan gum
2¼ teaspoons bread machine yeast

Directions

1. **Preparing the Ingredients.**
   Choose the size of loaf you would like to make and measure your ingredients.
   Add the ingredients to the bread pan in the order listed above.
   Place the pan in the bread machine and close the lid.
2. **Select the Bake cycle**
   Turn on the bread maker. Select the White/Basic or Gluten-Free (if your machine has this setting) setting, then the loaf size, and finally the crust color. Start the cycle.
   When the cycle is finished and the bread is baked, carefully remove the pan from the machine. Use a potholder as the handle will be very hot. Let rest for a few minutes.
   Remove the bread from the pan and allow to cool on a wire rack for at least 10 minutes before slicing.

Sourdough Cheddar Bread

PREP: 10 MINUTES /MAKES 1 LOAF/12 SLICE BREAD (1½ pounds)

Ingredients

1 cup Simple Sourdough Starter or No-Yeast Sourdough Starter, fed, active, and at room temperature
⅓ cup water, at 80°F to 90°F
4 teaspoons sugar
1 teaspoon salt
½ cup (2 ounces) grated aged Cheddar cheese
⅔ cup whole-wheat flour
¼ cup oat bran
1⅓ cups white bread flour
1½ teaspoons bread machine or instant yeast

Directions

1. **Preparing the Ingredients.**
   Place the ingredients in your bread machine as recommended by the manufacturer. Program the machine for Whole-Wheat/Whole-Grain bread, select light or medium crust, and press Start.
2. **Select the Bake cycle**
   When the loaf is done, remove the bucket from the machine.
   Let the loaf cool for 5 minutes. Gently shake the bucket to remove the loaf, and turn it out onto a rack to cool.

Herb Sourdough
PREP: 10 MINUTES /MAKES 1 LOAF/8 SLICE BREAD (1 pound)

Ingredients

1⅓ cups No-Yeast Sourdough Starter, fed, active, and at room temperature
4 teaspoons water, at 80°F to 90°F
4 teaspoons melted butter, cooled
1⅓ teaspoons sugar
1 teaspoon salt
1 teaspoon chopped fresh basil
1 teaspoon chopped fresh oregano
½ teaspoon chopped fresh thyme
1⅔ cups white bread flour
1 teaspoon bread machine or instant yeast

Directions

1.   **Preparing the Ingredients.**
     Place the ingredients in your bread machine as recommended by the manufacturer. Program the machine for Whole-Wheat/Whole-Grain bread, select light or medium crust, and press Start.

2.   **Select the Bake cycle**
     When the loaf is done, remove the bucket from the machine.
     Let the loaf cool for 5 minutes. Gently shake the bucket to remove the loaf, and turn it out onto a rack to cool.

Cranberry Pecan Sourdough
PREP: 10 MINUTES /MAKES 1 LOAF/12 SLICE BREAD (1½ pounds)

Ingredients

2 cups No-Yeast Sourdough Starter, fed, active, and at room temperature
2 tablespoons water, at 80°F to 90°F
2 tablespoons melted butter, cooled
2 teaspoons sugar
1½ teaspoons salt
⅓ teaspoon ground cinnamon
2½ cups white bread flour
1½ teaspoons bread machine or instant yeast
⅓ cup dried cranberries
⅓ cup chopped pecans

Directions

1.   **Preparing the Ingredients.**
     Place the ingredients in your bread machine as recommended by the manufacturer.
2.   **Select the Bake cycle**
     Program the machine for Whole-Wheat/Whole-Grain bread, select light or medium crust, and press Start.
     When the loaf is done, remove the bucket from the machine.
     Let the loaf cool for 5 minutes. Gently shake the bucket to remove the loaf, and turn it out onto a rack to cool.

Dark Chocolate Sourdough

PREP: 10 MINUTES /MAKES 1 LOAF/12 SLICE BREAD (1½ pounds)

Ingredients

2 cups No-Yeast Sourdough Starter, fed, active, and at room temperature
2 tablespoons water, at 80°F to 90°F
2 tablespoons melted butter, cooled
¾ teaspoon pure vanilla extract
2 teaspoons sugar
1½ teaspoons salt
⅓ teaspoon ground cinnamon
¼ cup unsweetened cocoa powder
2½ cups white bread flour
1½ teaspoons bread machine or instant yeast
½ cup semisweet chocolate chips
⅓ cup chopped pistachios
⅓ cup raisins

Directions

1. **Preparing the Ingredients.**
   Place the ingredients in your bread machine as recommended by the manufacturer. Program the machine for Whole-Wheat/Whole-Grain bread, select light or medium crust, and press Start.

2. **Select the Bake cycle**
   When the loaf is done, remove the bucket from the machine. Let the loaf cool for 5 minutes.
   Gently shake the bucket to remove the loaf, and turn it out onto a rack to cool.

FRUIT BREADS

Cinnamon Apple Bread
PREP: 10 MINUTES /MAKES 1 LOAF/16 SLICE BREAD (1½ pounds)

Ingredients

1⅓ cups lukewarm milk
3⅓ tablespoons butter, melted
2⅔ tablespoons sugar
2 teaspoons table salt
1⅓ teaspoons cinnamon, ground
A pinch ground cloves
4 cups white bread flour
2¼ teaspoons bread machine yeast
1⅓ cups peeled apple, finely diced

Directions

1. **Preparing the Ingredients.**

Choose the size of loaf you would like to make and measure your ingredients.

Add all of the ingredients except for the apples to the bread pan in the order listed above.

Place the pan in the bread machine and close the lid.

2. **Select the Bake cycle**

Turn on the bread maker. Select the White/Basic or Fruit/Nut (if your machine has this setting) setting, then the loaf size, and finally the crust color. Start the cycle.

When the machine signals to add ingredients, add the apples. (Some machines have a fruit/nut hopper where you can add the apples when you start the machine. The machine will automatically add them to the dough during the baking process.)

When the cycle is finished and the bread is baked, carefully remove the pan from the machine. Use a potholder as the handle will be very hot. Let rest for a few minutes.

Remove the bread from the pan and allow to cool on a wire rack for at least 10 minutes before slicing.

Candied Fruits Bread
PREP: 10 MINUTES /MAKES 1 LOAF

Ingredients

Orange juice - 1 cup
Lukewarm water - ½ cup
Butter - 2½ tbsp., softened
Powdered milk - 2 tbsp.
Brown sugar - 2½ tbsp.
Kosher salt - 1 tsp.
Whole-grain flour - 4 cups
Bread machine yeast - 1½ tsp.
Candied fruits - ¾ cup (pineapple, coconut, papaya)
Walnuts - ¼ cup, chopped
All-purpose flour - 1 tbsp. for packing candied fruits
Almond flakes - ¼ cup

Directions

1. **Preparing the Ingredients**

   Put the candied fruit water, then dry on a paper towel and roll in flour.

   Add everything in the bread machine pan (except almonds and fruit) according to bread machine recommendations.

2. **Select the Bake cycle**

   Select Basic and Medium crust. Add the almonds and fruit after the beep. Remove the bread when done.

   Cool, slice, and serve.

Fragrant Orange Bread

PREP: 10 MINUTES /MAKES 1 LOAF/12 SLICE BREAD (1½ pounds)

Ingredients

1 cup milk, at 80°F to 90°F

3 tablespoons freshly squeezed orange juice, at room temperature

3 tablespoons sugar

1 tablespoon melted butter, cooled

1 teaspoon salt

3 cups white bread flour

Zest of 1 orange

1¼ teaspoons bread machine or instant yeast

Directions

1. **Preparing the Ingredients.**

   Place the ingredients in your bread machine as recommended by the manufacturer.

2. **Select the Bake cycle**

   Program the machine for Basic/White bread, select light or medium crust, and press Start.

   When the loaf is done, remove the bucket from the machine.

   Let the loaf cool for 5 minutes. Gently shake the bucket to remove the loaf, and turn it out onto a rack to cool.

Banana Bread

PREP: 10 MINUTES /MAKES 1 LOAF

Ingredients

1¼ cups sugar

½ cup butter, softened

2 eggs

1½ cups mashed very ripe bananas (3 medium)

½ cup buttermilk

1 teaspoon vanilla

2½ cups all-purpose flour

1 teaspoon baking soda

1 teaspoon salt

1 cup chopped nuts, if desired

Directions

1. **Preparing the Ingredients.**

Place the banana, eggs, sugar, and vanilla in your bread machine.

Program the machine for Quick/Rapid bread and press Start.

While the wet ingredients are mixing, stir together the flour, nuts, salt, and baking soda in a small bowl.

2. **Select the Bake cycle**

After the first fast mixing is done and the machine signals, add the dry ingredients.

When the loaf is done, remove the bucket from the machine.

Let the loaf cool for 5 minutes.

Gently shake the bucket to remove the loaf, and turn it out onto a rack to cool.

Cool completely, about 2 hours, before slicing. Wrap tightly and store at room temperature up to 4 days, or refrigerate.

Blueberry Honey Bread

PREP: 10 MINUTES /MAKES 1 LOAF/16 SLICE BREAD (2 pounds)

Ingredients

1 cup plain yogurt
⅔ cup lukewarm water
¼ cup honey
4 teaspoons unsalted butter, melted
2 teaspoons table salt
1½ teaspoons lime zest
⅔ teaspoon lemon extract
4 cups white bread flour
2¼ teaspoons bread machine yeast
1⅓ cups dried blueberries

Directions

1. **Preparing the Ingredients.**

Choose the size of loaf you would like to make and measure your ingredients.

Add all of the ingredients except for the blueberries to the bread pan in the order listed above.

Place the pan in the bread machine and close the lid.

2. **Select the Bake cycle**

Turn on the bread maker. Select the White/Basic or Fruit/Nut (if your machine has this setting) setting, then the loaf size, and finally the crust color. Start the cycle. When the machine signals to add ingredients, add the blueberries. (Some machines have a fruit/nut hopper where you can add the blueberries when you start the machine. The machine will automatically add them to the dough during the baking process.)

When the cycle is finished and the bread is baked, carefully remove the pan from the machine. Use a potholder as the handle will be very hot. Let rest for a few minutes.

Remove the bread from the pan and allow to cool on a wire rack for at least 10 minutes before slicing.

Cranberry Orange Breakfast Bread

PREP: 10 MINUTES /MAKES 14 SLICES

Ingredients

1⅛ cup orange juice
2 Tbsp vegetable oil
2 Tbsp honey
3 cups bread flour
1 Tbsp dry milk powder
½ tsp ground cinnamon
½ tsp ground allspice
1 tsp salt
1 (.25 ounce) package active dry yeast
1 Tbsp grated orange zest
1 cup sweetened dried cranberries
⅓ cup chopped walnuts

Directions

1. **Preparing the Ingredients.**

   Add each ingredient to the bread machine in the order and at the temperature recommended by your bread machine manufacturer.

2. **Select the Bake cycle**

   Close the lid, select the basic bread, low crust setting on your bread machine, and press start.

   Add the cranberries and chopped walnuts 5 to 10 minutes before last kneading cycle ends.

   When the bread machine has finished baking, remove the bread and put it on a cooling rack.

Moist Oatmeal Apple Bread

PREP: 10 MINUTES /MAKES 1 LOAF/12 SLICE BREAD (1½ pounds)

Ingredients

⅔ cup milk, at 80°F to 90°F

¼ cup unsweetened applesauce, at room temperature

1 tablespoon melted butter, cooled

1 tablespoon sugar

1 teaspoon salt

½ teaspoon ground cinnamon

Pinch ground nutmeg

¼ cup quick oats

2¼ cups white bread flour

2¼ teaspoons bread machine or active dry yeast

Directions

1.   Preparing the Ingredients.

Place the ingredients in your bread machine as recommended by the manufacturer.

Program the machine for Basic/White bread, select light or medium crust, and press Start.

When the loaf is done, remove the bucket from the machine.

2.   Select the Bake cycle

Let the loaf cool for 5 minutes.

Gently shake the bucket to remove the loaf, and turn it out onto a rack to cool.

Chai-Spiced Bread

PREP: 10 MINUTES /MAKES 1 LOAF

Ingredients

¾ cup granulated sugar

½ cup butter, softened

½ cup cold brewed tea or water

⅓ cup milk

2 teaspoons vanilla

2 eggs

2 cups all-purpose flour

2 teaspoons baking powder

¾ teaspoon ground cardamom

½ teaspoon salt

¼ teaspoon ground cinnamon

1/8 teaspoon ground cloves

glaze

1 cup powdered sugar

¼ teaspoon vanilla

3 to 5 teaspoons milk

Additional ground cinnamon

Directions

1.   Preparing the Ingredients.

Place the ingredients in your bread machine as recommended by the manufacturer.

Program the machine for Basic/White bread, select light or medium crust, and press Start.

2.   Select the Bake cycle

When the loaf is done, remove the bucket from the machine.

Let the loaf cool for 5 minutes.

Gently shake the bucket to remove the loaf, and turn it out onto a rack to cool completely, about 2 hours, before slicing. Wrap tightly and store at room temperature up to 4 days, or refrigerate.

Raisin Candied Fruit Bread

PREP: 10 MINUTES /MAKES 1 LOAF/16 SLICE BREAD (2 pounds)

Ingredients

1 egg, beaten
1½ cups + 1 tablespoon lukewarm water
⅔ teaspoon ground cardamom
1¼ teaspoons table salt
2 tablespoons sugar
⅓ cup butter, melted
4 cups bread flour
1¼ teaspoons bread machine yeast
½ cup raisins
½ cup mixed candied fruit

Directions

1. Preparing the Ingredients.

Choose the size of loaf you would like to make and measure your ingredients. Add all of the ingredients except for the candied fruits and raisins to the bread pan in the order listed above. Place the pan in the bread machine and close the lid.

2. Select the Bake cycle

Turn on the bread maker. Select the White/Basic or Fruit/Nut (if your machine has this setting) setting, then the loaf size, and finally the crust color. Start the cycle. When the machine signals to add ingredients, add the candied fruits and raisins. (Some machines have a fruit/nut hopper where you can add the fruits and raisins when you start the machine. The machine will automatically add them to the dough during the baking process.)

When the cycle is finished and the bread is baked, carefully remove the pan from the machine. Use a potholder as the handle will be very hot. Let rest for a few minutes.

Remove the bread from the pan and allow to cool on a wire rack for at least 10 minutes before slicing.

Strawberry Shortcake Bread

PREP: 10 MINUTES /MAKES 1 LOAF/12 SLICE BREAD (1½ pounds)

Ingredients

1⅛ cups milk, at 80°F to 90°F
3 tablespoons melted butter, cooled
3 tablespoons sugar
1½ teaspoons salt
¾ cup sliced fresh strawberries
1 cup quick oats
2¼ cups white bread flour
1½ teaspoons bread machine or instant yeast

Directions

1. Preparing the Ingredients.

Place the ingredients in your bread machine as recommended by the manufacturer.
Program the machine for Basic/White bread, select light or medium crust, and press Start.
When the loaf is done, remove the bucket from the machine.

2. Select the Bake cycle

Let the loaf cool for 5 minutes.
Gently shake the bucket to remove the loaf, and turn it out onto a rack to cool.

Chocolate-Pistachio Bread

PREP: 10 MINUTES / MAKES ⅔ CUP (24 SLICES)

Ingredients

⅔ cup granulated sugar
½ cup butter, melted
¾ cup milk
1 egg
1½ cups all-purpose flour
1 cup chopped pistachio nuts
½ cup semisweet chocolate chips
⅓cup unsweetened baking cocoa
2 teaspoons baking powder
¼ teaspoon salt
Decorator sugar crystals, if desired

Directions

1. **Preparing the Ingredients.**

Place the ingredients in your bread machine as recommended by the manufacturer.
Program the machine for Basic/White bread, select light or medium crust, and press Start.
When the loaf is done, remove the bucket from the machine.

2. **Select the Bake cycle**

Let the loaf cool for 5 minutes.
Gently shake the bucket to remove the loaf. Cool in pan on cooling rack 10 minutes.
Cool completely, about 3 hours, before slicing. Wrap tightly and store at room temperature up to 4 days, or refrigerate.

Cinnamon-Raisin Bread

PREP: 10 MINUTES / MAKES 14 SLICES

Ingredients

1 cup water
2 Tbsp butter, softened
3 cups Gold Medal Better for Bread flour
3 Tbsp sugar
1½ tsp salt
1 tsp ground cinnamon
2½ tsp bread machine yeast
¾ cup raisins

Directions

1. **Preparing the Ingredients**

   Add each ingredient except the raisins to the bread machine in the order and at the temperature recommended by your bread machine manufacturer.

2. **Select the Bake cycle**

   Close the lid, select the sweet or basic bread, medium crust setting on your bread machine and press start.
   Add raisins 10 minutes before the last kneading cycle ends.
   When the bread machine has finished baking, remove the bread and put it on a cooling rack.

Spice Peach Bread

Ingredients

½ cup lukewarm heavy whipping cream
1 egg, beaten
1½ tablespoons unsalted butter, melted
3 tablespoons sugar
1½ teaspoons table salt
¼ teaspoon nutmeg, ground
½ teaspoon cinnamon, ground
3½ cups white bread flour
½ cup whole-wheat flour
1½ teaspoons bread machine yeast
1 cup canned peaches, drained and chopped

Directions

1. Preparing the Ingredients.

Choose the size of loaf you would like to make and measure your ingredients. Add all of the ingredients except for the peach to the bread pan in the order listed above. Place the pan in the bread machine and close the lid.

2. Select the Bake cycle

Turn on the bread maker. Select the White/Basic or Fruit/Nut (if your machine has this setting) setting, then the loaf size, and finally the crust color. Start the machine.

When the machine signals to add ingredients, add the peaches. (Some machines have a fruit/nut hopper where you can add the peaches when you start the machine. The machine will automatically add them to the dough during the baking process.) When the cycle is finished and the bread is baked, carefully remove the pan from the machine. Use a potholder as the handle will be very hot. Let rest for a few minutes.

Remove the bread from the pan and allow to cool on a wire rack for at least 10 minutes before slicing.

Pineapple Coconut Bread

Ingredients

6 tablespoons butter, at room temperature
2 eggs, at room temperature
½ cup coconut milk, at room temperature
½ cup pineapple juice, at room temperature
1 cup sugar
1½ teaspoons coconut extract
2 cups all-purpose flour
¾ cup shredded sweetened coconut
1 teaspoon baking powder
½ teaspoon salt

Directions

1. Preparing the Ingredients.

Place the butter, eggs, coconut milk, pineapple juice, sugar, and coconut extract in your bread machine.
Program the machine for Quick/Rapid bread and press Start.
While the wet ingredients are mixing, stir together the flour, coconut, baking powder, and salt in a small bowl.

2. Select the Bake cycle

After the first fast mixing is done and the machine signals, add the dry ingredients.
When the loaf is done, remove the bucket from the machine.
Let the loaf cool for 5 minutes.
Gently shake the bucket to remove the loaf, and turn it out onto a rack to cool.

Chocolate-Cherry Bread

PREP: 10 MINUTES /MAKES 1 LOAF

Ingredients

1½ teaspoons baking powder
½ teaspoon baking soda
¼ teaspoon salt
¾ cup sugar
½ cup butter, softened
2 eggs
1 teaspoon almond extract
1 teaspoon vanilla
1 container (8 oz) sour cream
½ cup chopped dried cherries
½ cup bittersweet or dark chocolate chips

Directions

1. Preparing the Ingredients.

Place the ingredients in your bread machine as recommended by the manufacturer.

Program the machine for Basic/White bread, select light or medium crust, and press Start. When the loaf is done, remove the bucket from the machine.

2. Select the Bake cycle

Let the loaf cool for 5 minutes. Gently shake the bucket to remove the loaf, and turn it out onto a rack to cool.

Cool completely, about 1 hour. Wrap tightly and store at room temperature up to 4 days, or refrigerate.

Cocoa Date Bread

PREP: 10 MINUTES /MAKES 1 LOAF/12 SLICE BREAD (1½ pounds)

Ingredients

¾ cup lukewarm water
½ cup lukewarm milk
2 tablespoons unsalted butter, melted
¼ cup honey
3 tablespoons molasses
1 tablespoon sugar
2 tablespoons skim milk powder
1 teaspoon table salt
1¼ cups white bread flour
2¼ cups whole-wheat flour
1 tablespoon cocoa powder, unsweetened
1½ teaspoons bread machine yeast
¾ cup dates, chopped

Directions

1. Preparing the Ingredients.

Choose the size of loaf you would like to make and measure your ingredients.

Add all of the ingredients except for the dates to the bread pan in the order listed above.

Place the pan in the bread machine and close the lid.

2. Select the Bake cycle

Turn on the bread maker. Select the White/Basic or Fruit/Nut (if your machine has this setting) setting, then the loaf size, and finally the crust color. Start the cycle.

When the machine signals to add ingredients, add the dates. (Some machines have a fruit/nut hopper where you can add the dates when you start the machine. The machine will automatically add them to the dough during the baking process.)

When the cycle is finished and the bread is baked, carefully remove the pan from the machine. Use a potholder as the handle will be very hot. Let rest for a few minutes.

Remove the bread from the pan and allow to cool on a wire rack for at least 10 minutes before slicing.

Warm Spiced Pumpkin Bread

PREP: 10 MINUTES /MAKES 1 LOAF/12 SLICE BREAD (1½ pounds)

Ingredients

Butter for greasing the bucket
1½ cups pumpkin purée
3 eggs, at room temperature
⅓ cup melted butter, cooled
1 cup sugar
3 cups all-purpose flour
1½ teaspoons baking powder
¾ teaspoon ground cinnamon
½ teaspoon baking soda
¼ teaspoon ground nutmeg
¼ teaspoon ground ginger
¼ teaspoon salt
Pinch ground cloves

Directions

1. **Preparing the Ingredients.**

Lightly grease the bread bucket with butter. Add the pumpkin, eggs, butter, and sugar.

2. **Select the Bake cycle**

Program the machine for Quick/Rapid bread and press Start. Let the wet ingredients be mixed by the paddles until the first fast mixing cycle is finished, about 10 minutes into the cycle. While the wet ingredients are mixing, stir together the flour, baking powder, cinnamon, baking soda, nutmeg, ginger, salt, and cloves until well blended. Add the dry ingredients to the bucket when the second fast mixing cycle starts. Scrape down the sides of the bucket once after the dry ingredients are mixed into the wet. When the loaf is done, remove the bucket from the machine. Let the loaf cool for 5 minutes. Gently shake the bucket to remove the loaf, and turn it out onto a rack to cool.

Ginger-Topped Pumpkin Bread

PREP: 10 MINUTES / MAKES 2 LOAVES (24 SLICES EACH)

Ingredients

1 can (15 oz) pumpkin (not pumpkin pie mix)
1⅔ cups granulated sugar
⅔ cup unsweetened applesauce
½ cup milk
2 teaspoons vanilla
1 cup fat-free egg product or 2 eggs plus 4 egg whites 3 cups all-purpose flour
2 teaspoons baking soda
1 teaspoon salt
1 teaspoon ground cinnamon
½ teaspoon baking powder
½ teaspoon ground cloves
glaze and topping
⅔ cup powdered sugar
2 to 3 teaspoons warm water
¼ teaspoon vanilla
3 tablespoons finely chopped crystallized ginger

Directions

1. **Preparing the Ingredients.**

Place the ingredients in your bread machine as recommended by the manufacturer. Program the machine for Basic/White bread, select light or medium crust, and press Start. When the loaf is done, remove the bucket from the machine.

2. **Select the Bake cycle**

Let the loaf cool for 5 minutes. Gently shake the bucket to remove the loaf, and turn it out onto a rack to cool. Cool completely, about 1 hour. In small bowl, mix powdered sugar, water and ¼ teaspoon vanilla until thin enough to drizzle. Drizzle over loaves. Sprinkle with ginger. Wrap tightly and store at room temperature up to 4 days, or refrigerate up to 10 days.

Strawberry Oat Bread
PREP: 10 MINUTES /MAKES 1 LOAF/16 SLICE BREAD (2 pounds)

Ingredients

1½ cups lukewarm milk
¼ cup unsalted butter, melted
¼ cup sugar
2 teaspoons table salt
1½ cups quick oats
3 cups white bread flour
2 teaspoons bread machine yeast
1 cup strawberries, sliced

Directions

1. **Preparing the Ingredients.**

Choose the size of loaf you would like to make and measure your ingredients.

Add all of the ingredients except for the strawberries to the bread pan in the order listed above.

Place the pan in the bread machine and close the lid.

2. **Select the Bake cycle**

Turn on the bread maker. Select the White/Basic or Fruit/Nut (if your machine has this setting) setting, then the loaf size, and finally the crust color. Start the cycle.

When the machine signals to add ingredients, add the strawberries. (Some machines have a fruit/nut hopper where you can add the strawberries when you start the machine. The machine will automatically add them to the dough during the baking process.)

When the cycle is finished and the bread is baked, carefully remove the pan from the machine. Use a potholder as the handle will be very hot. Let rest for a few minutes.

Remove the bread from the pan and allow to cool on a wire rack for at least 10 minutes before slicing.

Black Olive Bread
PREP: 10 MINUTES /MAKES 1 LOAF/12 SLICE BREAD (1½ pounds)

Ingredients

1 cup milk, at 80°F to 90°F
1½ tablespoons melted butter, cooled
1 teaspoon minced garlic
1½ tablespoons sugar
1 teaspoon salt
3 cups white bread flour
1 teaspoon bread machine or instant yeast
⅓ cup chopped black olives

Directions

1. **Preparing the Ingredients.**

Place the ingredients in your bread machine as recommended by the manufacturer.

Program the machine for Basic/White bread, select light or medium crust, and press Start.

When the loaf is done, remove the bucket from the machine.

2. **Select the Bake cycle**

Let the loaf cool for 5 minutes.

Gently shake the bucket to remove the loaf, and turn it out onto a rack to cool.

Cranberry & Golden Raisin Bread
PREP: 10 MINUTES /MAKES 14 SLICES

Ingredients

1⅓ cups water

4 Tbsp sliced butter

3 cups flour

1 cup old fashioned oatmeal

⅓ cup brown sugar

1 tsp salt

4 Tbsp dried cranberries

4 Tbsp golden raisins

2 tsp bread machine yeast

Directions

1. **Preparing the Ingredients**
   Add each ingredient except cranberries and golden raisins to the bread machine one by one, according to the manufacturer's instructions.
2. **Select the Bake cycle**
   Close the lid, select the sweet or basic bread, medium crust setting on your bread machine and press start.
   Add the cranberries and golden raisins 5 to 10 minutes before the last kneading cycle ends.
   When the bread machine has finished baking, remove the bread and put it on a cooling rack.

Zucchini Bread
PREP: 10 MINUTES / MAKES 2 LOAVES

Ingredients

3 cups shredded zucchini (2 to 3 medium)

1⅔ cups sugar

⅔ cup vegetable oil

2 teaspoons vanilla

4 eggs

3 cups all-purpose or whole wheat flour

2 teaspoons baking soda

1 teaspoon salt

1 teaspoon ground cinnamon

½ teaspoon baking powder

½ teaspoon ground cloves

½ cup chopped nuts

½ cup raisins, if desired

Directions

1. **Preparing the Ingredients.**

Place the ingredients in your bread machine as recommended by the manufacturer.

Program the machine for Basic/White bread, select light or medium crust, and press Start.

When the loaf is done, remove the bucket from the machine.

2. **Select the Bake cycle**

Let the loaf cool for 5 minutes. Gently shake the bucket to remove the loaf, and turn it out onto a rack to cool. Cool completely, about 2 hours, before slicing. Wrap tightly and store at room temperature up to 4 days, or refrigerate up to 10 days.

Cinnamon Figs Bread

PREP: 10 MINUTES /MAKES 1 LOAF/16 SLICE BREAD (2 pounds)

Ingredients

1⅛ cups lukewarm water

2¼ tablespoons unsalted butter, melted

3 tablespoons sugar

¾ teaspoon table salt

⅓ teaspoon cinnamon, ground

¾ teaspoon orange zest

Pinch ground nutmeg

1⅞ cups whole-wheat flour

1⅛ cups white bread flour

1½ teaspoons bread machine yeast

1 cup chopped plums or sliced figs

Directions

1. Preparing the Ingredients.

Choose the size of loaf you would like to make and measure your ingredients. Add all of the ingredients except for the plums to the bread pan in the order listed above. Place the pan in the bread machine and close the lid.

2. Select the Bake cycle

Turn on the bread maker. Select the White/Basic or Fruit/Nut (if your machine has this setting) setting, then the loaf size, and finally the crust color. Start the cycle.

When the machine signals to add ingredients, add the plums. (Some machines have a fruit/nut hopper where you can add the plums when you start the machine. The machine will automatically add them to the dough during the baking process.)

When the cycle is finished and the bread is baked, carefully remove the pan from the machine. Use a potholder as the handle will be very hot. Let rest for a few minutes.

Remove the bread from the pan and allow to cool on a wire rack for at least 10 minutes before slicing.

Robust Date Bread

PREP: 10 MINUTES /MAKES 1 LOAF/12 SLICE BREAD (1½ pounds)

Ingredients

¾ cup water, at 80°F to 90°F

½ cup milk, at 80°F

2 tablespoons melted butter, cooled

¼ cup honey

3 tablespoons molasses

1 tablespoon sugar

2 tablespoons skim milk powder

1 teaspoon salt

2¼ cups whole-wheat flour

1¼ cups white bread flour

1 tablespoon unsweetened cocoa powder

1½ teaspoons bread machine or instant yeast

¾ cup chopped dates

Directions

1. Preparing the Ingredients.

Place the ingredients, except the dates, in your bread machine as recommended by the manufacturer.

Program the machine for Basic/White bread, select light or medium crust, and press Start. When the machine signals, add the chopped dates, or put them in the nut/raisin hopper and let the machine add them automatically.

2. Select the Bake cycle

When the loaf is done, remove the bucket from the machine. Let the loaf cool for 5 minutes. Gently shake the bucket to remove the loaf, and turn it out onto a rack to cool.

Whole Wheat Banana Bread with Caramel Glaze

PREP: 10 MINUTES /MAKES 1 LOAF

Ingredients

2 cups white whole wheat flour
1 teaspoon baking soda
½ teaspoon baking powder
½ teaspoon salt
½ cup butter, softened
½ cup granulated sugar
½ cup packed brown sugar
2 eggs
1⅓ cups mashed very ripe bananas (3 medium)
½ cup chopped pecans, toasted glaze
½ cup packed brown sugar
3 tablespoons whipping cream
2 tablespoons butter, cut up
1 tablespoon light corn syrup
½ cup chopped pecans, toasted

Directions

1. Preparing the Ingredients.

Place the ingredients in your bread machine as recommended by the manufacturer. Program the machine for Basic/White bread, select light or medium crust, and press Start. When the loaf is done, remove the bucket from the machine. Let the loaf cool for 5 minutes. Gently shake the bucket to remove the loaf, and turn it out onto a rack to cool.

2. Select the Bake cycle

Cool completely, about 2 hours. Meanwhile, in 1-quart saucepan, combine all glaze ingredients except pecans. Bring to a boil over medium heat, stirring frequently, until sugar has melted. Boil, without stirring, 45 to 60 seconds or until thickened. Pour into small bowl; refrigerate 30 to 40 minutes or until cool enough to spread, stirring occasionally. Spread caramel over top of cooled bread; sprinkle ½ cup chopped pecans over caramel. Let stand until set. To toast pecans, bake in ungreased shallow pan at 325°F for 7 to 11 minutes, stirring occasionally, until light brown. When stirring the caramel, make sure all of the sugar is dissolved before it boils and thickens, or crystallization can occur. If there is sugar that has not dissolved on the side of the pan, use a pastry brush dipped in water to wash the sugar crystals down into the caramel before boiling.

Cranberry Honey Bread

PREP: 10 MINUTES /MAKES 1 LOAF/16 SLICE BREAD (2 pounds)

Ingredients

1¼ cups + 1 tablespoon lukewarm water

¼ cup unsalted butter, melted

3 tablespoons honey or molasses

4 cups white bread flour

½ cup cornmeal

2 teaspoons table salt

2½ teaspoons bread machine yeast

¾ cup cranberries, dried

Directions

1. **Preparing the Ingredients.**

Choose the size of loaf you would like to make and measure your ingredients.

Add all of the ingredients except for the dried cranberries to the bread pan in the order listed above.

Place the pan in the bread machine and close the lid.

2. **Select the Bake cycle**

Turn on the bread maker. Select the White/Basic or Fruit/Nut (if your machine has this setting) setting, then the loaf size, and finally the crust color. Start the cycle.

When the machine signals to add ingredients, add the dried cranberries. (Some machines have a fruit/nut hopper where you can add the dried cranberries when you start the machine. The machine will automatically add them to the dough during the baking process.)

When the cycle is finished and the bread is baked, carefully remove the pan from the machine. Use a potholder as the handle will be very hot. Let rest for a few minutes.

Remove the bread from the pan and allow to cool on a wire rack for at least 10 minutes before slicing.

Apple Spice Bread

PREP: 10 MINUTES /MAKES 1 LOAF/16 SLICE BREAD (2 pounds)

Ingredients

1⅓ cup milk, at 80°F to 90°F

3⅓ tablespoons melted butter, cooled

2⅔ tablespoons sugar

2 teaspoons salt

1⅓ teaspoons ground cinnamon

Pinch ground cloves

4 cups white bread flour

2¼ teaspoons bread machine or active dry yeast

1⅓ cups finely diced peeled apple

Directions

1. **Preparing the Ingredients.**

Place the ingredients, except the apple, in your bread machine as recommended by the manufacturer.

Program the machine for Basic/White bread, select light or medium crust, and press Start.

When the machine signals, add the apple to the bucket, or add it just before the end of the second kneading cycle if your machine does not have a signal.

When the loaf is done, remove the bucket from the machine.

2. **Select the Bake cycle**

Let the loaf cool for 5 minutes.

Gently shake the bucket to remove the loaf, and turn it out onto a rack to cool.

Poppy Seed–Lemon Bread

PREP: 10 MINUTES /MAKES 1 LOAF

Ingredients

1 cup sugar

¼ cup grated lemon peel

1 cup milk

¾ cup vegetable oil

2 tablespoons poppy seed

2 teaspoons baking powder

½ teaspoon salt

2 eggs, slightly beaten

Directions

1. Preparing the Ingredients.

Place the ingredients in your bread machine as recommended by the manufacturer.

Program the machine for Basic/White bread, select light or medium crust, and press Start.

When the loaf is done, remove the bucket from the machine.

2. Select the Bake cycle

Let the loaf cool for 5 minutes.

Gently shake the bucket to remove the loaf, and turn it out onto a rack to cool.

Cool completely, about 2 hours. Wrap tightly and store at room temperature up to 4 days, or refrigerate.

Ginger-Carrot-Nut Bread

PREP: 10 MINUTES /MAKES 1 LOAF

Ingredients

2 eggs

¾ cup packed brown sugar

⅓cup vegetable oil

½ cup milk

1 teaspoon vanilla

2 cups all-purpose flour

2 teaspoons baking powder

1 teaspoon ground ginger

½ teaspoon salt

1 cup shredded carrots (2 medium)

½ cup chopped nuts

Directions

1. Preparing the Ingredients.

Place the ingredients in your bread machine as recommended by the manufacturer.

Program the machine for Basic/White bread, select light or medium crust, and press Start.

When the loaf is done, remove the bucket from the machine.

2. Select the Bake cycle

Let the loaf cool for 5 minutes.

Gently shake the bucket to remove the loaf, and turn it out onto a rack to cool.

Cool completely, about 2 hours, before slicing. Wrap tightly and store at room temperature up to 4 days, or refrigerate.

Orange Bread

Ingredients

1¼ cups lukewarm milk

¼ cup orange juice

¼ cup sugar

1½ tablespoons unsalted butter, melted

1¼ teaspoons table salt

4 cups white bread flour

Zest of 1 orange

1¾ teaspoons bread machine yeast

Directions

1. Preparing the Ingredients.

Choose the size of loaf you would like to make and measure your ingredients.

Add the ingredients to the bread pan in the order listed above.

Place the pan in the bread machine and close the lid.

2. Select the Bake cycle

Turn on the bread maker. Select the White/Basic setting, then the loaf size, and finally the crust color. Start the cycle.

When the cycle is finished and the bread is baked, carefully remove the pan from the machine. Use a potholder as the handle will be very hot. Let rest for a few minutes.

Remove the bread from the pan and allow to cool on a wire rack for at least 10 minutes before slicing.

Lemon-Lime Blueberry Bread

Ingredients

¾ cup plain yogurt, at room temperature

½ cup water, at 80°F to 90°F

3 tablespoons honey

1 tablespoon melted butter, cooled

1½ teaspoons salt

½ teaspoon lemon extract

1 teaspoon lime zest

1 cup dried blueberries

3 cups white bread flour

2¼ teaspoons bread machine or instant yeast

Directions

1. Preparing the Ingredients.

Place the ingredients in your bread machine as recommended by the manufacturer.

Program the machine for Basic/White bread, select light or medium crust, and press Start.

When the loaf is done, remove the bucket from the machine.

2. Select the Bake cycle

Let the loaf cool for 5 minutes.

Gently shake the bucket to remove the loaf, and turn it out onto a rack to cool.

Apple-Fig Bread with Honey Glaze
PREP: 10 MINUTES /MAKES 1 LOAF

Ingredients

1½ cups all-purpose flour

1½ teaspoons ground cinnamon

1 teaspoon baking powder

½ teaspoon salt

½ teaspoon ground nutmeg

¼ teaspoon ground allspice

⅔ cup granulated sugar

½ cup vegetable oil

1 egg

1 egg yolk

1½ teaspoons vanilla

½ cup milk

1 cup chopped peeled apples

½ cup dried figs, chopped glaze

⅓to ½ cup powdered sugar

2 tablespoons honey

1 tablespoon butter, softened

Dash ground allspice

Directions

1. **Preparing the Ingredients.**

Place the ingredients in your bread machine as recommended by the manufacturer. Program the machine for Basic/White bread, select light or medium crust, and press Start. When the loaf is done, remove the bucket from the machine.

2. **Select the Bake cycle**

Let the loaf cool for 5 minutes. Gently shake the bucket to remove the loaf, and turn it out onto a rack to cool.

Cool completely, about 2 hours. In small bowl, beat ⅓cup powdered sugar, the honey, butter and dash of allspice until smooth, slowly adding additional powdered sugar for desired glaze consistency. Spread glaze over top of loaf. Let stand until set. (Glaze will remain slightly tacky to the touch.) Wrap tightly and store in refrigerator.

Honey Banana Bread
PREP: 10 MINUTES /MAKES 1 LOAF/12 SLICE BREAD (1½ pounds)

Ingredients

½ cup lukewarm milk

1 cup banana, mashed

1 egg, beaten

1½ tablespoons unsalted butter, melted

3 tablespoons honey

1 teaspoon pure vanilla extract

½ teaspoon table salt

1 cup whole-wheat flour

1¼ cups white bread flour

1½ teaspoons bread machine yeast

Directions

1. **Preparing the Ingredients.**

Choose the size of loaf you would like to make and measure your ingredients.

Add the ingredients to the bread pan in the order listed above.

Place the pan in the bread machine and close the lid.

2. **Select the Bake cycle**

Turn on the bread maker. Select the Sweet setting, then the loaf size, and finally the crust color. Start the cycle.

When the cycle is finished and the bread is baked, carefully remove the pan from the machine. Use a potholder as the handle will be very hot. Let rest for a few minutes.

Remove the bread from the pan and allow to cool on a wire rack for at least 10 minutes before slicing.

Banana Whole-Wheat Bread
PREP: 10 MINUTES /MAKES 1 LOAF/12 SLICE BREAD (1½ pounds)

Ingredients

½ cup milk, at 80°F to 90°F

1 cup mashed banana

1 egg, at room temperature

1½ tablespoons melted butter, cooled

3 tablespoons honey

1 teaspoon pure vanilla extract

½ teaspoon salt

1 cup whole-wheat flour

1¼ cups white bread flour

1½ teaspoons bread machine or instant yeast

Directions

1. **Preparing the Ingredients.**

Place the ingredients in your bread machine as recommended by the manufacturer. When the loaf is done, remove the bucket from the machine.

2. **Select the Bake cycle**

Program the machine for Sweet bread and press Start Let the loaf cool for 5 minutes. Gently shake the bucket to remove the loaf, and turn it out onto a rack to cool.

Oatmeal-Streusel Bread
PREP: 10 MINUTES /MAKES 1 LOAF

Ingredients

Streusel

¼ cup packed brown sugar

¼ cup chopped walnuts, toasted

2 teaspoons ground cinnamon

Bread

1 cup all-purpose flour

½ cup whole wheat flour

½ cup old-fashioned oats

2 tablespoons ground flaxseed or flaxseed meal

1 teaspoon baking powder

½ teaspoon salt

¼ teaspoon baking soda

¾ cup packed brown sugar

⅔ cup vegetable oil

2 eggs

¼ cup sour cream

2 teaspoons vanilla

½ cup milk

Icing

¾ to 1 cup powdered sugar

1 tablespoon milk

2 teaspoons light corn syrup

Directions

1. **Preparing the Ingredients.** Place the ingredients in your bread machine as recommended by the manufacturer. Program the machine for Basic/White bread, select light or medium crust, and press Start. When the loaf is done, remove the bucket from the machine. Let the loaf cool for 5 minutes.

2. **Select the Bake cycle.** Gently shake the bucket to remove the loaf, and turn it out onto a rack to cool. Cool on cooling rack 10 minutes. Cool completely, about 2 hours. In small bowl, beat all icing ingredients, adding enough of the powdered sugar for desired drizzling consistency. Drizzle icing over bread. Let stand until set. Wrap tightly and store at room temperature up to 4 days, or refrigerate. To toast walnuts, bake in ungreased shallow pan at 350°F for 7 to 11 minutes, stirring occasionally, until light brown.

Garlic Olive Bread

PREP: 10 MINUTES /MAKES 1 LOAF/12 SLICE BREAD (1½ pounds)

Ingredients

1 cup lukewarm milk

1½ tablespoons unsalted butter, melted

1 teaspoon garlic, minced

1½ tablespoons sugar

1 teaspoon table salt

3 cups white bread flour

1 teaspoon bread machine yeast

⅓ cup black olives, chopped

16 slice bread (2 pounds)

1⅓ cups lukewarm milk

2 tablespoons unsalted butter, melted

1⅓ teaspoons garlic, minced

2 tablespoons sugar

1⅓ teaspoons table salt

4 cups white bread flour

1½ teaspoons bread machine yeast

½ cup black olives, chopped

Directions

1. **Preparing the Ingredients.** Choose the size of loaf you would like to make and measure your ingredients. Add all of the ingredients except for the olives to the bread pan in the order listed above. Place the pan in the bread machine and close the lid.

2. **Select the Bake cycle** Turn on the bread maker. Select the White/Basic or Fruit/Nut (if your machine has this setting) setting, then the loaf size, and finally the crust color. Start the machine. When the machine signals to add ingredients, add the olives. (Some machines have a fruit/nut hopper where you can add the olives when you start the machine. The machine will automatically add them to the dough during the baking process.) When the cycle is finished and the bread is baked, carefully remove the pan from the machine. Use a potholder as the handle will be very hot. Let rest for a few minutes. Remove the bread from the pan and allow to cool on a wire rack for at least 10 minutes before slicing.

Orange Cranberry Bread

PREP: 10 MINUTES /MAKES 1 LOAF/12 SLICE BREAD (1½ pounds)

Ingredients

¾ cup milk, at 80°F to 90°F

¾ cup sugar

⅔ cup melted butter, cooled

2 eggs, at room temperature

¼ cup freshly squeezed orange juice, at room temperature

1 tablespoon orange zest

1 teaspoon pure vanilla extract

2¼ cups all-purpose flour

1 cup sweetened dried cranberries

1½ teaspoons baking powder

½ teaspoon baking soda

½ teaspoon salt

¼ teaspoon ground nutmeg

Directions

1. **Preparing the Ingredients.** Place the milk, sugar, butter, eggs, orange juice, zest, and vanilla in your bread machine.

2. **Select the Bake cycle.** Program the machine for Quick/Rapid bread and press Start.

While the wet ingredients are mixing, stir together the flour, cranberries, baking powder, baking soda, salt, and nutmeg in a medium bowl. After the first fast mixing is done and the machine signals, add the dry ingredients.

When the loaf is done, remove the bucket from the machine. Let the loaf cool for 5 minutes. Gently shake the bucket to remove the loaf, and turn it out onto a rack to cool.

Brown Bread with Raisins

PREP: 10 MINUTES /MAKES 1 LOAF/16 SLICE BREAD (2 pounds)

Ingredients

1 cup all-purpose flour
1 cup whole wheat flour
1 cup whole-grain cornmeal
1 cup raisins
2 cups buttermilk
¾ cup molasses
2 teaspoons baking soda
1 teaspoon salt

Directions

1. **Preparing the Ingredients.**

Place the ingredients in your bread machine as recommended by the manufacturer.
Program the machine for Basic/White bread, select light or medium crust, and press Start.
When the loaf is done, remove the bucket from the machine.

2. **Select the Bake cycle**

Let the loaf cool for 5 minutes.
Gently shake the bucket to remove the loaf, and turn it out onto a rack to cool.
Cool 30 minutes on cooling rack before slicing. Serve warm.

Cinnamon Pumpkin Bread

PREP: 10 MINUTES /MAKES 1 LOAF/16 SLICE BREAD (2 pounds)

Ingredients

2 cups pumpkin puree
4 eggs, slightly beaten
½ cup unsalted butter, melted
1¼ cups sugar
½ teaspoon table salt
4 cups white bread flour
1 teaspoon cinnamon, ground
¾ teaspoon baking soda
½ teaspoon nutmeg, ground
½ teaspoon ginger, ground
Pinch ground cloves
2 teaspoons baking powder

Directions

1. **Preparing the Ingredients.**

Choose the size of loaf you would like to make and measure your ingredients.
Add the ingredients to the bread pan in the order listed above.
Place the pan in the bread machine and close the lid.

2. **Select the Bake cycle**

Turn on the bread maker. Select the Quick/Rapid setting, then the loaf size, and finally the crust color. Start the cycle.
When the cycle is finished and the bread is baked, carefully remove the pan from the machine. Use a potholder as the handle will be very hot. Let rest for a few minutes.
Remove the bread from the pan and allow to cool on a wire rack for at least 10 minutes before slicing.

Plum Orange Bread
PREP: 10 MINUTES /MAKES 1 LOAF/12 SLICE BREAD (1½ pounds)

Ingredients
1⅛ cup water, at 80°F to 90°F
2¼ tablespoons melted butter, cooled
3 tablespoons sugar
¾ teaspoon salt
¾ teaspoon orange zest
⅓ teaspoon ground cinnamon
Pinch ground nutmeg
1¾ cups plus 2 tablespoons whole-wheat flour
1⅛ cups white bread flour
1½ teaspoons bread machine or instant yeast
1 cup chopped fresh plums

Directions
1. Preparing the Ingredients.
Place the ingredients, except the plums, in your bread machine as recommended by the manufacturer.
Program the machine for Basic/White bread, select light or medium crust, and press Start.
When the machine signals, add the chopped plums.
When the loaf is done, remove the bucket from the machine.
2. Select the Bake cycle
Let the loaf cool for 5 minutes.
Gently shake the bucket to remove the loaf, and turn it out onto a rack to cool.

Blueberries 'n Orange Bread
PREP: 10 MINUTES /MAKES 1 LOAF/16 SLICE BREAD (2 pounds)

Ingredients
3 cups Original Bisquick mix
½ cup granulated sugar
1 tablespoon grated orange peel
½ cup milk
3 tablespoons vegetable oil
2 eggs
1 cup fresh or frozen (rinsed and drained) blueberries glaze
½ cup powdered sugar
3 to 4 teaspoons orange juice
Additional grated orange peel, if desired

Directions
1. Preparing the Ingredients.
Place the ingredients in your bread machine as recommended by the manufacturer.
2. Select the Bake cycle
Program the machine for Basic/White bread, select light or medium crust, and press Start. When the loaf is done, remove the bucket from the machine. Let the loaf cool for 5 minutes.
Gently shake the bucket to remove the loaf, and turn it out onto a rack to cool. Cool completely, about 45 minutes.
In small bowl, mix powdered sugar and orange juice until smooth and thin enough to drizzle. Drizzle glaze over bread; sprinkle with additional orange peel.

Peaches and Cream Bread
PREP: 10 MINUTES /MAKES 1 LOAF/12 SLICE BREAD (1½ pounds)

Ingredients
¾ cup canned peaches, drained and chopped

⅓ cup heavy whipping cream, at 80°F to 90°F

1 egg, at room temperature

1 tablespoon melted butter, cooled

2¼ tablespoons sugar

1⅛ teaspoons salt

⅓ teaspoon ground cinnamon

⅛ teaspoon ground nutmeg

⅓ cup whole-wheat flour

2⅔ cups white bread flour

1⅛ teaspoons bread machine or instant yeast

Directions
1. Preparing the Ingredients.
Place the ingredients in your bread machine as recommended by the manufacturer.

Select the Bake cycle
Program the machine for Basic/White bread, select light or medium crust, and press Start. When the loaf is done, remove the bucket from the machine. Let the loaf cool for 5 minutes. Gently shake the bucket to remove the loaf, and turn it out onto a rack to cool.

Gluten-Free Glazed Lemon-Pecan Bread
PREP: 10 MINUTES /MAKES 1 LOAF/12 SLICE BREAD (1½ pounds)

Ingredients
½ cup white rice flour

½ cup tapioca flour

½ cup potato starch

¼ cup sweet white sorghum flour

¼ cup garbanzo and fava flour

1 teaspoon xanthan gum

1 teaspoon gluten-free baking powder

1 teaspoon baking soda

½ teaspoon salt

2 eggs

½ cup sunflower or canola oil or melted ghee

¼ cup almond milk, soymilk or regular milk

½ teaspoon cider vinegar

1 tablespoon grated lemon peel

¼ cup fresh lemon juice

⅔ cup granulated sugar

½ cup chopped pecans

glaze

2 tablespoons fresh lemon juice

1 cup gluten-free powdered sugar

Directions
1. Preparing the Ingredients.
Place the ingredients in your bread machine as recommended by the manufacturer.

2. Select the Bake cycle
Program the machine for Basic/White bread, select light or medium crust, and press Start. When the loaf is done, remove the bucket from the machine. Let the loaf cool for 5 minutes. Gently shake the bucket to remove the loaf, and turn it out onto a rack to cool.

In small bowl, stir all glaze ingredients until smooth. With fork, poke holes in top of loaf; drizzle glaze over loaf. Serve warm.

Fresh Blueberry Bread

Ingredients

1 cup plain Greek yogurt, at room temperature
½ cup milk, at room temperature
3 tablespoons butter, at room temperature
2 eggs, at room temperature
½ cup sugar
¼ cup light brown sugar
1 teaspoon pure vanilla extract
½ teaspoon lemon zest
2 cups all-purpose flour
1 tablespoon baking powder
¾ teaspoon salt
¼ teaspoon ground nutmeg
1 cup blueberries

Directions

1. **Preparing the Ingredients.**

Place the yogurt, milk, butter, eggs, sugar, brown sugar, vanilla, and zest in your bread machine.

2. **Select the Bake cycle**

Program the machine for Quick/Rapid bread and press Start. While the wet ingredients are mixing, stir together the flour, baking powder, salt, and nutmeg in a medium bowl. After the first fast mixing is done and the machine signals, add the dry ingredients. When the second mixing cycle is complete, stir in the blueberries. When the loaf is done, remove the bucket from the machine. Let the loaf cool for 5 minutes. Gently shake the bucket to remove the loaf, and turn it out onto a rack to cool.

Gluten-Free Best-Ever Banana Bread

Ingredients

½ cup tapioca flour
½ cup white rice flour
½ cup potato starch
¼ cup garbanzo and fava flour
¼ cup sweet white sorghum flour
1 teaspoon xanthan gum
½ teaspoon guar gum
1 teaspoon gluten-free baking powder
1 teaspoon baking soda
1 teaspoon salt
1 teaspoon ground cinnamon
¾ cup packed brown sugar
1 cup mashed very ripe bananas (2 medium)
½ cup ghee (measured melted)
¼ cup almond milk, soymilk or regular milk
1 teaspoon gluten-free vanilla
2 eggs

Directions

1. **Preparing the Ingredients.**

Place the ingredients in your bread machine as recommended by the manufacturer. Program the machine for Basic/White bread, select light or medium crust, and press Start. When the loaf is done, remove the bucket from the machine.

2. **Select the Bake cycle**

Let the loaf cool for 5 minutes. Gently shake the bucket to remove the loaf, and turn it out onto a rack to cool.
Cool completely, about 1 hour. Store tightly wrapped in refrigerator.

Blueberry Oatmeal Bread

PREP: 10 MINUTES /MAKES 1 LOAF/12 SLICE BREAD (1½ pounds)

Ingredients

¾ cup milk, at 80°F to 90°F

1 egg, at room temperature

2¼ tablespoons melted butter, cooled

1½ tablespoons honey

½ cup rolled oats

2⅓ cups white bread flour

1⅛ teaspoons salt

1½ teaspoons bread machine or instant yeast

½ cup dried blueberries

Directions

1. **Preparing the Ingredients.**

Place the ingredients, except the blueberries, in your bread machine as recommended by the manufacturer.

Program the machine for Basic/White bread, select light or medium crust, and press Start.

Add the blueberries when the machine signals or 5 minutes before the second kneading cycle is finished.

2. **Select the Bake cycle**

When the loaf is done, remove the bucket from the machine.

Let the loaf cool for 5 minutes.

Gently shake the bucket to remove the loaf, and turn it out onto a rack to cool.

Blueberry-Basil Loaf

PREP: 10 MINUTES /MAKES 1 LOAF/12 SLICE BREAD (1½ pounds)

Ingredients

1¼ cups fresh blueberries

1 tablespoon all-purpose flour

2¼ cups all-purpose flour

1 cup granulated sugar

2 teaspoons baking powder

1 teaspoon grated lemon peel

½ teaspoon salt

1 cup buttermilk

6 tablespoons butter, melted

1 teaspoon vanilla

2 eggs

¼ cup coarsely chopped fresh basil leaves

Topping

½ cup packed brown sugar

¼ cup butter, melted

⅔ cup all-purpose flour

Directions

1. **Preparing the Ingredients.**

Place the ingredients in your bread machine as recommended by the manufacturer.

Program the machine for Basic/White bread, select light or medium crust, and press Start.

2. **Select the Bake cycle**

When the loaf is done, remove the bucket from the machine.

Let the loaf cool for 5 minutes. Gently shake the bucket to remove the loaf, and turn it out onto a rack to cool.

Cool completely, about 1 hour.

Savory Sweet Potato Pan Bread

PREP: 10 MINUTES /MAKES 1 LOAF/8 SLICE BREAD (1 pound)

Ingredients

1½ cups uncooked shredded dark-orange sweet potato (about ½ potato) ½ cup sugar

¼ cup vegetable oil

2 eggs

¾ cup all-purpose flour

¾ cup whole wheat flour

2 teaspoons dried minced onion

1 teaspoon dried rosemary leaves, crumbled

1 teaspoon baking soda

½ teaspoon salt

¼ teaspoon baking powder

2 teaspoons sesame seed

Directions

1. Preparing the Ingredients.

Place the ingredients in your bread machine as recommended by the manufacturer.

Program the machine for Basic/White bread, select light or medium crust, and press Start.

When the loaf is done, remove the bucket from the machine.

2. Select the Bake cycle

Let the loaf cool for 5 minutes.

Gently shake the bucket to remove the loaf, and turn it out onto a rack to cool.

Serve warm.

Cardamom Cranberry Bread

PREP: 10 MINUTES /MAKES 1 LOAF

Ingredients

1¾ cups water

2 Tbsp brown sugar

1½ tsp salt

2 Tbsp coconut oil

4 cups flour

2 tsp cinnamon

2 tsp cardamom

1 cup dried cranberries

2 tsp yeast

Directions

1. **Preparing the Ingredients**

   Add each ingredient except the dried cranberries to the bread machine in the order and at the temperature recommended by your bread machine manufacturer.

2. **Select the Bake cycle**

   Close the lid, select the basic bread, medium crust setting on your bread machine and press start.

   Add the dried cranberries 5 to 10 minutes before the last kneading cycle ends.

   When the bread machine has finished baking, remove the bread and put it on a cooling rack.

Rosemary Cranberry Pecan Bread

PREP: 10 MINUTES / MAKES 14 SLICES

Ingredients

1⅓ cups water, plus

2 Tbsp water

2 Tbsp butter

2 tsp salt

4 cups bread flour

¾ cup dried sweetened cranberries

¾ cup toasted chopped pecans

2 Tbsp non-fat powdered milk

¼ cup sugar

2 tsp yeast

Directions

1. **Preparing the Ingredients**

   Add each ingredient to the bread machine in the order and at the temperature recommended by your bread machine manufacturer.

2. **Select the Bake cycle**

   Close the lid, select the basic bread, medium crust setting on your bread machine and press start.

   When the bread machine has finished baking, remove the bread and put it on a cooling rack.

Harvest Fruit Bread

PREP: 10 MINUTES / MAKES 14 SLICES

Ingredients

1 cup plus 2 Tbsp water (70°F to 80°F)

1 egg

3 Tbsp butter, softened

¼ cup packed brown sugar

1½ tsp salt

¼ tsp ground nutmeg

Dash allspice

3¾ cups plus 1 Tbsp bread flour

2 tsp active dry yeast

1 cup dried fruit (dried cherries, cranberries and/or raisins)

⅓ cup chopped pecans

Directions

1. **Preparing the Ingredients**

   Add each ingredient except the fruit and pecans to the bread machine in the order and at the temperature recommended by your bread machine manufacturer.

2. **Select the Bake cycle**

   Close the lid, select the basic bread, medium crust setting on your bread machine, and press start.

   Just before the final kneading, add the fruit and pecans.

   When the bread machine has finished baking, remove the bread and put it on a cooling rack.

Cranberry Walnut Wheat Bread

PREP: 10 MINUTES /MAKES 14 SLICES

Ingredients

1 cup warm water

1 tablespoon molasses

2 tablespoons butter

1 teaspoon salt

2 cups 100% whole wheat flour

1 cup unbleached flour

2 tablespoons dry milk

1 cup cranberries

1 cup walnuts, chopped

2 teaspoons active dry yeast

Directions

1. **Preparing the Ingredients**

   Add the liquid ingredients to the bread maker pan.

   Add the dry ingredients, except the yeast, walnuts and cranberries.

   Make a well in the center of the bread flour and add the yeast.

   Insert the pan into your bread maker and secure the lid.

2. **Select the Bake cycle**

   Select Wheat Bread setting, choose your preferred crust color, and press Start.

   Add cranberries and walnuts after first kneading cycle is finished.

   Remove the bread from the oven and turn it out of the pan onto a cooling rack and allow it to cool completely before slicing.

SPICE AND NUT BREAD

Super Spice Bread
PREP: 10 MINUTES /MAKES 1 LOAF/16 SLICE BREAD (2 pounds)

Ingredients

1⅓ cups lukewarm milk

2 eggs, at room temperature

2 tablespoons unsalted butter, melted

2⅔ tablespoons honey

1⅓ teaspoons table salt

4 cups white bread flour

1⅓ teaspoons ground cinnamon

⅔ teaspoon ground cardamom

⅔ teaspoon ground nutmeg

2¼ teaspoons bread machine yeast

Directions
1. Preparing the Ingredients.
Choose the size of loaf you would like to make and measure your ingredients.

Add the ingredients to the bread pan in the order listed above.

Place the pan in the bread machine and close the lid.

Turn on the bread maker. Select the White/Basic setting, then the loaf size, and finally the crust color. Start the cycle.

2. Select the Bake cycle
When the cycle is finished and the bread is baked, carefully remove the pan from the machine. Use a potholder as the handle will be very hot. Let rest for a few minutes.

Remove the bread from the pan and allow to cool on a wire rack for at least 10 minutes before slicing.

Fragrant Herb Bread
PREP: 10 MINUTES /MAKES 1 LOAF/12 SLICE BREAD (1½ pounds)

Ingredients

1⅛ cups water, at 80°F to 90°F

1½ tablespoons melted butter, cooled

1½ tablespoons sugar

1 teaspoon salt

3 tablespoons skim milk powder

1 teaspoon dried thyme

1 teaspoon dried chives

1 teaspoon dried oregano

3 cups white bread flour

1¼ teaspoons bread machine or instant yeast

Directions
1. Preparing the Ingredients.
Place the ingredients in your bread machine as recommended by the manufacturer.

Program the machine for Basic/White bread, select light or medium crust, and press Start.

2. Select the Bake cycle
When the loaf is done, remove the bucket from the machine.

Let the loaf cool for 5 minutes.

Gently shake the bucket to remove the loaf, and turn it out onto a rack to cool.

Citrus and Walnut Bread
PREP: 10 MINUTES   PLUS FERMENTING TIME /MAKES 14 SLICES

Ingredients
¾ cup lemon yogurt
½ cup orange juice
5 tsp caster sugar
1 tsp salt
2.5 Tbsp butter
2 cups unbleached white bread flour
1½ tsp easy blend dried yeast
⅓ cup chopped walnuts
2 tsp grated lemon rind
2 tsp grated orange rind

Directions
1. **Preparing the Ingredients.**
    Add each ingredient except the walnuts and orange and lemon rind to the bread machine one by one, as per the manufacturer's instructions.
2. **Select the Bake cycle**
    Close the lid, select the basic bread, medium crust setting on your bread machine, and press start.
    Add the walnuts, and orange and lemon rind during the 2nd kneading cycle:
    When the bread machine has finished baking, remove the bread and put it on a cooling rack.

Almond Milk Bread
PREP: 10 MINUTES /MAKES 1 LOAF/12 SLICE BREAD (1½ pounds)

Ingredients
¾ cup lukewarm milk
2 eggs, at room temperature
2 tablespoons butter, melted and cooled
¼ cup sugar
1 teaspoon table salt
2 teaspoons lemon zest
3 cups white bread flour
2 teaspoons bread machine yeast
⅓ cup slivered almonds, chopped
⅓ cup golden raisins, chopped

Directions
1. **Preparing the Ingredients.**
Choose the size of loaf you would like to make and measure your ingredients.
Add all of the ingredients except for the raisins and almonds to the bread pan in the order listed above.
Place the pan in the bread machine and close the lid.

2. **Select the Bake cycle**
Turn on the bread maker. Select the White/Basic or Fruit/Nut (if your machine has this setting) setting, then the loaf size, and finally the crust color. Start the cycle.
When the machine signals to add ingredients, add the raisins and almonds. (Some machines have a fruit/nut hopper where you can add the raisins and almonds when you start the machine. The machine will automatically add them to the dough during the baking process.)
When the cycle is finished and the bread is baked, carefully remove the pan from the machine. Use a potholder as the handle will be very hot. Let rest for a few minutes.
Remove the bread from the pan and allow to cool on a wire rack for at least 10 minutes before slicing.

Rosemary Bread
PREP: 10 MINUTES /MAKES 1 LOAF/12 SLICE BREAD (1½ pounds)

Ingredients
1¼ cups water, at 80°F to 90°F

2½ tablespoons melted butter, cooled

1 tablespoon sugar

1½ teaspoons salt

1½ tablespoons finely chopped fresh rosemary

3 cups white bread flour

2 teaspoons bread machine or instant yeast

Directions
1. Preparing the Ingredients.
Place the ingredients in your bread machine as recommended by the manufacturer.

Program the machine for Basic/White bread, select light or medium crust, and press Start.

When the loaf is done, remove the bucket from the machine.

2. Select the Bake cycle
Let the loaf cool for 5 minutes.

Gently shake the bucket to remove the loaf, and turn it out onto a rack to cool.

Cinnamon Milk Bread
PREP: 10 MINUTES /MAKES 1 LOAF/12 SLICE BREAD (1½ pounds)

Ingredients
1 cup lukewarm milk

1 egg, at room temperature

¼ cup unsalted butter, melted

½ cup sugar

½ teaspoon table salt

3 cups white bread flour

1½ teaspoons ground cinnamon

2 teaspoons bread machine yeast

Directions
1. Preparing the Ingredients.
Choose the size of loaf you would like to make and measure your ingredients.

Add the ingredients to the bread pan in the order listed above.

Place the pan in the bread machine and close the lid.

Turn on the bread maker. Select the White/Basic setting, then the loaf size, and finally the crust color. Start the cycle.

2. Select the Bake cycle
When the cycle is finished and the bread is baked, carefully remove the pan from the machine. Use a potholder as the handle will be very hot. Let rest for a few minutes.

Remove the bread from the pan and allow to cool on a wire rack for at least 10 minutes before slicing.

Spicy Cajun Bread

PREP: 10 MINUTES /MAKES 1 LOAF/12 SLICE BREAD (1½ pounds)

Ingredients

1⅛ cups water, at 80°F to 90°F

1½ tablespoons melted butter, cooled

1 tablespoon tomato paste

1½ tablespoons sugar

1½ teaspoons salt

3 tablespoons skim milk powder

¾ tablespoon Cajun seasoning

¼ teaspoon onion powder

3 cups white bread flour

1¼ teaspoons bread machine or instant yeast

Directions

1. Preparing the Ingredients.

Place the ingredients in your bread machine as recommended by the manufacturer.

Program the machine for Basic/White bread, select light or medium crust, and press Start.

When the loaf is done, remove the bucket from the machine.

2. Select the Bake cycle

Let the loaf cool for 5 minutes.

Gently shake the bucket to remove the loaf, and turn it out onto a rack to cool.

Oat Nut Bread

PREP: 10 MINUTES PLUS FERMENTING TIME /MAKES 1 LOAF

Ingredients

1¼ cups water

½ cup quick oats

¼ cup brown sugar, firmly packed

1 Tbsp butter

1½ tsp salt

3 cups bread flour

¾ cup chopped walnuts

1 package dry bread yeast

Directions

1. **Preparing the Ingredients**

   Add each ingredient to the bread machine in the order and at the temperature recommended by your bread machine manufacturer.

2. **Select the Bake cycle**

   Close the lid, select the rapid rise, medium crust setting on your bread machine, and press start.

   When the bread machine has finished baking, remove the bread and put it on a cooling rack.

Hazelnut Honey Bread

PREP: 10 MINUTES /MAKES 1 LOAF/16 SLICE BREAD (2 pounds)

Ingredients

1⅓ cups lukewarm milk

2 eggs, at room temperature

5 tablespoons unsalted butter, melted

¼ cup honey

1 teaspoon pure vanilla extract

1 teaspoon table salt

4 cups white bread flour

1 cup toasted hazelnuts, finely ground

2 teaspoons bread machine yeast

Directions

1. Preparing the Ingredients.

Choose the size of loaf you would like to make and measure your ingredients.

Add the ingredients to the bread pan in the order listed above.

Place the pan in the bread machine and close the lid.

Turn on the bread maker. Select the White/Basic setting, then the loaf size, and finally the crust color. Start the cycle.

2. Select the Bake cycle

When the cycle is finished and the bread is baked, carefully remove the pan from the machine. Use a potholder as the handle will be very hot. Let rest for a few minutes.

Remove the bread from the pan and allow to cool on a wire rack for at least 10 minutes before slicing.

Aromatic Lavender Bread

PREP: 10 MINUTES /MAKES 1 LOAF/16 SLICE BREAD (2 pounds)

Ingredients

1½ cups milk, at 80°F to 90°F

2 tablespoons melted butter, cooled

2 tablespoons sugar

2 teaspoons salt

2 teaspoons chopped fresh lavender flowers

1 teaspoon lemon zest

½ teaspoon chopped fresh thyme

4 cups white bread flour

1½ teaspoons bread machine or instant yeast

Directions

1. Preparing the Ingredients.

Place the ingredients in your bread machine as recommended by the manufacturer.

Program the machine for Basic/White bread, select light or medium crust, and press Start.

When the loaf is done, remove the bucket from the machine.

2. Select the Bake cycle

Let the loaf cool for 5 minutes.

Gently shake the bucket to remove the loaf, and turn it out onto a rack to cool.

Cardamom Honey Bread

PREP: 10 MINUTES /MAKES 1 LOAF/16 SLICE BREAD (2 pounds)

Ingredients

1⅛ cups lukewarm milk
1 egg, at room temperature
2 teaspoons unsalted butter, melted
¼ cup honey
1⅓ teaspoons table salt
4 cups white bread flour
1⅓ teaspoons ground cardamom
1⅔ teaspoons bread machine yeast

Directions

1.   Preparing the Ingredients.

Choose the size of loaf you would like to make and measure your ingredients.
Add the ingredients to the bread pan in the order listed above.
Place the pan in the bread machine and close the lid.

2.   Select the Bake cycle

Turn on the bread maker. Select the White/Basic setting, then the loaf size, and finally the crust color. Start the cycle.
When the cycle is finished and the bread is baked, carefully remove the pan from the machine. Use a potholder as the handle will be very hot. Let rest for a few minutes.
Remove the bread from the pan and allow to cool on a wire rack for at least 10 minutes before slicing.

Cracked Black Pepper Bread

PREP: 10 MINUTES /MAKES 1 LOAF/12 SLICE BREAD (1½ pounds)

Ingredients

1⅛ cups water, at 80°F to 90°F
1½ tablespoons melted butter, cooled
1½ tablespoons sugar
1 teaspoon salt
3 tablespoons skim milk powder
1½ tablespoons minced chives
¾ teaspoon garlic powder
¾ teaspoon freshly cracked black pepper
3 cups white bread flour
1¼ teaspoons bread machine or instant yeast

Directions

1.   Preparing the Ingredients.

Place the ingredients in your bread machine as recommended by the manufacturer.
Program the machine for Basic/White bread, select light or medium crust, and press Start.
When the loaf is done, remove the bucket from the machine.

2.   Select the Bake cycle

Let the loaf cool for 5 minutes.
Gently shake the bucket to remove the loaf, and turn it out onto a rack to cool.

Pistachio Cherry Bread
PREP: 10 MINUTES /MAKES 1 LOAF/16 SLICE BREAD (2 pounds)

Ingredients

1⅛ cups lukewarm water

1 egg, at room temperature

¼ cup butter, softened

¼ cup packed dark brown sugar

1½ teaspoons table salt

3¾ cups white bread flour

½ teaspoon ground nutmeg

Dash allspice

2 teaspoons bread machine yeast

1 cup dried cherries

½ cup unsalted pistachios, chopped

Directions

1.   Preparing the Ingredients.

Choose the size of loaf you would like to make and measure your ingredients.

Add all of the ingredients except for the pistachios and cherries to the bread pan in the order listed above.

Place the pan in the bread machine and close the lid.

2.   Select the Bake cycle

Turn on the bread maker. Select the White/Basic or Fruit/Nut (if your machine has this setting) setting, then the loaf size, and finally the crust color. Start the cycle.

When the machine signals to add ingredients, add the pistachios and cherries. (Some machines have a fruit/nut hopper where you can add the pistachios and cherries when you start the machine. The machine will automatically add them to the dough during the baking process.)

When the cycle is finished and the bread is baked, carefully remove the pan from the machine. Use a potholder as the handle will be very hot. Let rest for a few minutes.

Remove the bread from the pan and allow to cool on a wire rack for at least 10 minutes before slicing.

Herb and Garlic Cream Cheese Bread
PREP: 10 MINUTES /MAKES 1 LOAF/12 SLICE BREAD (1½ pounds)

Ingredients

½ cup water, at 80°F to 90°F

½ cup herb and garlic cream cheese, at room temperature

1 egg, at room temperature

2 tablespoons melted butter, cooled

3 tablespoons sugar

1 teaspoon salt

3 cups white bread flour

1½ teaspoons bread machine or instant yeast

Directions

1.   Preparing the Ingredients.

Place the ingredients in your bread machine as recommended by the manufacturer.

Program the machine for Basic/White bread, select light or medium crust, and press Start.

When the loaf is done, remove the bucket from the machine.

2.   Select the Bake cycle

Let the loaf cool for 5 minutes.

Gently shake the bucket to remove the loaf, and turn it out onto a rack to cool.

Mix Seed Raisin Bread

PREP: 10 MINUTES /MAKES 1 LOAF/16 SLICE BREAD (2 pounds)

Ingredients

1½ cups lukewarm milk
2 tablespoons unsalted butter, melted
2 tablespoons honey
1 teaspoon table salt
2½ cups white bread flour
¼ cup flaxseed
¼ cup sesame seeds
1½ cups whole-wheat flour
2¼ teaspoons bread machine yeast
½ cup raisins

Directions

1. Preparing the Ingredients.

Choose the size of loaf you would like to make and measure your ingredients.

Add the ingredients to the bread pan in the order listed above. Place the pan in the bread machine and close the lid.

2. Select the Bake cycle

Turn on the bread maker. Select the White/Basic setting, then the loaf size, and finally the crust color. Start the cycle.

When the cycle is finished and the bread is baked, carefully remove the pan from the machine. Use a potholder as the handle will be very hot. Let rest for a few minutes.

Remove the bread from the pan and allow to cool on a wire rack for at least 10 minutes before slicing.

Grain, Seed And Nut Bread

PREP: 10 MINUTES /MAKES 1 LOAF

Ingredients

¼ cup water
1 egg
3 Tbsp honey
1½ tsp butter, softened
3¼ cups bread flour
1 cup milk
1 tsp salt
¼ tsp baking soda
1 tsp ground cinnamon
2½ tsp active dry yeast
¾ cup dried cranberries
½ cup chopped walnuts
1 Tbsp white vinegar
½ tsp sugar

Directions

1. Preparing the Ingredients.

Add each ingredient except the berries and nuts to the bread machine in the order and at the temperature recommended by your bread machine manufacturer.

2. Select the Bake cycle

Close the lid, select the basic bread, medium crust setting on your bread machine, and press start.

Add the cranberries and walnuts around 5 minutes before the kneading cycle has finished

Honey-Spice Egg Bread

PREP: 10 MINUTES /MAKES 1 LOAF/12 SLICE BREAD (1½ pounds)

Ingredients

1 cup milk, at 80°F to 90°F

2 eggs, at room temperature

1½ tablespoons melted butter, cooled

2 tablespoons honey

1 teaspoon salt

1 teaspoon ground cinnamon

½ teaspoon ground cardamom

½ teaspoon ground nutmeg

3 cups white bread flour

2 teaspoons bread machine or instant yeast

Directions

1. Preparing the Ingredients.

Place the ingredients in your bread machine as recommended by the manufacturer.

Program the machine for Basic/White bread, select light or medium crust, and press Start. When the loaf is done, remove the bucket from the machine.

2. Select the Bake cycle

Let the loaf cool for 5 minutes.

Gently shake the bucket to remove the loaf, and turn it out onto a rack to cool.

Anise Honey Bread

PREP: 10 MINUTES /MAKES 1 LOAF/16 SLICE BREAD (2 pounds)

Ingredients

1 cup + 1 tablespoon lukewarm water

1 egg, at room temperature

⅓ cup butter, melted and cooled

⅓ cup honey

⅔ teaspoon table salt

4 cups white bread flour

1⅓ teaspoons anise seed

1⅓ teaspoons lemon zest

2½ teaspoons bread machine yeast

Directions

1. Preparing the Ingredients.

Choose the size of loaf you would like to make and measure your ingredients.

Add the ingredients to the bread pan in the order listed above.

Place the pan in the bread machine and close the lid.

Turn on the bread maker. Select the White/Basic setting, then the loaf size, and finally the crust color. Start the cycle.

2. Select the Bake cycle

When the cycle is finished and the bread is baked, carefully remove the pan from the machine. Use a potholder as the handle will be very hot. Let rest for a few minutes.

Remove the bread from the pan and allow to cool on a wire rack for at least 10 minutes before slicing.

Cinnamon Bread

PREP: 10 MINUTES /MAKES 1 LOAF/12 SLICE BREAD (1½ pounds)

Ingredients

1 cup milk, at 80°F to 90°F

1 egg, at room temperature

¼ cup melted butter, cooled

½ cup sugar

½ teaspoon salt

1½ teaspoons ground cinnamon

3 cups white bread flour

2 teaspoons bread machine or active dry yeast

Directions

1. Preparing the Ingredients.

Place the ingredients in your bread machine as recommended by the manufacturer.

Program the machine for Basic/White bread, select light or medium crust, and press Start.

When the loaf is done, remove the bucket from the machine.

2. Select the Bake cycle

Let the loaf cool for 5 minutes.

Gently shake the bucket to remove the loaf, and turn it out onto a rack to cool.

Basic Pecan Bread

PREP: 10 MINUTES /MAKES 1 LOAF/16 SLICE BREAD (2 pounds)

Ingredients

1⅓ cups lukewarm milk

2⅔ tablespoons unsalted butter, melted

1 egg, at room temperature

2⅔ tablespoons sugar

1⅓ teaspoons table salt

4 cups white bread flour

2 teaspoons bread machine yeast

1⅓ cups chopped pecans, toasted

Directions

1. Preparing the Ingredients.

Choose the size of loaf you would like to make and measure your ingredients.

Add all of the ingredients except for the toasted pecans to the bread pan in the order listed above.

Place the pan in the bread machine and close the lid.

Turn on the bread maker. Select the White/Basic or Fruit/Nut (if your machine has this setting) setting, then the loaf size, and finally the crust color. Start the cycle.

2. Select the Bake cycle

When the machine signals to add ingredients, add the toasted pecans. (Some machines have a fruit/nut hopper where you can add the toasted pecans when you start the machine. The machine will automatically add them to the dough during the baking process.)

When the cycle is finished and the bread is baked, carefully remove the pan from the machine. Use a potholder as the handle will be very hot. Let rest for a few minutes.

Remove the bread from the pan and allow to cool on a wire rack for at least 10 minutes before slicing.

Apple Walnut Bread

PREP: 10 MINUTES PLUS FERMENTING TIME /MAKES 1 LOAF

Ingredients

¾ cup unsweetened applesauce

4 cups apple juice

1 tsp salt

3 Tbsp butter

1 large egg

4 cups bread flour

¼ cup brown sugar, packed

1¼ tsp cinnamon

½ tsp baking soda

2 tsp active dry yeast

½ cup chopped walnuts

½ cup chopped dried cranberries

Directions

1. **Preparing the Ingredients**
   Add each ingredient to the bread machine in the order and at the temperature recommended by your bread machine manufacturer.
2. **Select the Bake cycle**
   Close the lid, select the basic bread, medium crust setting on your bread machine, and press start.
   When the bread machine has finished baking, remove the bread and put it on a cooling rack.

Simple Garlic Bread

PREP: 10 MINUTES /MAKES 1 LOAF/12 SLICE BREAD (1½ pounds)

Ingredients

1 cup milk, at 70°F to 80°F

1½ tablespoons melted butter, cooled

1 tablespoon sugar

1½ teaspoons salt

2 teaspoons garlic powder

2 teaspoons chopped fresh parsley

3 cups white bread flour

1¾ teaspoons bread machine or instant yeast

Directions

1. **Preparing the Ingredients.**

Place the ingredients in your bread machine as recommended by the manufacturer.

Program the machine for Basic/White bread, select light or medium crust, and press Start.

When the loaf is done, remove the bucket from the machine.

2. **Select the Bake cycle**

Let the loaf cool for 5 minutes.

Gently shake the bucket to remove the loaf, and turn it out onto a rack to cool.

Herbed Pesto Bread

PREP: 10 MINUTES /MAKES 1 LOAF/12 SLICE BREAD (1½ pounds)

Ingredients
1 cup water, at 80°F to 90°F
2¼ tablespoons melted butter, cooled
1½ teaspoons minced garlic
¾ tablespoon sugar
1 teaspoon salt
3 tablespoons chopped fresh parsley
1½ tablespoons chopped fresh basil
⅓ cup grated Parmesan cheese
3 cups white bread flour
1¼ teaspoons bread machine or active dry yeast

Directions
1. Preparing the Ingredients.
Place the ingredients in your bread machine as recommended by the manufacturer.
Program the machine for Basic/White bread, select light or medium crust, and press Start.
When the loaf is done, remove the bucket from the machine.

2. Select the Bake cycle
Let the loaf cool for 5 minutes.
Gently shake the bucket to remove the loaf, and turn it out onto a rack to cool.

Caraway Rye Bread

PREP: 10 MINUTES /MAKES 1 LOAF/12 SLICE BREAD (1½ pounds)

Ingredients
1⅛ cups water, at 80°F to 90°F
1¾ tablespoons melted butter, cooled
3 tablespoons dark brown sugar
1½ tablespoons dark molasses
1⅛ teaspoons salt
1½ teaspoons caraway seed
¾ cup dark rye flour
2 cups white bread flour
1⅛ teaspoons bread machine or instant yeast

Directions
1. Preparing the Ingredients.
Place the ingredients in your bread machine as recommended by the manufacturer.
Program the machine for Basic/White bread, select light or medium crust, and press Start.
When the loaf is done, remove the bucket from the machine.

2. Select the Bake cycle
Let the loaf cool for 5 minutes. Gently shake the bucket to remove the loaf, and turn it out onto a rack to cool.

Anise Lemon Bread

Ingredients
¾ cup water, at 80°F to 90°F
1 egg, at room temperature
¼ cup butter, melted and cooled
¼ cup honey
½ teaspoon salt
1 teaspoon anise seed
1 teaspoon lemon zest
3 cups white bread flour
2 teaspoons bread machine or instant yeast

Directions
1. **Preparing the Ingredients.**

Place the ingredients in your bread machine as recommended by the manufacturer.

2. **Select the Bake cycle**

Program the machine for Basic/White bread, select light or medium crust, and press Start.
When the loaf is done, remove the bucket from the machine.
Let the loaf cool for 5 minutes. Gently shake the bucket to remove the loaf, and turn it out onto a rack to cool.

Fragrant Cardamom Bread

Ingredients
¾ cup milk, at 80°F to 90°F
1 egg, at room temperature
1½ teaspoons melted butter, cooled
3 tablespoons honey
1 teaspoon salt
1 teaspoon ground cardamom
3 cups white bread flour
1¼ teaspoons bread machine or instant yeast

Directions
1. **Preparing the Ingredients.**

Place the ingredients in your bread machine as recommended by the manufacturer.
Program the machine for Basic/White bread, select light or medium crust, and press Start.
When the loaf is done, remove the bucket from the machine.
2. **Select the Bake cycle**

Let the loaf cool for 5 minutes.
Gently shake the bucket to remove the loaf, and turn it out onto a rack to cool.

Chocolate Mint Bread

PREP: 10 MINUTES /MAKES 1 LOAF/12 SLICE BREAD (1½ pounds)

Ingredients

1 cup milk, at 80°F to 90°F
⅛ teaspoon mint extract
1½ tablespoons butter, melted and cooled
¼ cup sugar
1 teaspoon salt
1½ tablespoons unsweetened cocoa powder
3 cups white bread flour
1¾ teaspoons bread machine or instant yeast
½ cup semisweet chocolate chips

Directions

1. Preparing the Ingredients.

Place the ingredients in your bread machine as recommended by the manufacturer.
Program the machine for Sweet bread, select light or medium crust, and press Start.
When the loaf is done, remove the bucket from the machine.

2. Select the Bake cycle

Gently shake the bucket to remove the loaf, and turn it out onto a rack to cool.
Let the loaf cool for 5 minutes.

Molasses Candied-Ginger Bread

PREP: 10 MINUTES /MAKES 1 LOAF/12 SLICE BREAD (1½ pounds)

Ingredients

1 cup milk, at 80°F to 90°F
1 egg, at room temperature
¼ cup dark molasses
3 tablespoons butter, melted and cooled
½ teaspoon salt
¼ cup chopped candied ginger
½ cup quick oats
3 cups white bread flour
2 teaspoons bread machine or instant yeast

Directions

1. Preparing the Ingredients.

Place the ingredients in your bread machine as recommended by the manufacturer.
Program the machine for Basic/White bread, select light or medium crust, and press Start.
When the loaf is done, remove the bucket from the machine.

2. Select the Bake cycle

Let the loaf cool for 5 minutes.
Gently shake the bucket to remove the loaf, and turn it out onto a rack to cool.

Whole-Wheat Seed Bread

PREP: 10 MINUTES /MAKES 1 LOAF/12 SLICE BREAD (1½ pounds)

Ingredients

1⅛ cups water, at 80°F to 90°F

1½ tablespoons honey

1½ tablespoons melted butter, cooled

¾ teaspoon salt

2½ cups whole-wheat flour

¾ cup white bread flour

3 tablespoons raw sunflower seeds

1 tablespoon sesame seeds

1½ teaspoons bread machine or instant yeast

Directions

1. Preparing the Ingredients.

Place the ingredients in your bread machine as recommended by the manufacturer.

Program the machine for Whole-Wheat/Whole-Grain bread, select light or medium crust, and press Start.

When the loaf is done, remove the bucket from the machine.

2. Select the Bake cycle

Let the loaf cool for 5 minutes.

Gently shake the bucket to remove the loaf, and turn it out onto a rack to cool.

Multigrain Bread

PREP: 10 MINUTES /MAKES 1 LOAF/12 SLICE BREAD (1½ pounds)

Ingredients

1 cup plus 2 tablespoons water, at 80°F to 90°F

2 tablespoons melted butter, cooled

1½ tablespoons honey

1½ teaspoons salt

1 cup plus 2 tablespoons multigrain flour

2 cups white bread flour

1½ teaspoons bread machine or active dry yeast

Directions

1. Preparing the Ingredients.

Place the ingredients in your bread machine as recommended by the manufacturer.

Program the machine for Basic/White bread, select light or medium crust, and press Start.

When the loaf is done, remove the bucket from the machine.

2. Select the Bake cycle

Let the loaf cool for 5 minutes.

Gently shake the bucket to remove the loaf, and turn it out onto a rack to cool.

Pecan Raisin Bread

PREP: 10 MINUTES PLUS FERMENTING TIME /MAKES 1 LOAF

Ingredients

1 cup plus 2 Tbsp water (70°F to 80°F)

8 tsp butter

1 egg

6 Tbsp sugar

¼ cup nonfat dry milk powder

1 tsp salt

4 cups bread flour

1 Tbsp active dry yeast

1 cup finely chopped pecans

1 cup raisins

Directions

1. **Preparing the Ingredients**

   Add each ingredient to the bread machine except the pecans and raisins in the order and at the temperature recommended by your bread machine manufacturer.

2. **Select the Bake cycle**

   Close the lid, select the basic bread, medium crust setting on your bread machine, and press start.

   Just before the final kneading, add the pecans and raisins.

   When the bread machine has finished baking, remove the bread and put it on a cooling rack.

Toasted Pecan Bread

PREP: 10 MINUTES /MAKES 1 LOAF/12 SLICE BREAD (1½ pounds)

Ingredients

1 cup milk, at 70°F to 80°F

2 tablespoons melted butter, cooled

1 egg, at room temperature

2 tablespoons sugar

1 teaspoon salt

3 cups white bread flour

1½ teaspoons bread machine or instant yeast

1 cup chopped pecans, toasted

Directions

1. **Preparing the Ingredients.**

Place the ingredients, except the pecans, in your bread machine as recommended by the manufacturer.

Program the machine for Basic/White bread, select light or medium crust, and press Start.

When the machine signals, add the pecans, or put them in a nut/raisin hopper and the machine will add them automatically.

2. **Select the Bake cycle**

When the loaf is done, remove the bucket from the machine.

Let the loaf cool for 5 minutes.

Gently shake the bucket to remove the loaf, and turn it out onto a rack to cool.

Quinoa Oatmeal Bread

PREP: 10 MINUTES /MAKES 1 LOAF

Ingredients

⅓ cup uncooked quinoa

⅔ cup water (for cooking quinoa)

1 cup buttermilk

1 tsp salt

1 Tbsp sugar

1 Tbsp honey

4 Tbsp unsalted butter

½ cup quick-cooking oats

½ cup whole wheat flour

1½ cups bread flour

Directions

1. **Preparing the Ingredients**

   Add quinoa to a saucepan. Cover it with water. Bring to boil. Cook for 5 minutes, covered. Turn off and leave the quinoa covered for 10 minutes. Add each ingredient to the bread machine in the order and at the temperature recommended by your bread machine manufacturer.

2. **Select the Bake cycle**

   Close the lid, select the whole grain, medium crust setting on your bread machine and press start. When the bread machine has finished baking, remove the bread and put it on a cooling rack.

Market Seed Bread

PREP: 10 MINUTES /MAKES 1 LOAF/12 SLICE BREAD (1½ pounds)

Ingredients

1 cup plus 2 tablespoons milk, at 80°F to 90°F

1½ tablespoons melted butter, cooled

1½ tablespoons honey

¾ teaspoon salt

3 tablespoons flaxseed

3 tablespoons sesame seeds

1½ tablespoons poppy seeds

1¼ cups whole-wheat flour

1¾ cups white bread flour

1¾ teaspoons bread machine or instant yeast

Directions

1. **Preparing the Ingredients.**

Place the ingredients in your bread machine as recommended by the manufacturer.

Program the machine for Basic/White bread, select light or medium crust, and press Start.

When the loaf is done, remove the bucket from the machine.

2. **Select the Bake cycle**

Let the loaf cool for 5 minutes.

Gently shake the bucket to remove the loaf, and turn it out onto a rack to cool.

Pesto Nut Bread

PREP: 10 MINUTES /MAKES 14 SLICES

Ingredients

1 cup plus 2 Tbsp water

3 cups Gold Medal Better for Bread flour

2 Tbsp sugar

1 tsp salt

1¼ tsp bread machine or quick active dry yeast

For the pesto filling:

⅓ cup basil pesto

2 Tbsp Gold Medal Better for Bread flour

⅓ cup pine nuts

Directions

1. **Preparing the Ingredients**

   Add each ingredient to the bread machine in the order and at the temperature recommended by your bread machine manufacturer.

2. **Select the Bake cycle**

   Close the lid, select the basic bread, medium crust setting on your bread machine, and press start.

   In a small bowl, combine pesto and 2 Tbsp of flour until well blended. Stir in the pine nuts. Add the filling 5 minutes before the last kneading cycle ends.

   When the bread machine has finished baking, remove the bread and put it on a cooling rack.

Cracked Wheat Bread

PREP: 10 MINUTES /MAKES 1 LOAF/12 SLICE BREAD (1½ pounds)

Ingredients

¼ cup cracked wheat

1¼ cups boiling water

¼ cup melted butter, cooled

3 tablespoons honey

1½ teaspoons salt

1 cup whole-wheat flour

2 cups white bread flour

2 teaspoons bread machine or instant yeast

Directions

1. **Preparing the Ingredients.**

Place the cracked wheat and water in the bucket of your bread machine for 30 minutes or until the liquid is 80°F to 90°F.

Place the remaining ingredients in your bread machine as recommended by the manufacturer.

Program the machine for Basic/White bread, select light or medium crust, and press Start.

2. **Select the Bake cycle**

When the loaf is done, remove the bucket from the machine.

Let the loaf cool for 5 minutes.

Gently shake the bucket to remove the loaf, and turn it out onto a rack to cool.

Double Coconut Bread

PREP: 10 MINUTES /MAKES 1 LOAF/12 SLICE BREAD (1½ pounds)

Ingredients
1 cup milk, at 80°F to 90°F
1 egg, at room temperature
1½ tablespoons melted butter, cooled
2 teaspoons pure coconut extract
2½ tablespoons sugar
¾ teaspoon salt
½ cup sweetened shredded coconut
3 cups white bread flour
1½ teaspoons bread machine or instant yeast

Directions
1. **Preparing the Ingredients.**
Place the ingredients in your bread machine as recommended by the manufacturer.
2. **Select the Bake cycle**
Program the machine for Sweet bread, select light or medium crust, and press Start.
When the loaf is done, remove the bucket from the machine.
Let the loaf cool for 5 minutes. Gently shake the bucket to remove the loaf, and turn it out onto a rack to cool.

Seed Bread

PREP: 10 MINUTES /MAKES 1 LOAF

Ingredients
3 Tbsp flax seed
1 Tbsp sesame seeds
1 Tbsp poppy seeds
¾ cup water
1 Tbsp honey
1 Tbsp canola oil
½ tsp salt
1½ cups bread flour
5 Tbsp whole meal flour
1¼ tsp dried active baking yeast

Directions
1. **Preparing the Ingredients**
Add each ingredient to the bread machine in the order and at the temperature recommended by your bread machine manufacturer.
2. **Select the Bake cycle**
Close the lid, select the basic bread, medium crust setting on your bread machine, and press start.
When the bread machine has finished baking, remove the bread and put it on a cooling rack.

Honeyed Bulgur Bread

PREP: 10 MINUTES /MAKES 1 LOAF/12 SLICE BREAD (1½ pounds)

Ingredients

¾ cup boiling water

3 tablespoons bulgur wheat

3 tablespoons quick oats

2 eggs, at room temperature

1½ tablespoons melted butter, cooled

2¼ tablespoons honey

1 teaspoon salt

2¼ cups white bread flour

1½ teaspoons bread machine or instant yeast

Directions

1. Preparing the Ingredients.

Place the water, bulgur, and oats in the bucket of your bread machine for 30 minutes or until the liquid is 80°F to 90°F.

Place the remaining ingredients in your bread machine as recommended by the manufacturer.

2. Select the Bake cycle

Program the machine for Basic/White bread, select light or medium crust, and press Start.

When the loaf is done, remove the bucket from the machine.

Let the loaf cool for 5 minutes. Gently shake the bucket to remove the loaf, and turn it out onto a rack to cool.

Chia Seed Bread

PREP: 10 MINUTES /MAKES 14 SLICES

Ingredients

¼ cup chia seeds

¾ cup hot water

2⅜ cups water

¼ cup oil

½ lemon, zest and juice

1¾ cups white flour

1¾ cups whole wheat flour

2 tsp baking powder

1 tsp salt

1 Tbsp sugar

2½ tsp quick rise yeast

Directions

1. **Preparing the Ingredients**

Add the chia seeds to a bowl, cover with hot water, mix well and let them stand until they are soaked and gelatinous, and don't feel warm to touch.

Add each ingredient to the bread machine in the order and at the temperature recommended by your bread machine manufacturer.

2. **Select the Bake cycle**

Close the lid, select the basic bread, medium crust setting on your bread machine, and press start.

When the mixing blade stops moving, open the machine and mix everything by hand with a spatula.

When the bread machine has finished baking, remove the bread and put it on a cooling rack.

Flaxseed Honey Bread

PREP: 10 MINUTES /MAKES 1 LOAF/12 SLICE BREAD (1½ pounds)

Ingredients

1⅛ cups milk, at 80°F to 90°F
1½ tablespoons melted butter, cooled
1½ tablespoons honey
1 teaspoon salt
¼ cup flaxseed
3 cups white bread flour
1¼ teaspoons bread machine or instant yeast

Directions

1. **Preparing the Ingredients.** Place the ingredients in your bread machine as recommended by the manufacturer. Program the machine for Basic/White bread, select light or medium crust, and press Start. When the loaf is done, remove the bucket from the machine.
2. **Select the Bake cycle.** Let the loaf cool for 5 minutes. Gently shake the bucket to remove the loaf, and turn it out onto a rack to cool.

Chia Sesame Bread

PREP: 10 MINUTES /MAKES 1 LOAF/12 SLICE BREAD (1½ pounds)

Ingredients

1 cup plus 2 tablespoons water, at 80°F to 90°F
1½ tablespoons melted butter, cooled
1½ tablespoons sugar
1⅛ teaspoons salt
½ cup ground chia seeds
1½ tablespoons sesame seeds
2½ cups white bread flour
1½ teaspoons bread machine or instant yeast

Directions

1. **Preparing the Ingredients.**

Place the ingredients in your bread machine as recommended by the manufacturer. Program the machine for Basic/White bread, select light or medium crust, and press Start. When the loaf is done, remove the bucket from the machine.

2. **Select the Bake cycle**

Let the loaf cool for 5 minutes. Gently shake the bucket to remove the loaf, and turn it out onto a rack to cool.

Sesame French Bread

PREP: 10 MINUTES /MAKES 1 LOAF

Ingredients

⅞ cup water
1 Tbsp butter, softened
3 cups bread flour
2 tsp sugar
1 tsp salt
2 tsp yeast
2 Tbsp sesame seeds toasted

Directions

Preparing the Ingredients

Add each ingredient to the bread machine in the order and at the temperature recommended by your bread machine manufacturer.

Select the Bake cycle

Close the lid, select the French bread, medium crust setting on your bread machine and press start.

When the bread machine has finished baking, remove the bread and put it on a cooling rack.

Quinoa Whole-Wheat Bread

PREP: 10 MINUTES /MAKES 1 LOAF/12 SLICE BREAD (1½ pounds)

Ingredients

1 cup milk, at 80°F to 90°F

⅔ cup cooked quinoa, cooled

¼ cup melted butter, cooled

1 tablespoon sugar

1 teaspoon salt

¼ cup quick oats

¾ cup whole-wheat flour

1½ cups white bread flour

1½ teaspoons bread machine or instant yeast

Directions

1. **Preparing the Ingredients.**

Place the ingredients in your bread machine as recommended by the manufacturer.

Program the machine for Basic/White bread, select light or medium crust, and press Start.

When the loaf is done, remove the bucket from the machine.

2. **Select the Bake cycle**

Let the loaf cool for 5 minutes.

Gently shake the bucket to remove the loaf, and turn it out onto a rack to cool.

Peanut Butter Bread

PREP: 10 MINUTES /MAKES 1 LOAF

Ingredients

1 cup peanut butter

1 cup milk, at 70°F to 80°F

½ cup packed light brown sugar

¼ cup sugar

¼ cup (½ stick) butter, at room temperature

1 egg, at room temperature

2 teaspoons pure vanilla extract

2 cups all-purpose flour

1 tablespoon baking powder

½ teaspoon salt

Directions

1. **Preparing the Ingredients.**

Place the peanut butter, milk, brown sugar, sugar, butter, egg, and vanilla in your bread machine.

Program the machine for Quick/Rapid bread and press Start.

While the wet ingredients are mixing, stir together the flour, baking powder, and salt in a small bowl.

2. **Select the Bake cycle**

After the first fast mixing is done and the machine signals, add the dry ingredients.

When the loaf is done, remove the bucket from the machine.

Let the loaf cool for 5 minutes.

Gently shake the bucket to remove the loaf, and turn it out onto a rack to cool.

Toasted Hazelnut Bread

PREP: 10 MINUTES /MAKES 1 LOAF/12 SLICE BREAD (1½ pounds)

Ingredients

1 cup milk, at 70°F to 80°F

1 egg, at room temperature

3¾ tablespoons melted butter, cooled

3 tablespoons honey

¾ teaspoon pure vanilla extract

¾ teaspoon salt

¾ cup finely ground toasted hazelnuts

3 cups white bread flour

1½ teaspoons bread machine or instant yeast

Directions

1. **Preparing the Ingredients.**

Place the ingredients in your bread machine as recommended by the manufacturer.

2. **Select the Bake cycle**

Program the machine for Basic/White bread, select light or medium crust, and press Start.

When the loaf is done, remove the bucket from the machine.

Let the loaf cool for 5 minutes.

Gently shake the bucket to remove the loaf, and turn it out onto a rack to cool.

Oatmeal Seed Bread

PREP: 10 MINUTES /MAKES 1 LOAF/12 SLICE BREAD (1½ pounds)

Ingredients

1⅛ cups water, at 80°F to 90°F

3 tablespoons melted butter, cooled

3 tablespoons light brown sugar

1½ teaspoons salt

3 tablespoons raw sunflower seeds

3 tablespoons pumpkin seeds

2 tablespoons sesame seeds

1 teaspoon anise seeds

1 cup quick oats

2¼ cups white bread flour

1½ teaspoons bread machine or instant yeast

Directions

1. **Preparing the Ingredients.**

Place the ingredients in your bread machine as recommended by the manufacturer.

Program the machine for Basic/White bread, select light or medium crust, and press Start.

When the loaf is done, remove the bucket from the machine.

2. **Select the Bake cycle**

Let the loaf cool for 5 minutes.

Gently shake the bucket to remove the loaf, and turn it out onto a rack to cool.

Nutty Wheat Bread

PREP: 10 MINUTES /MAKES 1 LOAF/12 SLICE BREAD (1½ pounds)

Ingredients

1½ cups water, at 80°F to 90°F

2 tablespoons melted butter, cooled

1 tablespoon sugar

1½ teaspoons salt

1¼ cups whole-wheat flour

2 cups white bread flour

1¼ teaspoons bread machine or instant yeast

2 tablespoons chopped almonds

2 tablespoons chopped pecans

2 tablespoons sunflower seeds

Directions

1. Preparing the Ingredients.

Place the ingredients, except the almonds, pecans, and seeds, in your bread machine as recommended by the manufacturer.

2. Select the Bake cycle

Program the machine for Basic/White bread, select light or medium crust, and press Start.

When the machine signals, add the nuts and seeds, or put them in the nut/raisin hopper and let the machine add them automatically. When the loaf is done, remove the bucket from the machine.

Let the loaf cool for 5 minutes.

Gently shake the bucket to remove the loaf, and turn it out onto a rack to cool.

Sunflower Bread

PREP: 10 MINUTES /MAKES 1 LOAF/12 SLICE BREAD (1½ pounds)

Ingredients

1 cup water, at 80°F to 90°F

1 egg, at room temperature

3 tablespoons melted butter, cooled

3 tablespoons skim milk powder

1½ tablespoons honey

1½ teaspoons salt

¾ cup raw sunflower seeds

3 cups white bread flour

1 teaspoon bread machine or instant yeast

Directions

1. Preparing the Ingredients.

Place the ingredients in your bread machine as recommended by the manufacturer.

Program the machine for Basic/White bread, select light or medium crust, and press Start.

When the loaf is done, remove the bucket from the machine.

2. Select the Bake cycle

Let the loaf cool for 5 minutes.

Gently shake the bucket to remove the loaf, and turn it out onto a rack to cool.

Raisin Seed Bread

PREP: 10 MINUTES /MAKES 1 LOAF/12 SLICE BREAD (1½ pounds)

Ingredients

1 cup plus 2 tablespoons milk, at 80°F to 90°F

1½ tablespoons melted butter, cooled

1½ tablespoons honey

¾ teaspoon salt

3 tablespoons flaxseed

3 tablespoons sesame seeds

1¼ cups whole-wheat flour

1¾ cups white bread flour

1¾ teaspoons bread machine or instant yeast

⅓ cup raisins

Directions

1.   Preparing the Ingredients.

Place the ingredients, except the raisins, in your bread machine as recommended by the manufacturer.

Program the machine for Basic/White bread, select light or medium crust, and press Start.

Add the raisins when your bread machine signals, or place the raisins in the raisin/nut hopper and let the machine add them.

2.   Select the Bake cycle

When the loaf is done, remove the bucket from the machine.

Let the loaf cool for 5 minutes.

Gently shake the bucket to remove the loaf, and turn it out onto a rack to cool.

Rosemary Bread

PREP: 10 MINUTES /MAKES 14 SLICES

Ingredients

1⅓ cups milk

4 Tbsp butter

3 cups bread flour

1 cup one minute oatmeal

1 tsp salt

6 tsp white granulated sugar

1 Tbsp onion powder

1 Tbsp dried rosemary

1½ tsp bread machine yeast

Directions

1. **Preparing the Ingredients**

    Add each ingredient to the bread machine in the order and at the temperature recommended by your bread machine manufacturer.

2. **Select the Bake cycle**

    Close the lid, select the basic bread, medium crust setting on your bread machine and press start.

    After the bread machine has finished kneading, sprinkle some rosemary on top of the bread dough.

    When the bread machine has finished baking, remove the bread and put it on a cooling rack.

Cajun Bread

PREP: 10 MINUTES /MAKES 14 SLICES

Ingredients
½ cup water

¼ cup chopped onion

¼ cup chopped green bell pepper

2 tsp finely chopped garlic

2 tsp soft butter

2 cups bread flour

1 Tbsp sugar

1 tsp Cajun

½ tsp salt

1 tsp active dry yeast

Directions
1. **Preparing the Ingredients**

   Add each ingredient to the bread machine in the order and at the temperature recommended by your bread machine manufacturer.

2. **Select the Bake cycle**

   Close the lid, select the basic bread, medium crust setting on your bread machine and press start.

   When the bread machine has finished baking, remove the bread and put it on a cooling rack.

Turmeric Bread

PREP: 10 MINUTES /MAKES 14 SLICES

Ingredients
1 tsp dried yeast

4 cups strong white flour

1 tsp turmeric powder

2 tsp beetroot powder

2 Tbsp olive oil

1.5 tsp salt

1 tsp chili flakes

1⅜ water

Directions
1. **Preparing the Ingredients**

   Add each ingredient to the bread machine in the order and at the temperature recommended by your bread machine manufacturer.

2. **Select the Bake cycle**

   Close the lid, select the basic bread, medium crust setting on your bread machine and press start.

   When the bread machine has finished baking, remove the bread and put it on a cooling rack.

Rosemary Bread

PREP: 10 MINUTES /MAKES 12 SLICES

Ingredients

1 cup warm water, about 105°F

2 tablespoons butter, softened

1 egg

3 cups all-purpose flour

¼cup whole wheat flour

⅓cup sugar

1 teaspoon salt

3 teaspoons bread maker yeast

2 tablespoons rosemary, freshly chopped

For the topping:

1 egg, room temperature

1 teaspoon milk, room temperature

Garlic powder

Sea salt

Directions

1. **Preparing the Ingredients**

   Place all of the ingredients in the bread maker pan in the order listed above.

2. **Select the Bake cycle**

   Select Dough cycle.

   When dough is kneaded, place on parchment paper on a flat surface and roll into two loaves; set aside and allow to rise for 30 minutes. Preheat a pizza stone in an oven on 375°F for 30 minutes.

   For the topping, add the egg and milk to a small mixing bowl and whisk to create an egg wash. Baste the formed loaves and sprinkle evenly with garlic powder and sea salt.

   Allow to rise for 40 minutes, lightly covered, in a warm area.

   Bake for 15 to 18 minutes or until golden brown. Serve warm.

VEGETABLE BREAD

Beetroot Bread
PREP: 10 MINUTES /MAKES 1 LOAF/16 SLICE BREAD (2 pounds)

Ingredients

1 cup lukewarm water

1 cup grated raw beetroot

2 tablespoons unsalted butter, melted

2 tablespoons sugar

2 teaspoons table salt

4 cups white bread flour

1⅔ teaspoons bread machine yeast

Directions
1.   Preparing the Ingredients.
Choose the size of loaf you would like to make and measure your ingredients.

Add the ingredients to the bread pan in the order listed above.

Place the pan in the bread machine and close the lid.

2.   Select the Bake cycle
Turn on the bread maker. Select the White/Basic setting, then the loaf size, and finally the crust color. Start the cycle.

When the cycle is finished and the bread is baked, carefully remove the pan from the machine. Use a potholder as the handle will be very hot. Let rest for a few minutes.

Remove the bread from the pan and allow to cool on a wire rack for at least 10 minutes before slicing.

Yeasted Carrot Bread
PREP: 10 MINUTES /MAKES 1 LOAF/12 SLICE BREAD (1½ pounds)

Ingredients

¾ cup milk, at 80°F to 90°F

3 tablespoons melted butter, cooled

1 tablespoon honey

1½ cups shredded carrot

¾ teaspoon ground nutmeg

½ teaspoon salt

3 cups white bread flour

2¼ teaspoons bread machine or active dry yeast

Directions
1.   Preparing the Ingredients.
Choose the size of loaf you would like to make and measure your ingredients.

Add the ingredients to the bread pan in the order listed above.

Program the machine for Quick/Rapid bread and press Start.

2.   Select the Bake cycle
When the loaf is done, remove the bucket from the machine.

Let the loaf cool for 5 minutes.

Gently shake the bucket to remove the loaf, and turn it out onto a rack to cool.

Sweet Potato Bread

PREP: 10 MINUTES /MAKES 1 LOAF/12 SLICE BREAD (1½ pounds)

Ingredients
⅓ cup + 2 tablespoons lukewarm water
¾ cup plain sweet potatoes, peeled and mashed
1½ tablespoons unsalted butter, melted
¼ cup dark brown sugar
1 teaspoon table salt
3 cups bread flour
⅛ teaspoon ground nutmeg
⅛ teaspoon cinnamon
¾ teaspoon vanilla extract
1½ tablespoons dry milk powder
1½ teaspoons bread machine yeast

Directions
1. Preparing the Ingredients.
Choose the size of loaf you would like to make and measure your ingredients.

Add the ingredients to the bread pan in the order listed above.

Place the pan in the bread machine and close the lid.

Turn on the bread maker. Select the White/Basic setting, then the loaf size, and finally the crust color. Start the cycle.

2. Select the Bake cycle
When the cycle is finished, and the bread is baked, carefully remove the pan from the machine. Use a potholder as the handle will be very hot. Let rest for a few minutes.

Remove the bread from the pan and allow to cool on a wire rack for at least 10 minutes before slicing.

Sauerkraut Rye Bread

PREP: 10 MINUTES /MAKES 1 LOAF/12 SLICE BREAD (1½ pounds)

Ingredients
1 cup water, at 80°F to 90°F
1½ tablespoons melted butter, cooled
⅓ cup molasses
½ cup drained sauerkraut
⅓ teaspoon salt
1½ tablespoons unsweetened cocoa powder
Pinch ground nutmeg
¾ cup rye flour
2 cups white bread flour
1⅔ teaspoons bread machine or instant yeast

Directions
1. Preparing the Ingredients.
Place the ingredients in your bread machine as recommended by the manufacturer.

Program the machine for Basic/White bread, select light or medium crust, and press Start.

2. Select the Bake cycle
When the loaf is done, remove the bucket from the machine.

Let the loaf cool for 5 minutes.

Gently shake the bucket to remove the loaf, and turn it out onto a rack to cool.

Garden Vegetable Bread

PREP: 10 MINUTES /MAKES 14 SLICES

Ingredients

½ cup warm buttermilk (70°F to 80°F)
3 Tbsp water (70°F to 80°F)
1 Tbsp canola oil
⅔ cup shredded zucchini
¼ cup chopped red sweet pepper
2 Tbsp chopped green onions
2 Tbsp grated parmesan cheese
2 Tbsp sugar
1 tsp salt
½ tsp lemon-pepper seasoning
½ cup old-fashioned oats
2½ cup bread flour
1½ tsp active dry yeast
Peppercorns

Directions

1. **Preparing the Ingredients.**
   Add each ingredient to the bread machine in the order and at the temperature recommended by your bread machine manufacturer.
2. **Select the Bake cycle**
   Close the lid, select the basic bread, medium crust setting on your bread machine and press start.
   When the bread machine has finished baking, remove the bread and put it on a cooling rack.

Carrot Coriander Bread

PREP: 10 MINUTES /MAKES 14 SLICES

Ingredients

2-3 freshly grated carrots,
1⅛ cup lukewarm water
2 Tbsp sunflower oil
4 tsp freshly chopped coriander
2½ cups unbleached white bread flour
2 tsp ground coriander
1 tsp salt
5 tsp sugar
4 tsp easy blend dried yeast

Directions

1. **Preparing the Ingredients.**
   Add each ingredient to the bread machine in the order and at the temperature recommended by your bread machine manufacturer.
2. **Select the Bake cycle**
   Close the lid, select the basic bread, medium crust setting on your bread machine, and press start.
   When the bread machine has finished baking, remove the bread and put it on a cooling rack.

Basil Tomato Bread

Ingredients
¾ cup lukewarm tomato sauce
¾ tablespoon olive oil
¾ tablespoon sugar
¾ teaspoon table salt
2¼ cups white bread flour
1½ tablespoons dried basil
¾ tablespoon dried oregano
3 tablespoons grated Parmesan cheese
2 teaspoons bread machine yeast

Directions
1. Preparing the Ingredients.
Choose the size of loaf you would like to make and measure your ingredients.
Add the ingredients to the bread pan in the order listed above.
Place the pan in the bread machine and close the lid.

2. Select the Bake cycle
Turn on the bread maker. Select the White/Basic setting, then the loaf size, and finally the crust color. Start the cycle.
When the cycle is finished and the bread is baked, carefully remove the pan from the machine. Use a potholder as the handle will be very hot. Let rest for a few minutes.
Remove the bread from the pan and allow to cool on a wire rack for at least 10 minutes before slicing.

Savory Onion Bread

Ingredients
1 cup water, at 80°F to 90°F
3 tablespoons melted butter, cooled
1½ tablespoons sugar
1⅛ teaspoons salt
3 tablespoons dried minced onion
1½ tablespoons chopped fresh chives
3 cups plus 2 tablespoons white bread flour
1⅔ teaspoons bread machine or instant yeast

Directions
1. Preparing the Ingredients.
Place the ingredients in your bread machine as recommended by the manufacturer.
2. Select the Bake cycle
Program the machine for Basic/White bread, select light or medium crust, and press Start.
When the loaf is done, remove the bucket from the machine.
Let the loaf cool for 5 minutes. Gently shake the bucket to remove the loaf, and turn it out onto a rack to cool.

Zucchini Spice Bread

PREP: 10 MINUTES PLUS FERMENTING TIME /MAKES 1 LOAF/12 SLICE BREAD (1½ pounds)

Ingredients

2 eggs, at room temperature
½ cup unsalted butter, melted
½ teaspoon table salt
¾ cup shredded zucchini
½ cup light brown sugar
2 tablespoons sugar
1½ cups all-purpose flour
½ teaspoon baking powder
½ teaspoon baking soda
¼ teaspoon ground allspice
1 teaspoon ground cinnamon
½ cup chopped pecans

Directions

1.   Preparing the Ingredients.

Choose the size of loaf you would like to make and measure your ingredients.

Add the ingredients to the bread pan in the order listed above.

Place the pan in the bread machine and close the lid.

Turn on the bread maker. Select the Quick/Rapid setting, then the loaf size, and finally the crust color. Start the cycle.

2.   Select the Bake cycle

When the cycle is finished and the bread is baked, carefully remove the pan from the machine. Use a potholder as the handle will be very hot. Let rest for a few minutes.

Remove the bread from the pan and allow to cool down on a wire rack for at least 10 minutes or more before slicing.

Tomato Herb Bread

PREP: 10 MINUTES /MAKES 1 LOAF/8 SLICE BREAD (1 pound)

Ingredients

½ cup tomato sauce, at 80°F to 90°F
½ tablespoon olive oil
½ tablespoon sugar
1 tablespoon dried basil
½ tablespoon dried oregano
½ teaspoon salt
2 tablespoons grated Parmesan cheese
1½ cups white bread flour
1⅛ teaspoons bread machine or instant yeast

Directions

1.   Preparing the Ingredients.

Place the ingredients in your bread machine as recommended by the manufacturer.

Program the machine for Basic/White bread, select light or medium crust, and press Start.

When the loaf is done, remove the bucket from the machine.

2.   Select the Bake cycle

Let the loaf cool for 5 minutes.

Gently shake the bucket to remove the loaf, and turn it out onto a rack to cool.

Potato Honey Bread

PREP: 10 MINUTES /MAKES 1 LOAF/12 SLICE BREAD (1½ pounds)

Ingredients

¾ cup lukewarm water

½ cup finely mashed potatoes, at room temperature

1 egg, at room temperature

¼ cup unsalted butter, melted

2 tablespoons honey

1 teaspoon table salt

3 cups white bread flour

2 teaspoons bread machine yeast

Directions

1. Preparing the Ingredients.

Choose the size of loaf you would like to make and measure your ingredients.

Add the ingredients to the bread pan in the order listed above.

Place the pan in the bread machine and close the lid.

2. Select the Bake cycle

Turn on the bread maker. Select the White/Basic setting, then the loaf size, and finally the crust color. Start the cycle.

When the cycle is finished and the bread is baked, carefully remove the pan from the machine. Use a potholder as the handle will be very hot. Let rest for a few minutes.

Remove the bread from the pan and allow to cool on a wire rack for at least 10 minutes before slicing.

Mashed Potato Bread

PREP: 10 MINUTES /MAKES 1 LOAF/12 SLICE BREAD (1½ pounds)

Ingredients

¾ cup water, at 80°F to 90°F

½ cup finely mashed potatoes, at room temperature

1 egg, at room temperature

¼ cup melted butter, cooled

2 tablespoons honey

1 teaspoon salt

3 cups white bread flour

2 teaspoons bread machine or instant yeast

Directions

1. Preparing the Ingredients.

Place the ingredients in your bread machine as recommended by the manufacturer.

Program the machine for Basic/White bread, select light or medium crust, and press Start.

When the loaf is done, remove the bucket from the machine.

2. Select the Bake cycle

Let the loaf cool for 5 minutes.

Gently shake the bucket to remove the loaf, and turn it out onto a rack to cool.

Dilly Onion Bread

PREP: 10 MINUTES /MAKES 14 SLICES

Ingredients

¾ cup water (70°F to 80°F)

1 Tbsp butter, softened

2 Tbsp sugar

3 Tbsp dried minced onion

2 Tbsp dried parsley flakes

1 Tbsp dill weed

1 tsp salt

1 garlic clove, minced

2 cups bread flour

⅓ cup whole wheat flour

1 Tbsp nonfat dry milk powder

2 tsp active dry yeast serving

Directions

1. **Preparing the Ingredients.**
   Add each ingredient to the bread machine in the order and at the temperature recommended by your bread machine manufacturer.

2. **Select the Bake cycle**
   Close the lid, select the basic bread, medium crust setting on your bread machine and press start.
   When the bread machine has finished baking, remove the bread and put it on a cooling rack.

Onion Chive Bread

PREP: 10 MINUTES /MAKES 1 LOAF/12 SLICE BREAD (1½ pounds)

Ingredients

1 cup lukewarm water

3 tablespoons unsalted butter, melted

1½ tablespoons sugar

1⅛ teaspoons table salt

3⅛ cups white bread flour

3 tablespoons dried minced onion

1½ tablespoons fresh chives, chopped

1⅔ teaspoons bread machine yeast

Directions

1. **Preparing the Ingredients.**

Choose the size of loaf you would like to make and measure your ingredients.

Add the ingredients to the bread pan in the order listed above.

Place the pan in the bread machine and close the lid.

2. **Select the Bake cycle**

Turn on the bread maker. Select the White/Basic setting, then the loaf size, and finally the crust color. Start the cycle.

When the cycle is finished and the bread is baked, carefully remove the pan from the machine. Use a potholder as the handle will be very hot. Let rest for a few minutes.

Remove the bread from the pan and allow to cool on a wire rack for at least 10 minutes before slicing.

Basil Tomato Bread
PREP: 10 MINUTES /MAKES 14 SLICES

Ingredients

2¼ tsp dried active baking yeast

1⅝ cups bread flour

3 Tbsp wheat bran

5 Tbsp quinoa

3 Tbsp dried milk powder

1 Tbsp dried basil

25g sun-dried tomatoes, chopped

1 tsp salt

1⅛ cups water

1 cup boiling water to cover tomatoes

Directions

1. **Preparing the Ingredients.**
   Cover dried tomatoes with boiling water in a bowl.
   Soak for 10 minutes, drain, and cool to room temperature.
   Snip tomatoes into small pieces, using scissors.
   Add each ingredient to the bread machine in the order and at the temperature recommended by your bread machine manufacturer.

2. **Select the Bake cycle**
   Close the lid, select the basic bread, medium crust setting on your bread machine and press start.
   When the bread machine has finished baking, remove the bread and put it on a cooling rack.

Confetti Bread
PREP: 10 MINUTES /MAKES 1 LOAF/8 SLICE BREAD (1pound)

Ingredients

⅓ cup milk, at 80°F to 90°F

2 tablespoons water, at 80°F to 90°F

2 teaspoons melted butter, cooled

⅔ teaspoon white vinegar

4 teaspoons sugar

⅔ teaspoon salt

4 teaspoons grated Parmesan cheese

⅓ cup quick oats

1⅔ cups white bread flour

1 teaspoon bread machine or instant yeast

⅓ cup finely chopped zucchini

¼ cup finely chopped yellow bell pepper

¼ cup finely chopped red bell pepper

4 teaspoons chopped chives

Directions

1. **Preparing the Ingredients.**

Place the ingredients, except the vegetables, in your bread machine as recommended by the manufacturer.

Program the machine for Basic/White bread, select light or medium crust, and press Start.

When the machine signals, add the chopped vegetables; if your machine has no signal, add the vegetables just before the second kneading is finished.

2. **Select the Bake cycle**

When the loaf is done, remove the bucket from the machine.

Let the loaf cool for 5 minutes.

Gently shake the bucket to remove the loaf, and turn it out onto a rack to cool.

Honey Potato Flakes Bread

PREP: 10 MINUTES /MAKES 1 LOAF/12 SLICE BREAD (1½ pounds)

Ingredients
1¼ cups lukewarm milk
2 tablespoons unsalted butter, melted
1 tablespoon honey
1½ teaspoons table salt
3 cups white bread flour
1 teaspoon dried thyme
½ cup instant potato flakes
2 teaspoons bread machine yeast

Directions
1. Preparing the Ingredients.
Choose the size of loaf you would like to make and measure your ingredients.
Add the ingredients to the bread pan in the order listed above.
Place the pan in the bread machine and close the lid.

2. Select the Bake cycle
Turn on the bread maker. Select the White/Basic setting, then the loaf size, and finally the crust color. Start the cycle.
When the cycle is finished and the bread is baked, carefully remove the pan from the machine. Use a potholder as the handle will be very hot. Let rest for a few minutes.
Remove the bread from the pan and allow to cool on a wire rack for at least 10 minutes before slicing.

Pretty Borscht Bread

PREP: 10 MINUTES /MAKES 1 LOAF/12 SLICE BREAD (1½ pounds)

Ingredients
¾ cups water, at 80°F to 90°F
¾ cup grated raw beetroot
1½ tablespoons melted butter, cooled
1½ tablespoons sugar
1¼ teaspoons salt
3 cups white bread flour
1¼ teaspoons bread machine or instant yeast

Directions
1. Preparing the Ingredients.
Place the ingredients in your bread machine as recommended by the manufacturer.
Program the machine for Basic/White bread, select light or medium crust, and press Start.

2. Select the Bake cycle
When the loaf is done, remove the bucket from the machine.
Let the loaf cool for 5 minutes.
Gently shake the bucket to remove the loaf, and turn it out onto a rack to cool.

Zucchini Lemon Bread
PREP: 10 MINUTES /MAKES 1 LOAF/12 SLICE BREAD (1½ pounds)

Ingredients
½ cup lukewarm milk
¾ cup finely shredded zucchini
¼ teaspoon lemon juice, at room temperature
1 tablespoon olive oil
1 tablespoon sugar
1 teaspoon table salt
¾ cup whole-wheat flour
1½ cups white bread flour
¾ cup quick oats
2¼ teaspoons bread machine yeast

Directions
   1. **Preparing the Ingredients.**
Choose the size of loaf you would like to make and measure your ingredients.
Add the ingredients to the bread pan in the order listed above. Place the pan in the bread machine and close the lid.

   2. **Select the Bake cycle**
Turn on the bread maker. Select the White/Basic setting, then the loaf size, and finally the crust color. Start the cycle.
When the cycle is finished and the bread is baked, carefully remove the pan from the machine. Use a potholder as the handle will be very hot. Let rest for a few minutes. Remove the bread from the pan and allow to cool on a wire rack for at least 10 minutes before slicing.

Yeasted Pumpkin Bread
PREP: 10 MINUTES /MAKES 1 LOAF/8 SLICE BREAD (1 pound)

Ingredients
⅓ cup milk, at 80°F to 90°F
⅔ cup canned pumpkin
2 tablespoons melted butter, cooled
⅔ teaspoon grated ginger
2¾ tablespoons sugar
½ teaspoon salt
⅔ teaspoon ground cinnamon
¼ teaspoon ground cloves
2 cups white bread flour
1⅛ teaspoons bread machine or instant yeast
Directions
   1. **Preparing the Ingredients.**
Place the ingredients in your bread machine as recommended by the manufacturer.
Program the machine for Basic/White bread, select light or medium crust, and press Start.

   2. **Select the Bake cycle**
When the loaf is done, remove the bucket from the machine.
Let the loaf cool for 5 minutes.
Gently shake the bucket to remove the loaf, and turn it out onto a rack to cool.

Oatmeal Zucchini Bread
PREP: 10 MINUTES /MAKES 1 LOAF/8 SLICE BREAD (1 pound)

Ingredients

⅓ cup milk, at 80°F to 90°F

½ cup finely shredded zucchini

¼ teaspoon freshly squeezed lemon juice, at room temperature

2 teaspoons olive oil

2 teaspoons sugar

⅔ teaspoon salt

½ cup quick oats

½ cup whole-wheat flour

1 cup white bread flour

1½ teaspoons bread machine or instant yeast

Directions

1. Preparing the Ingredients.

Place the ingredients in your bread machine as recommended by the manufacturer.

Program the machine for Basic/White bread, select light or medium crust, and press Start.

2. Select the Bake cycle

When the loaf is done, remove the bucket from the machine.

Let the loaf cool for 5 minutes.

Gently shake the bucket to remove the loaf, and turn it out onto a rack to cool.

Hot Red Pepper Bread
PREP: 10 MINUTES /MAKES 1 LOAF /12 SLICE BREAD (1½ pounds)

Ingredients

1¼ cups milk, at 80°F to 90°F

¼ cup red pepper relish

2 tablespoons chopped roasted red pepper

3 tablespoons melted butter, cooled

3 tablespoons light brown sugar

1 teaspoon salt

3 cups white bread flour

1½ teaspoons bread machine or instant yeast

Directions

1. Preparing the Ingredients.

Place the ingredients in your bread machine as recommended by the manufacturer.

Program the machine for Basic/White bread, select light or medium crust, and press Start.

2. Select the Bake cycle

When the loaf is done, remove the bucket from the machine.

Let the loaf cool for 5 minutes.

Gently shake the bucket to remove the loaf, and turn it out onto a rack to cool.

French Onion Bread

PREP: 10 MINUTES /MAKES 1 LOAF/12 SLICE BREAD (1½ pounds)

Ingredients

1¼ cups milk, at 80°F to 90°F
¼ cup melted butter, cooled
3 tablespoons light brown sugar
1 teaspoon salt
3 tablespoons dehydrated onion flakes
2 tablespoons chopped fresh chives
1 teaspoon garlic powder
3 cups white bread flour
1 teaspoon bread machine or instant yeast

Directions

1. Preparing the Ingredients.

Place the ingredients in your bread machine as recommended by the manufacturer.
Program the machine for Basic/White bread, select light or medium crust, and press Start.

2. Select the Bake cycle

When the loaf is done, remove the bucket from the machine.
Let the loaf cool for 5 minutes.
Gently shake the bucket to remove the loaf, and turn it out onto a rack to cool.

Golden Butternut Squash Raisin Bread

PREP: 10 MINUTES /MAKES 1 LOAF/16 SLICE BREAD (2 pounds)

Ingredients

2 cups cooked mashed butternut squash, at room temperature
1 cup (2 sticks) butter, at room temperature
3 eggs, at room temperature
1 teaspoon pure vanilla extract
2 cups sugar
½ cup light brown sugar
3 cups all-purpose flour
1 teaspoon baking soda
1 teaspoon ground cinnamon
½ teaspoon ground cloves
½ teaspoon ground nutmeg
½ teaspoon salt
½ teaspoon baking powder
½ cup golden raisins

Directions

1. Preparing the Ingredients.

Place the butternut squash, butter, eggs, vanilla, sugar, and brown sugar in your bread machine.
Program the machine for Quick/Rapid bread and press Start.
While the wet ingredients are mixing, stir together the flour, baking soda, cinnamon, cloves, nutmeg, salt, and baking powder in a small bowl.

2. Select the Bake cycle

After the first fast mixing is done and the machine signals, add the dry ingredients and raisins.
When the loaf is done, remove the bucket from the machine.
Let the loaf cool for 5 minutes.
Gently shake the bucket to remove the loaf, and turn it out onto a rack to cool.

Sweet Potato Bread

PREP: 10 MINUTES /MAKES 1 LOAF/12 SLICE BREAD (1½ pounds)

Ingredients
1½ cups mashed cooked sweet potato, at room temperature
¾ cup buttermilk, at room temperature
½ cup sugar
¼ cup melted butter, cooled
1 egg, at room temperature
1½ cups all-purpose flour
1 teaspoon ground cinnamon
½ teaspoon baking powder
½ teaspoon baking soda
¼ teaspoon ground cloves
¼ teaspoon salt

Directions
1. **Preparing the Ingredients.**
   Place the sweet potato, buttermilk, sugar, butter, and egg in your bread machine.
2. **Select the Bake cycle**
   Program the machine for Quick/Rapid bread and press Start. While the wet ingredients are mixing, stir together the flour, cinnamon, baking powder, baking soda, cloves, and salt in a small bowl.
   After the first fast mixing is done and the machine signals, add the dry ingredients.
   When the loaf is done, remove the bucket from the machine. Let the loaf cool for 5 minutes. Gently shake the bucket to remove the loaf, and turn it out onto a rack to cool.

Potato Thyme Bread

PREP: 10 MINUTES /MAKES 1 LOAF/12 SLICE BREAD (1½ pounds)

Ingredients
1¼ cups milk, at 80°F to 90°F
2 tablespoons melted butter, cooled
1 tablespoon honey
1½ teaspoons salt
1 teaspoon dried thyme
½ cup instant potato flakes
3 cups white bread flour
2 teaspoons bread machine or instant yeast

Directions
1. **Preparing the Ingredients.**
Place the ingredients in your bread machine as recommended by the manufacturer.
Program the machine for Basic/White bread, select light or medium crust, and press Start.

2. **Select the Bake cycle**
When the loaf is done, remove the bucket from the machine.
Let the loaf cool for 5 minutes.
Gently shake the bucket to remove the loaf, and turn it out onto a rack to cool.

Caramelized Onion Bread
PREP: 10 MINUTES /MAKES 14 SLICES

Ingredients
½ Tbsp butter
½ cup onions, sliced
1 cup water
1 Tbsp olive oil
3 cups Gold Medal Better for Bread flour
2 Tbsp sugar
1 tsp salt
1¼ tsp bread machine or quick active dry yeast

Directions
1. **Preparing the Ingredients**
   Melt the butter over medium-low heat in a skillet.
   Cook the onions in the butter for 10 to 15 minutes until they are brown and caramelized - then remove from the heat.
   Add each ingredient except the onions to the bread machine in the order and at the temperature recommended by your bread machine manufacturer.
2. **Select the Bake cycle**
   Close the lid, select the basic bread, medium crust setting on your bread machine and press start.
   Add ½ cup of onions 5 to 10 minutes before the last kneading cycle ends.
   When the bread machine has finished baking, remove the bread and put it on a cooling rack.

Light Corn Bread
PREP: 10 MINUTES /MAKES 1 LOAF/12 SLICE BREAD (1½ pounds)

Ingredients
¾ cup milk, at 80°F to 90°F
1 egg, at room temperature
2¼ tablespoons butter, melted and cooled
2¼ tablespoons honey
¾ teaspoon salt
⅓ cup cornmeal
2⅔ cups white bread flour
1¾ teaspoons bread machine or instant yeast

Directions
1. **Preparing the Ingredients.**
Place the ingredients in your bread machine as recommended by the manufacturer.
Program the machine for Basic/White bread, select light or medium crust, and press Start.

2. **Select the Bake cycle**
When the loaf is done, remove the bucket from the machine.
Let the loaf cool for 5 minutes.
Gently shake the bucket to remove the loaf, and turn it out onto a rack to cool.

Chive Bread
PREP: 10 MINUTES /MAKES 14 SLICES

Ingredients
⅔ cup milk (70°F to 80°F)
¼ cup water (70°F to 80°F)
¼ cup sour cream
2 Tbsp butter
1½ tsp sugar
1½ tsp salt
3 cups bread flour
⅛ tsp baking soda
¼ cup minced chives
2¼ tsp active dry yeast leaves

Directions
1. **Preparing the Ingredients**
   Add each ingredient to the bread machine in the order and at the temperature recommended by your bread machine manufacturer.
2. **Select the Bake cycle**
   Close the lid, select the basic bread, medium crust setting on your bread machine and press start.
   When the bread machine has finished baking, remove the bread and put it on a cooling rack.

Caramelized Onion Focaccia Bread
PREP: 10 MINUTES /MAKES 4

Ingredients
¾cup water
2 tablespoons olive oil
1 tablespoon sugar
1 teaspoon salt
2 cups flour
1 ½teaspoons yeast
¾cup mozzarella cheese, shredded
2 tablespoons parmesan cheese, shredded
Onion topping:
3 tablespoons butter
2 medium onions
2 cloves garlic, minced

Directions
Preparing the Ingredients
Place all ingredients, except cheese and onion topping, in your bread maker in the order listed above.   Grease a large baking sheet.   Pat dough into a 12-inch circle on the pan; cover and let rise in warm place for about 30 minutes.
 Melt butter in large frying pan over medium-low heat. Cook onions and garlic in butter 15 minutes, stirring often, until onions are caramelized.
Preheat an oven to 400°F.
Make deep depressions across the dough at 1-inch intervals with the handle of a wooden spoon.   Spread the onion topping over dough and sprinkle with cheeses.
Bake 15 to 20 minutes or until golden brown. Cut into wedges and serve warm.

Pumpkin Cinnamon Bread

PREP: 10 MINUTES / MAKES 14 SLICES

Ingredients

1 cup sugar
1 cup canned pumpkin
⅓ cup vegetable oil
1 tsp vanilla
2 eggs
1½ cups all-purpose bread flour
2 tsp baking powder
¼ tsp salt
1 tsp ground cinnamon
¼ tsp ground nutmeg
⅛ tsp ground cloves

Directions

1. **Preparing the Ingredients**

   Add each ingredient to the bread machine in the order and at the temperature recommended by your bread machine manufacturer.

2. **Select the Bake cycle**

   Close the lid, select the quick, medium crust setting on your bread machine and press start.

   When the bread machine has finished baking, remove the bread and put it on a cooling rack.

Potato Dill Bread

PREP: 10 MINUTES / MAKES 14 SLICES

Ingredients

1 (.25 oz) package active dry yeast
½ cup water
1 Tbsp sugar
1 tsp salt
2 Tbsp melted butter
1 package or bunch fresh dill
¾ cup room temperature mashed potatoes
2¼ cups bread flour

Directions

1. **Preparing the Ingredients**

   Add each ingredient to the bread machine in the order and at the temperature recommended by your bread machine manufacturer.

2. **Select the Bake cycle**

   Close the lid, select the basic bread, medium crust setting on your bread machine, and press start.

   When the bread machine has finished baking, remove the bread and put it on a cooling rack.

Tomato Basil Bread
PREP: 10 MINUTES /MAKES 16 SLICES

Ingredients
¾cup warm water
¼cup fresh basil, minced
¼cup parmesan cheese, grated
3 tablespoons tomato paste
1 tablespoon sugar
1 tablespoon olive oil
1 teaspoon salt
¼teaspoon crushed red pepper flakes
2 ½cups bread flour
1 package active dry yeast
Flour, for surface

Directions
1. **Preparing the Ingredients**
   Add ingredients, except yeast, to bread maker pan in above listed order.   Make a well in the flour; pour the yeast into the hole.
2. **Select the Bake cycle**
   Select Dough cycle and press Start. Turn finished dough out onto a floured surface and knead until smooth and elastic, about 3 to 5 minutes. Place in a greased bowl, turning once to grease top. Cover and let rise in a warm place until doubled, about 1 hour. Punch dough down and knead for 1 minute. Shape into a round loaf. Place on a greased baking sheet. Cover and let rise until doubled, about 1 hour. With a sharp knife, cut a large "X" in top of loaf. Bake at 375°F for 35-40 minutes or until golden brown. Remove from pan and cool on a cooling rack before serving.

CHEESE BREADS

Zesty Cheddar Bread
PREP: 10 MINUTES /MAKES 1 LOAF/12 SLICE BREAD (1½ pounds)

Ingredients
1 cup buttermilk
⅓cup butter, melted
1 tablespoon sugar
2 tablespoons finely chopped chipotle chiles in adobo sauce (from 7-oz can) 2 eggs
2 cups all-purpose flour
1 cup shredded Cheddar cheese (4 oz)
2 teaspoons baking powder
1 teaspoon baking soda
½ teaspoon salt

Directions
1. **Preparing the Ingredients.**
Place the ingredients in your bread machine as recommended by the manufacturer.
Program the machine for Basic/White bread, select light or medium crust, and press Start.
When the loaf is done, remove the bucket from the machine.

2. **Select the Bake cycle**
Let the loaf cool for 5 minutes.
Gently shake the bucket to remove the loaf, and turn it out onto a rack to cool.
Serve warm, if desired.

French Cheese Bread
PREP: 10 MINUTES /MAKES 14 SLICES

Ingredients
1 tsp sugar
2¼ tsp yeast
1¼ cup water
3 cups bread flour
2 Tbsp parmesan cheese
1 tsp garlic powder
1½ tsp salt
Directions
1. **Preparing the Ingredients**
   Add each ingredient to the bread machine in the order and at the temperature recommended by your bread machine manufacturer.
2. **Select the Bake cycle**
   Close the lid, select the basic bread, medium crust setting on your bread machine, and press start.
   When the bread machine has finished baking, remove the bread and put it on a cooling rack.

Romano Oregano Bread
PREP: 10 MINUTES /MAKES 1 LOAF/12 SLICE BREAD (1½ pounds)

Ingredients
1 cup lukewarm water
3 tablespoons sugar
1½ tablespoons olive oil
1 teaspoon table salt
1 tablespoon dried leaf oregano
½ cup cheese (Romano or Parmesan), freshly grated
3 cups white bread flour
2 teaspoons bread machine yeast

Directions
1. Preparing the Ingredients.
Choose the size of loaf you would like to make and measure your ingredients.
Add the ingredients to the bread pan in the order listed above.
Place the pan in the bread machine and close the lid.
Turn on the bread maker. Select the White/Basic setting, then the loaf size, and finally the crust color. Start the cycle.

2. Select the Bake cycle
When the cycle is finished and the bread is baked, carefully remove the pan from the machine. Use a potholder as the handle will be very hot. Let rest for a few minutes.
Remove the bread from the pan and allow to cool down on a wire rack for at least 10 minutes or more before slicing.

Jalapeno Cheese Bread
PREP: 10 MINUTES /MAKES 14 SLICES

Ingredients
3 cups bread flour
1½ tsp active dry yeast
1 cup water
2 Tbsp sugar
1 tsp salt
½ cup shredded cheddar cheese
¼ cup diced jalapeno peppers

Directions
1. **Preparing the Ingredients.**
   Add each ingredient to the bread machine in the order and at the temperature recommended by your bread machine manufacturer.
2. **Select the Bake cycle**
   Close the lid, select the basic bread, medium crust setting on your bread machine, and press start. When the bread machine has finished baking, remove the bread and put it on a cooling rack.

Cheesy Chipotle Bread
PREP: 10 MINUTES /MAKES 1 LOAF/8 SLICE BREAD (1 pound)

Ingredients
⅔ cup water, at 80°F to 90°F
1½ tablespoons sugar
1½ tablespoons powdered skim milk
¾ teaspoon salt
½ teaspoon chipotle chili powder
2 cups white bread flour
½ cup (2 ounces) shredded sharp Cheddar cheese
¾ teaspoon bread machine or instant yeast

Directions
1. **Preparing the Ingredients.**

Place the ingredients in your bread machine as recommended by the manufacturer.
Program the machine for Basic/White bread, select light or medium crust, and press Start.
When the loaf is done, remove the bucket from the machine.

2. **Select the Bake cycle**

Let the loaf cool for 5 minutes.
Gently shake the bucket to remove the loaf, and turn it out onto a rack to cool.

Cheddar Cheese Bread
PREP: 10 MINUTES /MAKES 1 LOAF

Ingredients
1 cup lukewarm milk
3 cups all-purpose flour
1¼ tsp salt
1 tsp tabasco sauce, optional
¼ cup Vermont cheese powder
1 Tbsp sugar
1 cup grated cheddar cheese, firmly packed
1½ tsp instant yeast

Directions
1. **Preparing the Ingredients**

    Add each ingredient to the bread machine in the order and at the temperature recommended by your bread machine manufacturer.

2. **Select the Bake cycle**

    Close the lid, select the basic bread, medium crust setting on your bread machine, and press start.
    When the bread machine has finished baking, remove the bread and put it on a cooling rack.

Apricot–Cream Cheese Ring
PREP: 10 MINUTES /MAKES 10 SERVINGS

Ingredients
⅓ cup water
2 tablespoons butter, softened
1 egg
2 cups bread flour
2 tablespoons sugar
½ teaspoon salt
1¾ teaspoons bread machine or fast-acting dry yeast
filling
1 package (3 oz) cream cheese, softened
1½ tablespoons bread flour
¼ cup apricot preserves
1 egg, beaten
2 tablespoons sliced almonds

Directions
1. Preparing the Ingredients.
Measure carefully, placing all bread dough ingredients in bread machine pan in the order recommended by the manufacturer. Select Dough/Manual cycle. Do not use delay cycle.
Remove dough from pan, using lightly floured hands. Cover and let rest 10 minutes on lightly floured surface. In small bowl, mix cream cheese and 1½ tablespoons flour.
4 Grease 9-inch round pan with shortening. Roll dough into 15-inch round.
Place in pan, letting side of dough hang over edge of pan. Spread cream cheese mixture over dough in pan; spoon apricot preserves onto cream cheese mixture.

2. Select the Bake cycle
Make cuts along edge of dough at 1-inch intervals to about ½ inch above cream cheese mixture. Twist pairs of dough strips and fold over cream cheese mixture.
Cover and let rise in warm place 40 to 50 minutes or until almost double.
5 Heat oven to 375°F. Brush beaten egg over dough. Sprinkle with almonds.
Bake 30 to 35 minutes or until golden brown. Cool at least 30 minutes before cutting.

Cottage Cheese and Chive Bread
PREP: 10 MINUTES /MAKES 14 SERVINGS

Ingredients
⅜ cup water
1 cup cottage cheese
1 large egg
2 Tbsp butter
1½ tsp salt
3¾ cups white bread flour
3 Tbsp dried chives
2½ Tbsp granulated sugar
2¼ tsp active dry yeast

Directions
1. Preparing the Ingredients
Add each ingredient to the bread machine in the order and at the temperature recommended by your bread machine manufacturer.
2. Select the Bake cycle
Close the lid, select the basic bread, medium crust setting on your bread machine, and press start.
When the bread machine has finished baking, remove the bread and put it on a cooling rack.

Mexican Style Jalapeno Cheese Bread
PREP: 10 MINUTES /MAKES 1 LOAF/12 SLICE BREAD (1½ pounds)

Ingredients
1 small jalapeno pepper, seeded and minced
¾ cup lukewarm water
2 tablespoons nonfat dry milk powder
1 tablespoon unsalted butter, melted
1 tablespoon sugar
1 teaspoon salt
3 tablespoons finely shredded cheese (Mexican blend or Monterrey Jack)
2 cups white bread flour
1½ teaspoons bread machine yeast

Directions
1. **Preparing the Ingredients.**

Choose the size of loaf you would like to make and measure your ingredients.

Add the ingredients to the bread pan in the order listed above.

Place the pan in the bread machine and close the lid.

Turn on the bread maker. Select the White/Basic setting, then the loaf size, and finally the crust color. Start the cycle.

2. **Select the Bake cycle**

When the cycle is finished and the bread is baked, carefully remove the pan from the machine. Use a potholder as the handle will be very hot. Let rest for a few minutes.

Remove the bread from the pan and allow to cool on a wire rack for at least 10 minutes before slicing.

Ricotta Bread
PREP: 10 MINUTES /MAKES 14 SLICES

Ingredients
3 Tbsp skim milk
⅔ cup ricotta cheese
4 tsp unsalted butter, softened to room temperature
1 large egg
2 Tbsp granulated sugar
½ tsp salt
1½ cups bread flour, + more flour, as needed
1 tsp active dry yeast

Directions
1. **Preparing the Ingredients**

   Add each ingredient to the bread machine in the order and at the temperature recommended by your bread machine manufacturer.
2. **Select the Bake cycle**

   Close the lid, select the basic bread, medium crust setting on your bread machine, and press start. When the bread machine has finished baking, remove the bread and put it on a cooling rack.

Roasted Garlic Asiago Bread

PREP: 10 MINUTES /MAKES 1 LOAF/12 SLICE BREAD (1½ pounds)

Ingredients

¾ cup plus 1 tablespoon milk, at 70°F to 80°F

¼ cup melted butter, cooled

1 teaspoon minced garlic

2 tablespoons sugar

1 teaspoon salt

½ cup (2 ounces) grated Asiago cheese

2¾ cups white bread flour

1½ teaspoons bread machine or instant yeast

½ cup mashed roasted garlic

Directions

1. Preparing the Ingredients.

Place the ingredients, except the roasted garlic, in your bread machine as recommended by the manufacturer.

Program the machine for Basic/White bread, select light or medium crust, and press Start.

Add the roasted garlic when your machine signals or 5 minutes before the last kneading is done.

2. Select the Bake cycle

Gently shake the bucket to remove the loaf, and turn it out onto a rack to cool.

When the loaf is done, remove the bucket from the machine.

Let the loaf cool for 5 minutes

Jalapeno Cheddar Bread

PREP: 10 MINUTES /MAKES 1 LOAF/12 SLICE BREAD (1½ pounds)

Ingredients

1 cup lukewarm buttermilk

¼ cup unsalted butter, melted

2 eggs, at room temperature

½ teaspoon table salt

1 jalapeno pepper, chopped

½ cup Cheddar cheese, shredded

¼ cup sugar

1⅓ cups all-purpose flour

1 cup cornmeal

1 tablespoon baking powder

Directions

1. Preparing the Ingredients.

Choose the size of loaf you would like to make and measure your ingredients.

Add the ingredients to the bread pan in the order listed above.

Place the pan in the bread machine and close the lid.

2. Select the Bake cycle

Turn on the bread maker. Select the Rapid/Quick setting, then the loaf size, and finally the crust color. Start the cycle.

When the cycle is finished and the bread is baked, carefully remove the pan from the machine. Use a potholder as the handle will be very hot. Let rest for a few minutes.

Remove the bread from the pan and allow to cool on a wire rack for at least 10 minutes before slicing.

Oregano Cheese Bread

PREP: 10 MINUTES /MAKES 1 LOAF

Ingredients

3 cups bread flour

1 cup water

½ cup freshly grated parmesan cheese

3 Tbsp sugar

1 Tbsp dried leaf oregano

1½ Tbsp olive oil

1 tsp salt

2 tsp active dry yeast

Directions

1. **Preparing the Ingredients**
   Add each ingredient to the bread machine in the order and at the temperature recommended by your bread machine manufacturer.

2. **Select the Bake cycle**
   Close the lid, select the basic bread, medium crust setting on your bread machine, and press start.
   When the bread machine has finished baking, remove the bread and put it on a cooling rack.

Cheddar Cheese Basil Bread

PREP: 10 MINUTES /MAKES 1 LOAF/8 SLICE BREAD (1 pound)

Ingredients

⅔ cup milk, at 80°F to 90°F

2 teaspoons melted butter, cooled

2 teaspoons sugar

⅔ teaspoon dried basil

½ cup (2 ounces) shredded sharp Cheddar cheese

½ teaspoon salt

2 cups white bread flour

1 teaspoon bread machine or active dry yeast

Directions

1. **Preparing the Ingredients.**

Place the ingredients in your bread machine as recommended by the manufacturer.

Program the machine for Basic/White bread, select light or medium crust, and press Start.

2. **Select the Bake cycle**

When the loaf is done, remove the bucket from the machine.

Let the loaf cool for 5 minutes.

Gently shake the bucket to remove the loaf, and turn it out onto a rack to cool.

Spinach and Feta Bread

PREP: 10 MINUTES /MAKES 14 SLICES

Ingredients

1 cup water

2 tsp butter

3 cups flour

1 tsp sugar

2 tsp instant minced onion

1 tsp salt

1¼ tsp instant yeast

1 cup crumbled feta

1 cup chopped fresh spinach leaves

Directions

1. **Preparing the Ingredients**

Add each ingredient except the cheese and spinach to the bread machine in the order and at the temperature recommended by your bread machine manufacturer.

2. **Select the Bake cycle**

Close the lid, select the basic bread, medium crust setting on your bread machine, and press start.
When only 10 minutes are left in the last kneading cycle add the spinach and cheese.
When the bread machine has finished baking, remove the bread and put it on a cooling rack.

Blue Cheese Bread

PREP: 10 MINUTES /MAKES 12 SLICES

Ingredients

¾cup warm water

1 large egg

1 teaspoon salt

3 cups bread flour

1 cup blue cheese, crumbled

2 tablespoons nonfat dry milk

2 tablespoons sugar

1 teaspoon bread machine yeast

Directions

1. **Preparing the Ingredients**

Add the ingredients to bread machine pan in the order listed above, (except yeast) ; be sure to add the cheese with the flour.
Make a well in the flour; pour the yeast into the hole.

2. **Select the Bake cycle**

Select Basic bread cycle, medium crust color, and press Start.
When finished, transfer to a cooling rack for 10 minutes and serve warm.

Parsley Garlic Bread

PREP: 10 MINUTES /MAKES 1 LOAF/12 SLICE BREAD (1½ pounds)

Ingredients

1 cup lukewarm milk

1½ tablespoons unsalted butter, melted

1 tablespoon sugar

1½ teaspoons table salt

2 teaspoons garlic powder

2 teaspoons fresh parsley, chopped

3 cups white bread flour

1¾ teaspoons bread machine yeast

Directions

1. **Preparing the Ingredients.**

Choose the size of loaf you would like to make and measure your ingredients.

Add the ingredients to the bread pan in the order listed above.

Place the pan in the bread machine and close the lid.

2. **Select the Bake cycle**

Turn on the bread maker. Select the White/Basic setting, then the loaf size, and finally the crust color. Start the cycle.

When the cycle is finished and the bread is baked, carefully remove the pan from the machine. Use a potholder as the handle will be very hot. Let rest for a few minutes.

Remove the bread from the pan and allow to cool on a wire rack for at least 10 minutes before slicing.

Prosciutto Parmesan Breadsticks

PREP: 10 MINUTES /MAKES 12

Ingredients

1 ⅓ cups warm water

1 tablespoon butter

1 ½ tablespoons sugar

1 ½ teaspoons salt

4 cups bread flour

2 teaspoons yeast

For the topping:

½ pound prosciutto, sliced very thin

½ cup of grated parmesan cheese

1 egg yolk

1 tablespoon of water

Directions

1. **Preparing the Ingredients**

   Place the first set of dough ingredients (except yeast) in the bread pan in the order indicated. Do not add any of the topping ingredients yet. Make a well in the center of the dry ingredients and add the yeast.

2. **Select the Bake cycle**

   Select the Dough cycle on the bread machine. When finished, drop the dough onto a lightly-floured surface.

   Roll the dough out flat to about ¼-inch thick, or about half a centimeter. Cover with plastic wrap and let rise for 20 to 30 minutes.

   Sprinkle dough evenly with parmesan and carefully lay the prosciutto slices on the surface of the dough to cover as much of it as possible. Preheat an oven to 400°F.

   Cut the dough into 12 long strips, about one inch wide. Twist each end in opposite directions, twisting the toppings into the bread stick. Place the breadsticks onto a lightly greased baking sheet. Whisk the egg yolk and water together in a small mixing bowl and lightly baste each breadstick. Bake for 8 to 10 minutes or until golden brown.

   Remove from oven and serve warm.

Jalapeño Corn Bread

PREP: 10 MINUTES /MAKES 1 LOAF/12 SLICE BREAD (1½ pounds)

Ingredients

1 cup buttermilk, at 80°F to 90°F
¼ cup melted butter, cooled
2 eggs, at room temperature
1 jalapeño pepper, chopped
1⅓ cups all-purpose flour
1 cup cornmeal
½ cup (2 ounces) shredded Cheddar cheese
¼ cup sugar
1 tablespoon baking powder
½ teaspoon salt

Directions
1. Preparing the Ingredients.
Place the buttermilk, butter, eggs, and jalapeño pepper in your bread machine.
Program the machine for Quick/Rapid bread and press Start.
While the wet ingredients are mixing, stir together the flour, cornmeal, cheese, sugar, baking powder, and salt in a small bowl.

2. Select the Bake cycle
After the first fast mixing is done and the machine signals, add the dry ingredients.
When the loaf is done, remove the bucket from the machine.
Let the loaf cool for 5 minutes.
Gently shake the bucket to remove the loaf, and turn it out onto a rack to cool.

Cheddar Bacon Bread

PREP: 10 MINUTES /MAKES 1 LOAF/12 SLICE BREAD (1½ pounds)

Ingredients

½ cup lukewarm milk
1½ teaspoons unsalted butter, melted
1½ tablespoons honey
1½ teaspoons table salt
½ cup green chilies, chopped
½ cup grated Cheddar cheese
½ cup cooked bacon, chopped
3 cups white bread flour
2 teaspoons bread machine yeast

Directions
1. Preparing the Ingredients.
Choose the size of loaf you would like to make and measure your ingredients.
Add the ingredients to the bread pan in the order listed above.
Place the pan in the bread machine and close the lid.

2. Select the Bake cycle
Turn on the bread maker. Select the White/Basic setting, then the loaf size, and finally the crust color. Start the cycle.
When the cycle is finished and the bread is baked, carefully remove the pan from the machine. Use a potholder as the handle will be very hot. Let rest for a few minutes.
Remove the bread from the pan and allow to cool on a wire rack for at least 10 minutes before slicing.

Italian Cheese Bread

PREP: 10 MINUTES /MAKES 14 SLICES

Ingredients
1¼ cups water
3 cups bread flour
½ shredded pepper jack cheese
2 tsp Italian seasoning
2 Tbsp brown sugar
1½ tsp salt
2 tsp active dry yeast

Directions
1. **Preparing the Ingredients.**
   Add each ingredient to the bread machine in the order and at the temperature recommended by your bread machine manufacturer.
2. **Select the Bake cycle**
   Close the lid, select the basic bread, medium crust setting on your bread machine, and press start.
   When the bread machine has finished baking, remove the bread and put it on a cooling rack.

Olive Cheese Bread

PREP: 10 MINUTES /MAKES 1 LOAF/12 SLICE BREAD (1½ pounds)

Ingredients
1 cup milk, at 80°F to 90°F
1½ tablespoons melted butter, cooled
1 teaspoon minced garlic
1½ tablespoons sugar
1 teaspoon salt
3 cups white bread flour
¾ cup (3 ounces) shredded Swiss cheese
1 teaspoon bread machine or instant yeast
⅓ cup chopped black olives

Directions
1. **Preparing the Ingredients.**
Place the ingredients in your bread machine as recommended by the manufacturer, tossing the flour with the cheese first.
2. **Select the Bake cycle**
Program the machine for Basic/White bread, select light or medium crust, and press Start. When the loaf is done, remove the bucket from the machine. Let the loaf cool for 5 minutes.
Gently shake the bucket to remove the loaf, and turn it out onto a rack to cool.
When the bread machine has finished baking, remove the bread and put it on a cooling rack.

Cheesy Sausage Loaf

PREP: 10 MINUTES /MAKES 1 LOAF

Ingredients

1 cup warm water
4 teaspoons butter, softened
1 ¼teaspoons salt
1 teaspoon sugar
3 cups bread flour
2 ¼teaspoons active dry yeast
1 pound pork sausage roll, cooked and drained
1 ½cups Italian cheese, shredded
¼teaspoon garlic powder
Pinch of black pepper
1 egg, lightly beaten
Flour, for surface

Directions

1. **Preparing the Ingredients**

   Add the first five ingredients to the bread maker pan in order listed above.

   Make a well in the flour; pour the yeast into the hole.

2. **Select the Bake cycle**

   Select Dough cycle and press Start.

   Turn kneaded dough onto a lightly floured surface and roll into a 16-by-10-inch rectangle. Cover with plastic wrap and let rest for 10 minutes Combine sausage, cheese, garlic powder and pepper in a mixing bowl.

   Spread sausage mixture evenly over the dough to within one ½inch of edges. Start with a long side and roll up like a jelly roll, pinch seams to seal, and tuck ends under. Place the loaf seam-side down on a greased baking sheet. Cover and let rise in a warm place for 30 minutes. Preheat an oven to 350°F and bake 20 minutes. Brush with egg and bake an additional 15 to 20 minutes until golden brown. Remove to a cooling rack and serve warm.

Mixed Herb Cheese Bread

PREP: 10 MINUTES PLUS FERMENTING TIME/MAKES 1 LOAF/12 SLICE BREAD (1½ pounds)

Ingredients
1 cup lukewarm water
1½ tablespoons olive oil
¾ teaspoon table salt
¾ tablespoon sugar
2 cloves garlic, crushed
2 tablespoons mixed fresh herbs (basil, chives, oregano, rosemary, etc.)
3 tablespoons Parmesan cheese, grated
3 cups white bread flour
1⅔ teaspoons bread machine yeast

Directions
1. **Preparing the Ingredients.**

Choose the size of loaf you would like to make and measure your ingredients.

Add the ingredients to the bread pan in the order listed above.

Place the pan in the bread machine and close the lid.

Turn on the bread maker. Select the White/Basic setting, then the loaf size, and finally the crust color. Start the cycle.

2. **Select the Bake cycle**

When the cycle is finished and the bread is baked, carefully remove the pan from the machine. Use a potholder as the handle will be very hot. Let rest for a few minutes.

Remove the bread from the pan and allow to cool on a wire rack for at least 10 minutes before slicing.

Blue Cheese Onion Bread

PREP: 10 MINUTES PLUS FERMENTING TIME /MAKES 1 LOAF/12 SLICE BREAD (1½ pounds)

Ingredients
1¼ cup water, at 80°F to 90°F
1 egg, at room temperature
1 tablespoon melted butter, cooled
¼ cup powdered skim milk
1 tablespoon sugar
¾ teaspoon salt
½ cup (2 ounces) crumbled blue cheese
1 tablespoon dried onion flakes
3 cups white bread flour
¼ cup instant mashed potato flakes
1 teaspoon bread machine or active dry yeast

Directions
1. **Preparing the Ingredients.**

Place the ingredients in your bread machine as recommended by the manufacturer.

2. **Select the Bake cycle**

Program the machine for Basic/White bread, select light or medium crust, and press Start.

When the loaf is done, remove the bucket from the machine.

Let the loaf cool for 5 minutes. Gently shake the bucket to remove the loaf, and turn it out onto a rack to cool.

Cheddar and Bacon Bread

PREP: 10 MINUTES PLUS FERMENTING TIME /MAKES 14 SLICES

Ingredients

1⅓ cups water

2 Tbsp vegetable oil

1¼ tsp salt

2 Tbsp plus 1½ tsp sugar

4 cups bread flour

3 Tbsp nonfat dry milk

2 tsp dry active yeast

2 cups cheddar

8 slices crumbled bacon

Directions

1. **Preparing the Ingredients**

   Add each ingredient to the bread machine except the cheese and bacon in the order and at the temperature recommended by your bread machine manufacturer.

2. **Select the Bake cycle**

   Close the lid, select the basic bread, medium crust setting on your bread machine, and press start.

   Add the cheddar cheese and bacon 30 to 40 minutes into the cycle. When the bread machine has finished baking, remove the bread and put it on a cooling rack.

Basil Cheese Bread

PREP: 10 MINUTES PLUS FERMENTING TIME /MAKES 1 LOAF/12 SLICE BREAD (1½ pounds)

Ingredients

1 cup lukewarm milk

1 tablespoon unsalted butter, melted

1 tablespoon sugar

1 teaspoon dried basil

¾ teaspoon table salt

¾ cup sharp Cheddar cheese, shredded

3 cups white bread flour

1½ teaspoons bread machine yeast

Directions

1. **Preparing the Ingredients.**

Choose the size of loaf you would like to make and measure your ingredients.

Add the ingredients to the bread pan in the order listed above.

Place the pan in the bread machine and close the lid.

2. **Select the Bake cycle**

Turn on the bread maker. Select the White/Basic setting, then the loaf size, and finally the crust color. Start the cycle.

When the cycle is finished and the bread is baked, carefully remove the pan from the machine. Use a potholder as the handle will be very hot. Let rest for a few minutes.

Remove the bread from the pan and allow to cool on a wire rack for at least 10 minutes before slicing.

Double Cheese Bread

PREP: 10 MINUTES PLUS FERMENTING TIME/MAKES 1 LOAF/8 SLICE BREAD (1 pound)

Ingredients
¾ cup plus 1 tablespoon milk, at 80°F to 90°F

2 teaspoons butter, melted and cooled

4 teaspoons sugar

⅔ teaspoon salt

⅓ teaspoon freshly ground black pepper

Pinch cayenne pepper

1 cup (4 ounces) shredded aged sharp Cheddar cheese

⅓ cup shredded or grated Parmesan cheese

2 cups white bread flour

¾ teaspoon bread machine or instant yeast

Directions
1. Preparing the Ingredients.
Place the ingredients in your bread machine as recommended by the manufacturer.

Program the machine for Basic/White bread, select light or medium crust, and press Start.

When the loaf is done, remove the bucket from the machine.

2. Select the Bake cycle
Let the loaf cool for 5 minutes.

Gently shake the bucket to remove the loaf, and turn it out onto a rack to cool.

American Cheese Beer Bread

PREP: 10 MINUTES PLUS FERMENTING TIME /MAKES 1 LOAF/16 SLICE BREAD (2 pounds)

Ingredients
1⅔ cups warm beer

1½ tablespoons sugar

2 teaspoons table salt

1½ tablespoons unsalted butter, melted

¾ cup American cheese, shredded

¾ cup Monterrey Jack cheese, shredded

4 cups white bread flour

2 teaspoons bread machine yeast

Directions
1. Preparing the Ingredients.
Choose the size of loaf you would like to make and measure your ingredients.

Add the ingredients to the bread pan in the order listed above.

Place the pan in the bread machine and close the lid.

2. Select the Bake cycle
Turn on the bread maker. Select the White/Basic setting, then the loaf size, and finally the crust color. Start the cycle.

When the cycle is finished and the bread is baked, carefully remove the pan from the machine. Use a potholder as the handle will be very hot. Let rest for a few minutes.

Remove the bread from the pan and allow to cool on a wire rack for at least 10 minutes before slicing.

Mozzarella and Salami Bread

PREP: 10 MINUTES PLUS FERMENTING TIME /MAKES 1 LOAF/12 SLICE BREAD (1½ pounds)

Ingredients

1 cup water plus 2 tablespoons, at 80°F to 90°F

½ cup (2 ounces) shredded mozzarella cheese

2 tablespoons sugar

1 teaspoon salt

1 teaspoon dried basil

¼ teaspoon garlic powder

3¼ cups white bread flour

1½ teaspoons bread machine or instant yeast

¾ cup finely diced hot German salami

Directions

1. Preparing the Ingredients.

Place the ingredients, except the salami, in your bread machine as recommended by the manufacturer.

Program the machine for Basic/White bread, select light or medium crust, and press Start.

When the loaf is done, remove the bucket from the machine.

2. Select the Bake cycle

Add the salami when your machine signals or 5 minutes before the second kneading cycle is finished.

Let the loaf cool for 5 minutes. Gently shake the bucket to remove the loaf, and turn it out onto a rack to cool.

Swiss Olive Bread

PREP: 10 MINUTES PLUS FERMENTING TIME/MAKES 1 LOAF/12 SLICE BREAD (1½ pounds)

Ingredients

1 cup lukewarm milk

1½ tablespoons unsalted butter, melted

1 teaspoon minced garlic

1½ tablespoons sugar

1 teaspoon table salt

¾ cup Swiss cheese, shredded

3 cups white bread flour

1 teaspoon bread machine yeast

⅓ cup chopped black olives

Directions

1. Preparing the Ingredients.

Choose the size of loaf you would like to make and measure your ingredients.

Add all of the ingredients except for the olives to the bread pan in the order listed above.

Place the pan in the bread machine and close the lid.

Turn on the bread maker

2. Select the Bake cycle

Select the White/Basic or Fruit/Nut (if your machine has this setting) setting, then the loaf size, and finally the crust color.

Start the cycle. When the machine signals to add ingredients, add the olives. (Some machines have a fruit/nut hopper where you can add the olives when you start the machine. The machine will automatically add them to the dough during the baking process.) When the cycle is finished and the bread is baked, carefully remove the pan from the machine. Use a potholder as the handle will be very hot. Let rest for a few minutes.

Remove the bread from the pan and allow to cool on a wire rack for at least 10 minutes before slicing.

Simple Cottage Cheese Bread
PREP: 10 MINUTES PLUS FERMENTING TIME /MAKES 1 LOAF/12 SLICE BREAD (1½ pounds)

Ingredients
½ cup water, at 80°F to 90°F
¾ cup cottage cheese, at room temperature
1 egg, at room temperature
2 tablespoons butter, melted and cooled
1 tablespoon sugar
1 teaspoon salt
¼ teaspoon baking soda
3 cups white bread flour
2 teaspoons bread machine or instant yeast

Directions
   1.   **Preparing the Ingredients.**
Place the ingredients in your bread machine as recommended by the manufacturer.
   2.   **Select the Bake cycle**
Program the machine for Basic/White bread, select light or medium crust, and press Start. When the loaf is done, remove the bucket from the machine. Let the loaf cool for 5 minutes.
Gently shake the bucket to remove the loaf, and turn it out onto a rack to cool.

Parmesan Cheddar Bread
PREP: 10 MINUTES PLUS FERMENTING TIME /MAKES 1 LOAF/12 SLICE BREAD (1½ pounds)

Ingredients
1¼ cups lukewarm milk
1 tablespoon unsalted butter, melted
2 tablespoons sugar
1 teaspoon table salt
½ teaspoon freshly ground black pepper
Pinch cayenne pepper
1½ cups shredded aged sharp Cheddar cheese
½ cup shredded or grated Parmesan cheese
3 cups white bread flour
1¼ teaspoons bread machine yeast

Directions
   1.   **Preparing the Ingredients.**
Choose the size of loaf you would like to make and measure your ingredients.
Add the ingredients to the bread pan in the order listed above.
Place the pan in the bread machine and close the lid.

   2.   **Select the Bake cycle**
Turn on the bread maker. Select the White/Basic setting, then the loaf size, and finally the crust color. Start the cycle.
When the cycle is finished and the bread is baked, carefully remove the pan from the machine. Use a potholder as the handle will be very hot. Let rest for a few minutes.
Remove the bread from the pan and allow to cool on a wire rack for at least 10 minutes before slicing.

Chile Cheese Bacon Bread

PREP: 10 MINUTES PLUS FERMENTING TIME /MAKES 1 LOAF/8 SLICE BREAD (1 pound)

Ingredients
⅓ cup milk, at 80°F to 90°F
1 teaspoon melted butter, cooled
1 tablespoon honey
1 teaspoon salt
⅓ cup chopped and drained green chiles
⅓ cup grated Cheddar cheese
⅓ cup chopped cooked bacon
2 cups white bread flour
1⅓ teaspoons bread machine or instant yeast

Directions
1. Preparing the Ingredients.
Place the ingredients in your bread machine as recommended by the manufacturer.

2. Select the Bake cycle
Program the machine for Basic/White bread, select light or medium crust, and press Start.
When the loaf is done, remove the bucket from the machine. Let the loaf cool for 5 minutes.
Gently shake the bucket to remove the loaf, and turn it out onto a rack to cool.

Honey Goat Cheese Bread

PREP: 10 MINUTES PLUS FERMENTING TIME /MAKES 1 LOAF/12 SLICE BREAD (1½ pounds)

Ingredients
1 cup lukewarm milk
1½ tablespoons honey
1 teaspoon table salt
1 teaspoon freshly cracked black pepper
¼ cup goat cheese, shredded or crumbled
3 cups white bread flour
1½ teaspoons bread machine yeast

Directions
1. Preparing the Ingredients.
Choose the size of loaf you would like to make and measure your ingredients.
Add the ingredients to the bread pan in the order listed above.
Place the pan in the bread machine and close the lid.
2. Select the Bake cycle
Turn on the bread maker. Select the White/Basic setting, then the loaf size, and finally the crust color. Start the cycle.
When the cycle is finished and the bread is baked, carefully remove the pan from the machine. Use a potholder as the handle will be very hot. Let rest for a few minutes.

Remove the bread from the pan and allow to cool on a wire rack for at least 10 minutes before slicing.

Italian Parmesan Bread

PREP: 10 MINUTES PLUS FERMENTING TIME /MAKES 1 LOAF/8 SLICE BREAD (1 pound)

Ingredients

¾ cup water, at 80°F to 90°F

2 tablespoons melted butter, cooled

2 teaspoons sugar

⅔ teaspoon salt

1⅓ teaspoons chopped fresh basil

2⅔ tablespoons grated Parmesan cheese

2⅓ cups white bread flour

1 teaspoon bread machine or instant yeast

Directions

1. **Preparing the Ingredients.**

Place the ingredients in your bread machine as recommended by the manufacturer.

2. **Select the Bake cycle**

Program the machine for Basic/White bread, select light or medium crust, and press Start. When the loaf is done, remove the bucket from the machine. Let the loaf cool for 5 minutes. Gently shake the bucket to remove the loaf, and turn it out onto a rack to cool.

Rich Cheddar Bread

PREP: 10 MINUTES PLUS FERMENTING TIME /MAKES 1 LOAF/12 SLICE BREAD (1½ pounds)

Ingredients

1 cup milk, at 80°F to 90°F

2 tablespoons butter, melted and cooled

3 tablespoons sugar

1 teaspoon salt

½ cup (2 ounces) grated aged Cheddar cheese

3 cups white bread flour

2 teaspoons bread machine or instant yeast

Directions

1. **Preparing the Ingredients.** Place the ingredients in your bread machine as recommended by the manufacturer.
2. **Select the Bake cycle** Program the machine for Basic/White bread, select light or medium crust, and press Start. When the loaf is done, remove the bucket from the machine. Let the loaf cool for 5 minutes. Gently shake the bucket to remove the loaf, and turn it out onto a rack to cool.

Feta Oregano Bread

PREP: 10 MINUTES PLUS FERMENTING TIME /MAKES 1 LOAF/8 SLICE BREAD (1 pound)

Ingredients

⅔ cup milk, at 80°F to 90°F

2 teaspoons melted butter, cooled

2 teaspoons sugar

⅔ teaspoon salt

2 teaspoons dried oregano

2 cups white bread flour

1½ teaspoons bread machine or instant yeast

⅔ cup (2½ ounces) crumbled feta cheese

Directions

1. **Preparing the Ingredients.**

Place the ingredients in your bread machine as recommended by the manufacturer.

Program the machine for Basic/White bread, select light or medium crust, and press Start.

2. **Select the Bake cycle**

When the loaf is done, remove the bucket from the machine.

Let the loaf cool for 5 minutes. Gently shake the bucket to remove the loaf, and turn it out onto a rack to cool.

Goat Cheese Bread

PREP: 10 MINUTES PLUS FERMENTING TIME /MAKES 1 LOAF/8 SLICE BREAD (1 pound)

Ingredients

⅔ cup milk, at 80°F to 90°F

2⅔ tablespoons goat cheese, at room temperature

1 tablespoon honey

⅔ teaspoon salt

⅔ teaspoon freshly cracked black pepper

2 cups white bread flour

1 teaspoon bread machine or instant yeast

Directions

1. **Preparing the Ingredients.**

Place the ingredients in your bread machine as recommended by the manufacturer.

Program the machine for Basic/White bread, select light or medium crust, and press Start.

2. **Select the Bake cycle**

When the loaf is done, remove the bucket from the machine.

Let the loaf cool for 5 minutes.

Gently shake the bucket to remove the loaf, and turn it out onto a rack to cool.

Mozzarella-Herb Bread

PREP: 10 MINUTES PLUS FERMENTING TIME /MAKES 1 LOAF/12 SLICE BREAD (1½ pounds)

Ingredients

1¼ cups milk, at 80°F to 90°F

1 tablespoon butter, melted and cooled

2 tablespoons sugar

1 teaspoon salt

2 teaspoons dried basil

1 teaspoon dried oregano

1½ cups (6 ounces) shredded mozzarella cheese

3 cups white bread flour

2¼ teaspoons bread machine or instant yeast

Directions

1. **Preparing the Ingredients.**

Place the ingredients in your bread machine as recommended by the manufacturer.

2. **Select the Bake cycle**

Program the machine for Basic/White bread, select light or medium crust, and press Start.

When the loaf is done, remove the bucket from the machine.

Let the loaf cool for 5 minutes. Gently shake the bucket to remove the loaf, and turn it out onto a rack to cool.

Olive Loaf

Ingredients
1 cup plus 2 tablespoons water
1 tablespoon olive oil
3 cups bread flour
2 tablespoons instant nonfat dry milk
1 tablespoon sugar
1 ¼ teaspoons salt
¼ teaspoon garlic powder
2 teaspoons active dry yeast
⅔ cup grated parmesan cheese
1 cup pitted Greek olives, sliced and drained

Directions
1. **Preparing the Ingredients**
   Add ingredients, except yeast, olives and cheese, to bread maker in order listed above. Make a well in the flour; pour the yeast into the hole.
2. **Select the Bake cycle**
   Select Basic cycle, light crust color, and press Start; do not use delay cycle.   Just before the final kneading, add the olives and cheese. Remove and allow to cool on a wire rack for 15 minutes before serving.

Wine and Cheese Bread

Ingredients
¾ cup white wine
½ cup white cheddar or gruyere cheese, shredded
1 ½ tablespoons butter
½ teaspoon salt
¾ teaspoon sugar
2 ¼ cups bread flour
1 ½ teaspoons active dry yeast

Directions
1. **Preparing the Ingredients**
   Add liquid ingredients to the bread maker pan.   Add dry ingredients, except yeast, to the bread pan.
   Use your fingers to form a well-like hole in the flour where you will pour the yeast; yeast must never come into contact with a liquid when you are adding the ingredients. Carefully pour the yeast into the well.
2. **Select the Bake cycle**
   Select Basic bread setting, light crust color, and press Start. Allow to cool on a wire rack before serving.

SWEET BREAD

Sugared Doughnuts
PREP: 30 MINUTES PLUS FERMENTING TIME /MAKES 20 DOUGHNUTS

Ingredients
⅔ cup milk
¼ cup water
¼ cup butter, softened
1 egg
3 cups bread flour
¼ cup sugar
1 teaspoon salt
2½ teaspoons bread machine or fast-acting dry yeast
Vegetable oil
Additional sugar, if desired

Directions
1. **Preparing the Ingredients.**
Measure carefully, placing all ingredients except vegetable oil and additional sugar in bread machine pan in the order recommended by the manufacturer.
2. **Select the Bake cycle**
Select Dough/Manual cycle. Do not use delay cycle. Remove dough from pan, using lightly floured hands. Cover and let rest 10 minutes on lightly floured board. Roll dough to 3/8-inch thickness on lightly floured board. Cut with floured doughnut cutter. Cover and let rise on board 35 to 45 minutes or until slightly raised.
In deep fryer or heavy Dutch oven, heat 2 to 3 inches oil to 375°F. Fry doughnuts in oil, 2 or 3 at a time, turning as they rise to the surface. Fry 2 to 3 minutes or until golden brown on both sides. Remove from oil with slotted spoon to cooling rack. Roll warm doughnuts in sugar.

Chocolate Cherry Bread
PREP: 30 MINUTES PLUS FERMENTING TIME /MAKES 14 SLICES

Ingredients
1 cup milk
1 egg
3 Tbsp water
4 tsp butter
½ tsp almond extract
4 cups bread flour
3 Tbsp sugar
1 tsp salt
1¼ tsp active dry yeast
½ cup dried cherries, snipped
½ cup semisweet chocolate pieces, chilled
Directions
1. **Preparing the Ingredients**
    Add each ingredient to the bread machine in the order and at the temperature recommended by your bread machine manufacturer.
2. **Select the Bake cycle**
    Close the lid, select the sweet loaf, low crust setting on your bread machine, and press start.
    When the bread machine has finished baking, remove the bread and put it on a cooling rack.

Apple Honey Bread

PREP: 10 MINUTES PLUS FERMENTING TIME /MAKES 1 LOAF/12 SLICE BREAD (1½ pounds)

Ingredients

5 tablespoons lukewarm milk

3 tablespoons apple cider, at room temperature

3 tablespoons sugar

2 tablespoons unsalted butter, melted

1½ tablespoons honey

¼ teaspoon table salt

3 cups white bread flour

1¼ teaspoons bread machine yeast

1 apple, peeled, cored, and finely diced

Directions

1. **Preparing the Ingredients.**

Choose the size of loaf you would like to make and measure your ingredients.

Add all of the ingredients except for the apples to the bread pan in the order listed above.

Place the pan in the bread machine and close the lid.

2. **Select the Bake cycle**

Turn on the bread maker. Select the White/Basic or Fruit/Nut (if your machine has this setting) setting, then the loaf size, and finally the crust color. Start the cycle.

When the machine signals to add ingredients, add the apples. (Some machines have a fruit/nut hopper where you can add the apples when you start the machine. The machine will automatically add them to the dough during the baking process.)

When the cycle is finished and the bread is baked, carefully remove the pan from the machine. Use a potholder as the handle will be very hot. Let rest for a few minutes. Remove the bread from the pan and allow to cool on a wire rack for at least 10 minutes before slicing.

Chocolate Chip Peanut Butter Banana Bread

PREP: 10 MINUTES PLUS FERMENTING TIME /MAKES 1 LOAF/12 SLICE BREAD (1½ pounds)

Ingredients

2 bananas, mashed

2 eggs, at room temperature

½ cup melted butter, cooled

2 tablespoons milk, at room temperature

1 teaspoon pure vanilla extract

2 cups all-purpose flour

½ cup sugar

1¼ teaspoons baking powder

½ teaspoon baking soda

½ teaspoon salt

½ cup peanut butter chips

½ cup semisweet chocolate chips

Directions

1. **Preparing the Ingredients.**

Stir together the bananas, eggs, butter, milk, and vanilla in the bread machine bucket and set it aside.

In a medium bowl, toss together the flour, sugar, baking powder, baking soda, salt, peanut butter chips, and chocolate chips.

Add the dry ingredients to the bucket.

2. **Select the Bake cycle**

Program the machine for Quick/Rapid bread, and press Start.

When the loaf is done, stick a knife into it, and if it comes out clean, the loaf is done.

If the loaf needs a few more minutes, check the control panel for a Bake Only button and extend the time by 10 minutes.

When the loaf is done, remove the bucket from the machine. Let the loaf cool for 5 minutes.

Gently shake the bucket to remove the loaf, and turn it out onto a rack to cool.

Easy Apple Coffee Cake
PREP: 10 MINUTES PLUS FERMENTING TIME /MAKES 10 SERVINGS

Ingredients
⅔ cup water
3 tablespoons butter, softened
2 cups bread flour
3 tablespoons granulated sugar
1 teaspoon salt
1½ teaspoons bread machine or fast-acting dry yeast
1 cup canned apple pie filling
Powdered sugar, if desired

Directions
1. Preparing the Ingredients.
Measure carefully, placing all ingredients except pie filling and powdered sugar in bread machine pan in the order recommended by the manufacturer. Remove dough from pan, using lightly floured hands. Cover and let rest 10 minutes on lightly floured surface.

2. Select the Bake cycle
Select Dough/Manual cycle. Do not use delay cycle. Grease large cookie sheet. Roll dough into 13×8-inch rectangle on lightly floured surface. Place on cookie sheet. Spoon pie filling lengthwise down center third of rectangle. On each 13-inch side, using sharp knife, make cuts from filling to edge of dough at 1-inch intervals. Fold ends up over filling. Fold strips diagonally over filling, alternating sides and overlapping in center. Cover and let rise in warm place 30 to 45 minutes or until doubled in size. Dough is ready if indentation remains when touched. Heat oven to 375°F. Bake 30 to 35 minutes or until golden brown. Remove from cookie sheet to cooling rack; cool. Sprinkle with powdered sugar.

White Chocolate Bread
PREP: 10 MINUTES PLUS FERMENTING TIME /MAKES 1 LOAF/12 SLICE BREAD (1½ pounds)

Ingredients
1 cup lukewarm milk
1 egg, at room temperature
2 tablespoons unsalted butter, melted
1½ teaspoons pure vanilla extract
3 tablespoons light brown sugar
4 teaspoons cocoa powder, unsweetened
¾ teaspoon table salt
3 cups white bread flour
1¼ teaspoons bread machine yeast
⅓ cup semisweet chocolate chips
⅓ cup white chocolate chips

Directions
1. Preparing the Ingredients.
Choose the size of loaf you would like to make and measure your ingredients. Take the bread pan; add the ingredients except both the chocolate chips to the bread pan in the order listed above. Place the pan in the bread machine and close the lid.

2. Select the Bake cycle
Turn on the bread maker. Select the White/Basic or Fruit/Nut (if your machine has this setting) setting, then the loaf size, and finally the crust color. Start the cycle. When the machine signals to add ingredients, add both the chocolate chips. (Some machines have a fruit/nut hopper where you can add both the chocolate chips when you start the machine. The machine will automatically add them to the dough during the baking process.)

When the cycle is finished and the bread is baked, carefully remove the pan from the machine. Use a potholder as the handle will be very hot. Let rest for a few minutes.

Remove the bread from the pan and allow to cool on a wire rack for at least 10 minutes before slicing.

Chocolate Sour Cream Bread

PREP: 20 MINUTES PLUS FERMENTING TIME /MAKES 1 LOAF/12 SLICE BREAD (1½ pounds)

Ingredients

1 cup sour cream
2 eggs, at room temperature
1 cup sugar
½ cup (1 stick) butter, at room temperature
¼ cup plain Greek yogurt
1¾ cups all-purpose flour
½ cup unsweetened cocoa powder
½ teaspoon baking powder
½ teaspoon salt
1 cup milk chocolate chips

Directions

1. Preparing the Ingredients.

In a small bowl, whisk together the sour cream, eggs, sugar, butter, and yogurt until just combined.

Transfer the wet ingredients to the bread machine bucket, and then add the flour, cocoa powder, baking powder, salt, and chocolate chips. Program the machine for Quick/Rapid bread, and press Start. When the loaf is done, stick a knife into it, and if it comes out clean, the loaf is done.

2. Select the Bake cycle

If the loaf needs a few more minutes, check the control panel for a Bake Only button and extend the time by 10 minutes.

When the loaf is done, remove the bucket from the machine. Let the loaf cool for 5 minutes. Gently shake the bucket to remove the loaf, and turn it out onto a rack to cool.

Chocolate Orange Bread

PREP: 10 MINUTES PLUS FERMENTING TIME /MAKES 14 SLICES

Ingredients

1⅝ cups strong white bread flour
2 Tbsp cocoa
1 tsp ground mixed spice
1 egg, beaten
½ cup water
¼ cup orange juice
2 Tbsp butter
3 Tbsp light muscovado sugar
1 tsp salt
1½ tsp easy bake yeast
¾ cup mixed peel
¾ cup chocolate chips

Directions

1. Preparing the Ingredients

Sift the flour, cocoa, and spices together in a bowl.

Add each ingredient to the bread machine in the order and at the temperature recommended by your bread machine manufacturer.

2. Select the Bake cycle

Close the lid, select the sweet loaf, medium crust setting on your bread machine, and press start.

Add the mixed peel and chocolate chips 5 to 10 minutes before the last kneading cycle ends.

When the bread machine has finished baking, remove the bread and put it on a cooling rack.

Cherry–White Chocolate Almond Twist
PREP: 25 MINUTES PLUS FERMENTING TIME /MAKES 16 SERVINGS

Ingredients
Bread dough

½ cup maraschino cherries

¾ cup plus 2 tablespoons water

1 teaspoon almond extract

2 tablespoons butter

3¼ cups bread flour

2 tablespoons sugar

1 teaspoon salt

2 teaspoons bread machine yeast or fast-acting dry yeast filling

½ cup chopped white baking chips

⅓cup chopped slivered almonds

2 tablespoons sugar

2 tablespoons butter, softened

¼ cup maraschino cherries, well drained

Glaze

½ cup powdered sugar

2 to 4 teaspoons reserved maraschino cherry juice

Directions
1. Preparing the Ingredients.

Drain ½ cup cherries thoroughly; reserve 2 to 4 teaspoons cherry juice for glaze. Measure carefully, placing ½ cup cherries and remaining bread dough ingredients in bread machine pan in the order recommended by the manufacturer.

2. Select the Bake cycle

Select Dough/Manual cycle. Do not use delay cycle. Remove dough from pan, using lightly floured hands. Cover and let rest 10 minutes on lightly floured surface. In small bowl, mix baking chips, almonds and 2 tablespoons sugar.

Grease large cookie sheet with shortening. On floured surface, roll dough into 15×10-inch rectangle. Spread 2 tablespoons butter over dough. Sprinkle with almond mixture and ¼ cup cherries; press into dough. Starting with 15-inch side, roll up dough; press to seal seam. Place, seam side down, on cookie sheet.

Cut roll lengthwise in half. Place halves, filling side up and side by side, on cookie sheet; twist together gently and loosely. Pinch ends to seal. Cover and let rise in warm place about 45 minutes or until doubled in size.

Heat oven to 350°F. Bake 30 to 35 minutes or until golden brown. Remove from cookie sheet to cooling rack. Cool 20 minutes. In small bowl, stir powdered sugar and enough cherry juice for drizzling consistency. Drizzle over coffee cake.

Coffee Cake Banana Bread

PREP: 10 MINUTES PLUS /MAKES 14 SLICES

Ingredients

4 medium bananas, mushed
2 Tbsp brown sugar
1½ tsp vanilla extract
¾ tsp ground cinnamon
½ cup butter, softened
1 cup sugar
2 eggs
2 cups all-purpose flour
1 tsp baking soda
¼ tsp salt
2 Tbsp Greek yogurt

Directions

1. **Preparing the Ingredients.**
   Add each ingredient to the bread machine in the order and at the temperature recommended by your bread machine manufacturer.
2. **Select the Bake cycle**
   Close the lid, select the sweet loaf, low crust setting on your bread machine, and press start.
   When the bread machine has finished baking, remove the bread and put it on a cooling rack.

Ginger Spiced Bread

PREP: 10 MINUTES PLUS FERMENTING TIME /MAKES 1 LOAF/12 SLICE BREAD (1½ pounds)

Ingredients

1 cup lukewarm buttermilk
1 egg, at room temperature
¼ cup dark molasses
1 tablespoon unsalted butter, melted
3 tablespoons sugar
1½ teaspoons table salt
3½ cups white bread flour
1 teaspoon ground cinnamon
½ teaspoon ground nutmeg
¼ teaspoon ground cloves
1½ teaspoons ground ginger
2 teaspoons bread machine yeast

Directions

1. **Preparing the Ingredients.**

Choose the size of loaf you would like to make and measure your ingredients.

Add the ingredients to the bread pan in the order listed above.

Place the pan in the bread machine and close the lid.

2. **Select the Bake cycle**

Turn on the bread maker. Select the Sweet setting, then the loaf size, and finally the crust color. Start the cycle.

When the cycle is finished and the bread is baked, carefully remove the pan from the machine. Use a potholder as the handle will be very hot. Let rest for a few minutes.

Remove the bread from the pan and allow to cool on a wire rack for at least 10 minutes before slicing.

Nectarine Cobbler Bread

PREP: 10 MINUTES PLUS FERMENTING TIME /MAKES 1 LOAF/12 SLICE BREAD (1½ pounds)

Ingredients

½ cup (1 stick) butter, at room temperature

2 eggs, at room temperature

1 cup sugar

¼ cup milk, at room temperature

1 teaspoon pure vanilla extract

1 cup diced nectarines

1¾ cups all-purpose flour

1 teaspoon baking soda

½ teaspoon salt

½ teaspoon ground nutmeg

¼ teaspoon baking powder

Directions

1. **Preparing the Ingredients.**

Place the butter, eggs, sugar, milk, vanilla, and nectarines in your bread machine.

2. **Select the Bake cycle**

Program the machine for Quick/Rapid bread and press Start.

While the wet ingredients are mixing, stir together the flour, baking soda, salt, nutmeg, and baking powder in a small bowl.

After the first fast mixing is done and the machine signals, add the dry ingredients.

When the loaf is done, remove the bucket from the machine.

Let the loaf cool for 5 minutes.

Gently shake the bucket to remove the loaf, and turn it out onto a rack to cool.

Almond Chocolate Chip Bread

PREP: 10 MINUTES PLUS FERMENTING TIME /MAKES 14 SLICES

Ingredients

1 cup plus 2 Tbsp water

2 Tbsp softened butter

½ tsp vanilla

3 cups Gold Medal Better for Bread flour

¾ cup semisweet chocolate chips

3 Tbsp sugar

1 Tbsp dry milk

¾ tsp salt

1½ tsp quick active dry yeast

⅓ cup sliced almonds

Directions

1. **Preparing the Ingredients**

   Add each ingredient except the almonds to the bread machine in the order and at the temperature recommended by your bread machine manufacturer.

2. **Select the Bake cycle**

   Close the lid, select the sweet loaf, low crust setting on your bread machine, and press start.

   Add almonds 10 minutes before last kneading cycle ends. When the bread machine has finished baking, remove the bread and put it on a cooling rack.

Swedish Coffee Bread

PREP: 10 MINUTES /MAKES 14 SLICES

Ingredients

1 cup milk

½ tsp salt

1 egg yolk

2 Tbsp softened butter

3 cups all-purpose flour

⅓ cup sugar

1 envelope active dry yeast

3 tsp ground cardamom

2 egg whites, slightly beaten

Directions

1. **Preparing the Ingredients**

   Add each ingredient to the bread machine in the order and at the temperature recommended by your bread machine manufacturer.

2. **Select the Bake cycle**

   Select the dough cycle and press start. Grease your baking sheet.

   When the dough cycle has finished, divide the dough into three equal parts. Roll each part into a rope 12-14" long. Lay 3 ropes side by side, and then braid them together.

   Tuck the ends underneath and put onto the sheet. Next, cover the bread, using kitchen towel, and let it rise until it has doubled in size. Brush your bread with beaten egg white and sprinkle with pearl sugar. Bake until golden brown at 375°F in a preheated oven for 20-25 minutes. When baked, remove the bread and put it on a cooling rack.

Pear Kuchen with Ginger Topping

PREP: 20 MINUTES PLUS FERMENTING TIME /MAKES 12 SERVINGS

Ingredients

Bread dough

½ cup milk

2 tablespoons butter, softened

1 egg

2 cups bread flour

2 tablespoons sugar

1 teaspoon salt

1¾ teaspoons bread machine or fast-acting dry yeast

Topping

3 cups sliced peeled pears

1 cup sugar

2 tablespoons butter, softened

1 tablespoon chopped crystallized ginger

½ cup whipping cream

1 egg yolk

Directions

1. **Preparing the Ingredients.**

Measure carefully, placing all bread dough ingredients in bread machine pan in the order recommended by the manufacturer.

2. **Select the Bake cycle**

Select Dough/Manual cycle. Do not use delay cycle.

Remove dough from pan, using lightly floured hands. Cover and let rest 10 minutes on lightly floured surface.

Grease 13×9-inch pan with shortening. Press dough evenly in bottom of pan.

Arrange pears on dough. In small bowl, mix 1 cup sugar, 2 tablespoons butter and the ginger. Reserve 2 tablespoons of the topping; sprinkle remaining topping over pears. Cover and let rise in warm place 30 to 45 minutes or until doubled in size. Dough is ready if indentation remains when touched.

Heat oven to 375°F. Bake 20 minutes. Mix whipping cream and egg yolk; pour over hot kuchen. Bake 15 minutes longer or until golden brown. Sprinkle with reserved 2 tablespoons topping. Serve warm.

Walnut Cocoa Bread

PREP: 20 MINUTES PLUS FERMENTING TIME /MAKES 14 SERVINGS

Ingredients

⅔ cup milk

⅓ cup water

5 Tbsp butter, softened

⅓ cup packed brown sugar

5 Tbsp baking cocoa

1 tsp salt

3 cups bread flour

2¼ tsp active dry yeast

⅔ cup chopped walnuts, toasted

Directions

1. **Preparing the Ingredients**

   Add each ingredient except the walnuts to the bread machine in the order and at the temperature recommended by your bread machine manufacturer.

2. **Select the Bake cycle**

   Close the lid, select the sweet loaf, low crust setting on your bread machine, and press start.

   Just before the final kneading, add the walnuts.

   When the bread machine has finished baking, remove the bread and put it on a cooling rack.

Sweet Applesauce Bread

PREP: 10 MINUTES PLUS FERMENTING TIME /MAKES 1 LOAF/12 SLICE BREAD (1½ pounds)

Ingredients

⅔ cup lukewarm milk

¼ cup unsweetened applesauce, at room temperature

1 tablespoon unsalted butter, melted

1 tablespoon sugar

1 teaspoon table salt

¼ cup quick oats

2¼ cups white bread flour

½ teaspoon ground cinnamon

Pinch ground nutmeg

2¼ teaspoons bread machine yeast

Directions

1. **Preparing the Ingredients.**

Choose the size of loaf you would like to make and measure your ingredients.

Add the ingredients to the bread pan in the order listed above.

Place the pan in the bread machine and close the lid.

2. **Select the Bake cycle**

Turn on the bread maker. Select the White/Basic setting, then the loaf size, and finally the crust color. Start the cycle.

When the cycle is finished and the bread is baked, carefully remove the pan from the machine. Use a potholder as the handle will be very hot. Let rest for a few minutes.

Remove the bread from the pan and allow to cool on a wire rack for at least 10 minutes before slicing.

Mexican Chocolate Bread

PREP: 10 MINUTES PLUS FERMENTING TIME /MAKES 1 LOAF

Ingredients

½ cup milk
½ cup orange juice
1 large egg plus 1 egg yolk
3 Tbsp unsalted butter cut into pieces
2½ cups bread flour
¼ cup light brown sugar
3 Tbsp unsweetened dutch-process cocoa powder
1 Tbsp gluten
1 tsp instant espresso powder
¾ tsp ground cinnamon
½ cup bittersweet chocolate chips
2½ tsp bread machine yeast

Directions

1. **Preparing the Ingredients.**
   Add each ingredient to the bread machine in the order and at the temperature recommended by your bread machine manufacturer.

2. **Select the Bake cycle**
   Close the lid, select the sweet loaf, low crust setting on your bread machine, and press start.
   When the bread machine has finished baking, remove the bread and put it on a cooling rack.

Sour Cream Maple Bread

PREP: 10 MINUTES PLUS FERMENTING TIME /MAKES 1 LOAF/8 SLICE BREAD (1 pound)

Ingredients

6 tablespoons water, at 80°F to 90°F
6 tablespoons sour cream, at room temperature
1½ tablespoons butter, at room temperature
¾ tablespoon maple syrup
½ teaspoon salt
1¾ cups white bread flour
1⅛ teaspoons bread machine or instant yeast

Directions

1. **Preparing the Ingredients.**

Place the ingredients in your bread machine as recommended by the manufacturer.
Program the machine for Basic/White bread, select light or medium crust, and press Start.

2. **Select the Bake cycle**

When the loaf is done, remove the bucket from the machine.
Let the loaf cool for 5 minutes.
Gently shake the bucket to remove the loaf, and turn it out onto a rack to cool.

Chocolate Chip Bread
PREP: 10 MINUTES PLUS FERMENTING TIME /MAKES 1 LOAF

Ingredients
¼ cup water
1 cup milk
1 egg
3 cups bread flour
3 Tbsp brown sugar
2 Tbsp white sugar
1 tsp salt
1 tsp ground cinnamon
1½ tsp active dry yeast
2 Tbsp margarine, softened
¾ cup semisweet chocolate chips

Directions

1. **Preparing the Ingredients**

   Add each ingredient except the chocolate chips to the bread machine in the order and at the temperature recommended by your bread machine manufacturer.

2. **Select the Bake cycle**

   Close the lid, select the sweet loaf, low crust setting on your bread machine, and press start.

   Add the chocolate chips about 5 minutes before the kneading cycle has finished. When the bread machine has finished baking, remove the bread and put it on a cooling rack.

Crunchy Wheat-and-Honey Twist
PREP: 10 MINUTES PLUS FERMENTING TIME /MAKES 1 LOAF/16 SLICE BREAD (2 pounds)

Ingredients
Bread dough
¾ cup plus 2 tablespoons water
2 tablespoons honey
1 tablespoon butter, softened
1¼ cups whole wheat flour
1 cup bread flour
⅓ cup slivered almonds, toasted
1 teaspoon salt
1 teaspoon bread machine or fast-acting dry yeast
Topping
Butter, melted
1 egg, slightly beaten
2 tablespoons sugar
¼ teaspoon ground cinnamon

Directions

1. **Preparing the Ingredients.**

Measure carefully, placing all bread dough ingredients in bread machine pan in the order recommended by the manufacturer. Select Dough/Manual cycle. Do not use delay cycle.

Remove dough from pan, using lightly floured hands. Cover and let rest 10 minutes on lightly floured surface.

Grease large cookie sheet with shortening. Divide dough in half. Roll each half into 15-inch rope. Place ropes side by side on cookie sheet; twist together gently and loosely. Pinch ends to seal. Brush melted butter lightly over dough.

2. **Select the Bake cycle**

Cover and let rise in warm place 45 to 60 minutes or until doubled in size.

Dough is ready if indentation remains when touched.

Heat oven to 375°F. Brush egg over dough. Mix sugar and cinnamon; sprinkle over dough. Bake 25 to 30 minutes or until twist is golden brown and sounds hollow when tapped. Remove from cookie sheet to cooling rack; cool 20 minutes.

To toast almonds, bake in ungreased shallow pan at 350°F for 6 to 10 minutes, stirring occasionally, until light brown.

Milk Sweet Bread

PREP: 10 MINUTES PLUS FERMENTING TIME /MAKES 1 LOAF/12 SLICE BREAD (1½ pounds)

Ingredients
1 cup lukewarm milk
1 egg, at room temperature
2 tablespoons butter, softened
½ cup sugar
1 teaspoon table salt
3 cups white bread flour
2¼ teaspoons bread machine yeast

Directions
1. Preparing the Ingredients.

Choose the size of loaf you would like to make and measure your ingredients.

Add the ingredients to the bread pan in the order listed above.

Place the pan in the bread machine and close the lid.

2. Select the Bake cycle

Turn on the bread maker. Select the Sweet setting, then the loaf size, and finally the crust color. Start the cycle.

When the cycle is finished and the bread is baked, carefully remove the pan from the machine. Use a potholder as the handle will be very hot. Let rest for a few minutes.

Remove the bread from the pan and allow to cool on a wire rack for at least 10 minutes before slicing.

Barmbrack Bread

PREP: 10 MINUTES PLUS FERMENTING TIME /MAKES 1 LOAF/8 SLICE BREAD (1 pound)

Ingredients
⅔ cup water, at 80°F to 90°F
1 tablespoon melted butter, cooled
2 tablespoons sugar
2 tablespoons skim milk powder
1 teaspoon salt
1 teaspoon dried lemon zest
¼ teaspoon ground allspice
⅛ teaspoon ground nutmeg
2 cups white bread flour
1½ teaspoons bread machine or active dry yeast
½ cup dried currants

Directions
1. Preparing the Ingredients.

Place the ingredients, except the currants, in your bread machine as recommended by the manufacturer.

2. Select the Bake cycle

Program the machine for Basic/White bread, select light or medium crust, and press Start.

Add the currants when your machine signals or when the second kneading cycle starts.

When the loaf is done, remove the bucket from the machine.

Let the loaf cool for 5 minutes.

Gently shake the bucket to remove the loaf, and turn it out onto a rack to cool.

Miniature Brioche

Ingredients

¼ cup water

3 tablespoons butter, softened

2 eggs

2½ cups bread flour

¼ cup sugar

¾ teaspoon salt

1 teaspoon grated orange or lemon peel

2½ teaspoons bread machine yeast

1 tablespoon milk

1 egg yolk

Coarse sugar crystals

Directions

1. Preparing the Ingredients.

Measure carefully, placing all ingredients except milk, egg yolk and sugar crystals in bread machine pan in the order recommended by the manufacturer.

Cover with plastic wrap; refrigerate at least 4 hours but no longer than 24 hours.

Grease 12 regular-size muffin cups. Punch down dough. Divide dough into 16 equal pieces. Roll each piece into a ball. Cut 4 balls into 3 pieces each; roll into small balls. Place 12 large balls in muffin cups. Flatten and make an indentation in center of each with thumb. Place 1 small ball in each indentation.

2. Select the Bake cycle

Select Dough/Manual cycle. Do not use delay cycle.

Grease medium bowl. Place dough in bowl, turning dough to grease all sides. Cover and let rise in warm place 50 to 60 minutes or until doubled in size. Heat oven to 350°F. Mix milk and egg yolk; gently brush over tops of rolls.

Sprinkle with sugar crystals. Bake 15 to 20 minutes or until golden brown. Remove from pan to cooling rack. Serve warm.

Pumpernickel Bread

Ingredients

1 cup plus 2 tablespoons water

1½ teaspoons salt

⅓ cup molasses

2 tablespoons vegetable oil

1 cup plus 1 tablespoon rye flour

1 cup plus 2 tablespoons whole wheat flour

1½ cups bread flour

3 tablespoons unsweetened baking cocoa

1½ teaspoons instant coffee granules or crystals

1 tablespoon caraway seed

1 teaspoon bread machine or fast-acting dry yeast

Directions

1. Preparing the Ingredients.

Measure carefully, placing all ingredients in bread machine pan in the order recommended by the manufacturer.

2. Select the Bake cycle

Select Whole Wheat or Basic/White cycle. Use Medium or Light crust color.

Remove baked bread from pan; cool on cooling rack.

Allspice Currant Bread
PREP: 10 MINUTES PLUS FERMENTING TIME /MAKES 1 LOAF/16 SLICE BREAD (2 pounds)

Ingredients

1½ cups lukewarm water
2 tablespoons unsalted butter, melted
¼ cup sugar
¼ cup skim milk powder
2 teaspoons table salt
4 cups white bread flour
1½ teaspoons dried lemon zest
¾ teaspoon ground allspice
¼ teaspoon ground nutmeg
2½ teaspoons bread machine yeast
1 cup dried currants

Directions

1. Preparing the Ingredients.

Choose the size of loaf you would like to make and measure your ingredients.

Add all of the ingredients except for the dried currants to the bread pan in the order listed above.

Place the pan in the bread machine and close the lid.

2. Select the Bake cycle

Turn on the bread maker. Select the White/Basic or Fruit/Nut (if your machine has this setting) setting, then the loaf size, and finally the crust color. Start the cycle.

When the machine signals to add ingredients, add the dried currants. (Some machines have a fruit/nut hopper where you can add the dried currants when you start the machine. The machine will automatically add them to the dough during the baking process.)

When the cycle is finished and the bread is baked, carefully remove the pan from the machine. Use a potholder as the handle will be very hot. Let rest for a few minutes.

Remove the bread from the pan and allow to cool on a wire rack for at least 10 minutes before slicing.

Apple Butter Bread
PREP: 10 MINUTES PLUS FERMENTING TIME /MAKES 1 LOAF/8 SLICE BREAD (1 pound)

Ingredients

⅔ cup milk, at 80°F to 90°F
⅓ cup apple butter, at room temperature
4 teaspoons melted butter, cooled
2 teaspoons honey
⅔ teaspoon salt
⅔ cup whole-wheat flour
1½ cups white bread flour
1 teaspoon bread machine or instant yeast

Directions

1. Preparing the Ingredients.

Place the ingredients in your bread machine as recommended by the manufacturer.

2. Select the Bake cycle

Program the machine for Basic/White bread, select light or medium crust, and press Start.

When the loaf is done, remove the bucket from the machine. Let the loaf cool for 5 minutes.

Gently shake the bucket to remove the loaf, and turn it out onto a rack to cool.

Beer and Pretzel Bread

PREP: 10 MINUTES PLUS FERMENTING TIME /MAKES 12 SLICES

Ingredients

¾ cup regular or nonalcoholic beer

⅓cup water

2 tablespoons butter, softened

3 cups bread flour

1 tablespoon packed brown sugar

1 teaspoon ground mustard

1 teaspoon salt

1½ teaspoons bread machine yeast

½ cup bite-size pretzel pieces, about 1×¾ inch, or pretzel rods, cut into 1-inch pieces

Directions

1. **Preparing the Ingredients.**

Measure carefully, placing all ingredients except pretzels in bread machine pan in order recommended by the manufacturer.

2. **Select the Bake cycle**

Select Basic/White cycle. Use Medium or Light crust color. Do not use delay cycle.

Add pretzels 5 minutes before the last kneading cycle ends. Remove baked bread from pan; cool on cooling rack.

Buttermilk Pecan Bread

PREP: 10 MINUTES PLUS FERMENTING TIME /MAKES 1 LOAF/12 SLICE BREAD (1½ pounds)

Ingredients

¾ cup buttermilk, at room temperature

¾ cup butter, at room temperature

1 tablespoon instant coffee granules

3 eggs, at room temperature

¾ cup sugar

2 cups all-purpose flour

½ tablespoon baking powder

½ teaspoon table salt

1 cup chopped pecans

Directions

1. **Preparing the Ingredients.**

Choose the size of loaf you would like to make and measure your ingredients.

Add the ingredients to the bread pan in the order listed above. Place the pan in the bread machine and close the lid.

2. **Select the Bake cycle**

Turn on the bread maker. Select the Quick/Rapid setting, then the loaf size, and finally the crust color. Start the cycle.

When the cycle is finished and the bread is baked, carefully remove the pan from the machine. Use a potholder as the handle will be very hot. Let rest for a few minutes.

Remove the bread from the pan and allow to cool on a wire rack for at least 10 minutes before slicing.

Crusty Honey Bread

PREP: 10 MINUTES PLUS FERMENTING TIME /MAKES 1 LOAF/12 SLICE BREAD (1½ pounds)

Ingredients

1 cup minus 1 tablespoon water, at 80°F to 90°F

1½ tablespoons honey

1⅛ tablespoons melted butter, cooled

¾ teaspoon salt

2⅔ cups white bread flour

1½ teaspoons bread machine or instant yeast

Directions

1. **Preparing the Ingredients.**

Place the ingredients in your bread machine as recommended by the manufacturer.

2. **Select the Bake cycle**

Program the machine for Basic/White bread, select light or medium crust, and press Start. When the loaf is done, remove the bucket from the machine. Let the loaf cool for 5 minutes. Gently shake the bucket to remove the loaf, and turn it out onto a rack to cool.

Brown Sugar Date Nut Swirl Bread

PREP: 10 MINUTES PLUS FERMENTING TIME /MAKES 1 LOAF

Ingredients

1 cup milk

1 large egg

4 tablespoons butter

4 tablespoons sugar

1 teaspoon salt

4 cups flour

1 ⅔teaspoons yeast

For the filling:

½cup packed brown sugar

1 cup walnuts, chopped

1 cup medjool dates, pitted and chopped

2 teaspoons cinnamon

2 teaspoons clove spice

1 ⅓tablespoons butter

Powdered sugar, sifted

Directions

1. **Preparing the Ingredients**

   Add wet ingredients to the bread maker pan. Mix flour, sugar and salt and add to pan.

   Make a well in the center of the dry ingredients and add the yeast.

2. **Select the Bake cycle**

   Select the Dough cycle and press Start.

   Punch the dough down and allow it to rest in a warm place.

   Mix the brown sugar with walnuts, dates and spices; set aside.

   Roll the dough into a rectangle, on a lightly floured surface.

   Baste with a tablespoon of butter, add the filling.

   Start from the short side and roll the dough to form a jelly roll shape.

   Place the roll into a greased loaf pan and cover.

   Let it rise in a warm place, until nearly doubled in size; about 30 minutes.

   Bake at 350°F for approximately 30 minutes.

   Cover with foil during the last 10 minutes of cooking.

   Transfer to a cooling rack for 15 minutes; sprinkle with the powdered sugar and serve.

Sage-Raisin Wheat Bread

PREP: 15 MINUTES PLUS FERMENTING TIME /MAKES 16 SLICES

Ingredients

1¼ cups water

2 tablespoons butter, softened

1½ cups bread flour

1½ cups whole wheat flour

2 tablespoons sugar

1½ teaspoons salt

¾ teaspoon crumbled dried sage leaves

1¾ teaspoons bread machine or fast-acting dry yeast

¾ cup golden raisins

1 egg, beaten

Directions

1. **Preparing the Ingredients.**

Measure carefully, placing all ingredients except raisins and egg in bread machine pan in the order recommended by the manufacturer. Add raisins at the Raisin/Nut signal.

Select Dough/Manual cycle. Do not use delay cycle.

Remove dough from pan, using lightly floured hands. Cover and let rest 10 minutes on lightly floured surface.

2. **Select the Bake cycle**

Grease large cookie sheet. Cut off one-third of the dough; shape into small ball (about 3 inches). Shape remaining dough into large ball (about 5 inches).

Place large ball on cookie sheet; place small ball on large ball. Holding thumb and first two fingers together, push into the middle of the small ball, pushing through center of dough until almost touching cookie sheet. Cover and let rise in warm place 30 to 45 minutes or until doubled in size. Dough is ready if indentation remains when touched.

Heat oven to 400°F. Brush egg over loaf. Using serrated knife, cut ¼-inch-deep vertical slashes on sides of each ball about 2 inches apart. Bake 18 to 20 minutes or until loaf is deep golden brown and sounds hollow when tapped.

Remove from cookie sheet to cooling rack; cool.

Cashew Butter/Peanut Butter Bread

PREP: 10 MINUTES PLUS FERMENTING TIME /MAKES 1 LOAF/12 SLICE BREAD (1½ pounds)

Ingredients

1 cup peanut butter or cashew butter

1 cup lukewarm milk

½ cup packed light brown sugar

¼ cup sugar

¼ cup butter, at room temperature

1 egg, at room temperature

2 teaspoons pure vanilla extract

2 cups all-purpose flour

1 tablespoon baking powder

½ teaspoon table salt

Directions

1. **Preparing the Ingredients.**

Choose the size of loaf you would like to make and measure your ingredients.

Add the ingredients to the bread pan in the order listed above.

Place the pan in the bread machine and close the lid.

2. **Select the Bake cycle**

Turn on the bread maker. Select the Quick/Rapid setting, then the loaf size, and finally the crust color. Start the cycle.

When the cycle is finished and the bread is baked, carefully remove the pan from the machine. Use a potholder as the handle will be very hot. Let rest for a few minutes.

Remove the bread from the pan and allow to cool down on a wire rack for at least 10 minutes or more before slicing.

Honey Granola Bread
PREP: 10 MINUTES PLUS FERMENTING TIME /MAKES 1 LOAF/12 SLICE BREAD (1½ pounds)

Ingredients
1⅛ cups milk, at 80°F to 90°F
3 tablespoons honey
1½ tablespoons butter, melted and cooled
1⅛ teaspoons salt
¾ cup whole-wheat flour
⅔ cup prepared granola, crushed
1¾ cups white bread flour
1½ teaspoons bread machine or instant yeast

Directions
1. Preparing the Ingredients.
Place the ingredients in your bread machine as recommended by the manufacturer.

2. Select the Bake cycle
Program the machine for Basic/White bread, select light or medium crust, and press Start.
When the loaf is done, remove the bucket from the machine. Let the loaf cool for 5 minutes.
Gently shake the bucket to remove the loaf, and turn it out onto a rack to cool.

Caramelized-Onion Bread
PREP: 15 MINUTES PLUS FERMENTING TIME /MAKES 12 SLICES

Ingredients
Caramelized onions
1 tablespoon butter
2 medium onions, sliced
Bread
1 cup water
1 tablespoon olive or vegetable oil
3 cups bread flour
2 tablespoons sugar
1 teaspoon salt
1¼ teaspoons bread machine or fast-acting dry yeast

Directions
1. Preparing the Ingredients.
In 10-inch skillet, melt butter over medium-low heat. Cook onions in butter 10 to 15 minutes, stirring occasionally, until onions are brown and caramelized; remove from heat.
Measure carefully, placing all ingredients except onions in bread machine pan in the order recommended by the manufacturer.

2. Select the Bake cycle
Select Basic/White cycle. Use Medium or Light crust color. Do not use delay cycle. Add ½ cup of the onions at the Raisin/Nut signal or 5 to 10 minutes before last kneading cycle ends. (Reserve any remaining onions for another use.) Remove baked bread from pan; cool on cooling rack.

Delicious Sour Cream Bread
PREP: 10 MINUTES PLUS FERMENTING TIME /MAKES 1 LOAF/12 SLICE BREAD (1½ pounds)

Ingredients
½ cup + 1 tablespoon lukewarm water
½ cup + 1 tablespoon sour cream, at room temperature
2¼ tablespoons butter, at room temperature
1 tablespoon maple syrup
¾ teaspoon table salt
2¾ cups white bread flour
1⅔ teaspoons bread machine yeast

Directions
1. Preparing the Ingredients.

Choose the size of loaf you would like to make and measure your ingredients. Add the ingredients to the bread pan in the order listed above. Place the pan in the bread machine and close the lid.

2. Select the Bake cycle

Turn on the bread maker. Select the White/Basic setting, then the loaf size, and finally the crust color. Start the cycle.

When the cycle is finished and the bread is baked, carefully remove the pan from the machine. Use a potholder as the handle will be very hot. Let rest for a few minutes.

Remove the bread from the pan and allow to cool down on a wire rack for at least 10 minutes or more before slicing.

Black Bread
PREP: 10 MINUTES PLUS FERMENTING TIME /MAKES 1 LOAF/12 SLICE BREAD (1½ pounds)

Ingredients
¾ cup water, at 80°F to 90°F
⅓ cup brewed coffee, at 80°F to 90°F
1½ tablespoons balsamic vinegar
1½ tablespoons olive oil
1½ tablespoons dark molasses
¾ tablespoon light brown sugar
¾ teaspoon salt
1½ teaspoons caraway seeds
3 tablespoons unsweetened cocoa powder
¾ cup dark rye flour
1¾ cups white bread flour
1½ teaspoons bread machine or instant yeast

Directions
1. Preparing the Ingredients.

Place the ingredients in your bread machine as recommended by the manufacturer.

2. Select the Bake cycle

Program the machine for Whole-Wheat/Whole-Grain bread, select light or medium crust, and press Start.

When the loaf is done, remove the bucket from the machine. Let the loaf cool for 5 minutes. Gently shake the bucket to remove the loaf, and turn it out onto a rack to cool.

Caramelized-Onion Focaccia
PREP: 10 MINUTES PLUS FERMENTING TIME /MAKES 8 SLICES

Ingredients
Dough
¾ cup water
2 tablespoons olive or vegetable oil
2 cups bread flour
1 tablespoon sugar
1 teaspoon salt
1½ teaspoons bread machine yeast
Onion topping
¼ cup butter
4 large onions, sliced
¾ cup shredded mozzarella cheese (3 oz)
2 tablespoons grated Parmesan cheese

Directions
1. Preparing the Ingredients.
Measure carefully, placing all dough ingredients in bread machine pan in the order recommended by the manufacturer.

2. Select the Bake cycle
Select Dough/Manual cycle. Do not use delay cycle.
Grease cookie sheet. Pat dough into 12-inch round on cookie sheet. Cover and let rise in warm place 30 minutes or until almost double Meanwhile, in 12-inch skillet, melt butter over medium heat. Cook onions in butter 25 to 30 minutes, stirring occasionally, until onions are brown and caramelized; remove from heat.
Heat oven to 400°F. With fingertips or handle of wooden spoon, make deep depressions in dough at 1-inch intervals. Spread onions over dough. Sprinkle with cheeses. Bake 15 to 18 minutes or until edge is golden brown. Remove from cookie sheet to cooling rack. Serve warm. Cut into wedges or squares.

Cinnamon Rum Bread
PREP: 10 MINUTES PLUS FERMENTING TIME /MAKES 1 LOAF/12 SLICE BREAD (1½ pounds)

Ingredients
¾ cup lukewarm water
1 egg, at room temperature
3 tablespoons butter, melted and cooled
3 tablespoons sugar
1 tablespoon rum extract
1¼ teaspoons table salt
3 cups white bread flour
1 teaspoon ground cinnamon
¼ teaspoon ground nutmeg
1 teaspoon bread machine yeast
Directions
1. Preparing the Ingredients.
Choose the size of loaf you would like to make and measure your ingredients.
Add the ingredients to the bread pan in the order listed above.
Place the pan in the bread machine and close the lid.

2. Select the Bake cycle
Turn on the bread maker. Select the Sweet setting, then the loaf size, and finally the crust color. Start the cycle.
When the cycle is finished and the bread is baked, carefully remove the pan from the machine. Use a potholder as the handle will be very hot. Let rest for a few minutes.
Remove the bread from the pan and allow to cool on a wire rack for at least 10 minutes before slicing.

Apple Cider Bread

PREP: 10 MINUTES PLUS FERMENTING TIME /MAKES 1 LOAF/8 SLICE BREAD (1 pound)

Ingredients

¼ cup milk, at 80°F to 90°F

2 tablespoons apple cider, at room temperature

2 tablespoons sugar

4 teaspoons melted butter, cooled

1 tablespoon honey

¼ teaspoon salt

2 cups white bread flour

¾ teaspoons bread machine or instant yeast

⅔ apple, peeled, cored, and finely diced

Directions

1. Preparing the Ingredients.

Place the ingredients, except the apple, in your bread machine as recommended by the manufacturer.

2. Select the Bake cycle

Program the machine for Basic/White bread, select light or medium crust, and press Start.

Add the apple when the machine signals or 5 minutes before the last kneading cycle is complete.

When the loaf is done, remove the bucket from the machine.

Let the loaf cool for 5 minutes. Gently shake the bucket to remove the loaf, and turn it out onto a rack to cool.

Whole Wheat–Cranberry Bread

PREP: 10 MINUTES PLUS FERMENTING TIME /MAKES 1 LOAF/12 SLICE BREAD (1½ pounds)

Ingredients

1 cup plus 2 tablespoons water

¼ cup honey

2 tablespoons butter, softened

2 cups bread flour

1¼ cups whole wheat flour

1½ teaspoons salt

¾ teaspoon ground mace

2 teaspoons bread machine or fast-acting dry yeast

½ cup sweetened dried cranberries or raisins

Cranberry-orange butter

½ cup butter, softened

2 tablespoons cranberry-orange relish or sauce

Directions

1. Preparing the Ingredients.

Measure carefully, placing all bread ingredients except cranberries in bread machine pan in the order recommended by the manufacturer. Add cranberries at the Raisin/Nut signal or 5 to 10 minutes before last kneading cycle ends.

2. Select the Bake cycle

Select Whole Wheat or Basic/White cycle. Use Medium or Light crust color. Do not use delay cycle. Remove baked bread from pan; cool on cooling rack.

In small bowl, mix butter and cranberry-orange relish until well blended. Serve with bread. Store butter in refrigerator.

Sweet Pineapple Bread

PREP: 10 MINUTES PLUS FERMENTING TIME /MAKES 1 LOAF/16 SLICE BREAD (2 pounds)

Ingredients

6 tablespoons unsalted butter, melted
2 eggs, at room temperature
½ cup coconut milk, at room temperature
½ cup pineapple juice, at room temperature
1 cup sugar
1½ teaspoons coconut extract
2 cups all-purpose flour
¾ cup shredded sweetened coconut
1 teaspoon baking powder
½ teaspoon table salt

Directions

1. Preparing the Ingredients.

Choose the size of loaf you would like to make and measure your ingredients. Add the ingredients to the bread pan in the order listed above. Place the pan in the bread machine and close the lid.

2. Select the Bake cycle

Turn on the bread maker. Select the Quick/Rapid setting, then the loaf size, and finally the crust color. Start the cycle. When the cycle is finished and the bread is baked, carefully remove the pan from the machine. Use a potholder as the handle will be very hot. Let rest for a few minutes.

Remove the bread from the pan and allow to cool on a wire rack for at least 10 minutes before slicing.

Coffee Cake

PREP: 10 MINUTES PLUS FERMENTING TIME /MAKES 1 LOAF/12 SLICE BREAD (1½ pounds)

Ingredients

¾ cup buttermilk, at room temperature
¾ cup (1½ sticks) butter, at room temperature
1 tablespoon instant coffee granules
3 eggs, at room temperature
¾ cup sugar
2 cups all-purpose flour
½ tablespoon baking powder
½ teaspoon salt
1 cup chopped pecans

Directions

1. Preparing the Ingredients.

Place the buttermilk, butter, coffee granules, eggs, and sugar in your bread machine.

2. Select the Bake cycle

Program the machine for Quick/Rapid bread and press Start. While the wet ingredients are mixing, stir together the flour, baking powder, salt, and pecans in a small bowl. After the first fast mixing is done and the machine signals, add the dry ingredients. When the loaf is done, remove the bucket from the machine.

Let the loaf cool for 5 minutes.

Gently shake the bucket to remove the loaf, and turn it out onto a rack to cool.

Caramel Apple and Pecan Bread
PREP: 10 MINUTES PLUS FERMENTING TIME /MAKES 1 LOAF/12 SLICE BREAD (1½ pounds)

Ingredients
1 cup water
2 tablespoons butter, softened
3 cups bread flour
¼ cup packed brown sugar
¾ teaspoon ground cinnamon
1 teaspoon salt
2 teaspoons bread machine or fast-acting dry yeast
½ cup chopped unpeeled apple
⅓ cup coarsely chopped pecans, toasted

Directions
1. Preparing the Ingredients.
Measure carefully, placing all ingredients except apple and pecans in bread machine pan in the order recommended by the manufacturer. Add apple and pecans at the Raisin/Nut signal or 5 to 10 minutes before last kneading cycle ends.
2. Select the Bake cycle
Select Sweet or Basic/White cycle. Use Light crust color. Do not use delay cycle. Remove baked bread from pan; cool on cooling rack.

Cocoa Banana Bread
PREP: 10 MINUTES PLUS FERMENTING TIME /MAKES 1 LOAF/12 SLICE BREAD (1½ pounds)

Ingredients
3 bananas, mashed
2 eggs, at room temperature
¾ cup packed light brown sugar
½ cup unsalted butter, melted
½ cup sour cream, at room temperature
¼ cup sugar
1½ teaspoons pure vanilla extract
1 cup all-purpose flour
½ cup quick oats
2 tablespoons unsweetened cocoa powder
1 teaspoon baking soda

Directions
1. Preparing the Ingredients.
Choose the size of loaf you would like to make and measure your ingredients.
Add the ingredients to the bread pan in the order listed above.
Place the pan in the bread machine and close the lid.
2. Select the Bake cycle
Turn on the bread maker. Select the Quick/Rapid setting, then the loaf size, and finally the crust color. Start the cycle.
When the cycle is finished and the bread is baked, carefully remove the pan from the machine. Use a potholder as the handle will be very hot. Let rest for a few minutes.

Remove the bread from the pan and allow to cool on a wire rack for at least 10 minutes before slicing.

Pumpkin Coconut Bread

PREP: 10 MINUTES PLUS FERMENTING TIME /MAKES 1 LOAF/12 SLICE BREAD (1½ pounds)

Ingredients

1 cup pure canned pumpkin
½ cup (1 stick) butter, at room temperature
1½ teaspoons pure vanilla extract
1 cup sugar
½ cup dark brown sugar
2 cups all-purpose flour
¾ cup sweetened shredded coconut
1½ teaspoons ground cinnamon
1 teaspoon baking soda
1 teaspoon baking powder
½ teaspoon ground nutmeg
½ teaspoon ground ginger
⅛ teaspoon ground allspice

Directions

1. **Preparing the Ingredients.**

Place the pumpkin, butter, vanilla, sugar, and dark brown sugar in your bread machine.

Program the machine for Quick/Rapid bread and press Start.

After the first fast mixing is done, add the flour, coconut, cinnamon, baking soda, baking powder, nutmeg, ginger, and allspice.

2. **Select the Bake cycle**

When the loaf is done, remove the bucket from the machine. Let the loaf cool for 5 minutes.

Gently shake the bucket to remove the loaf, and turn it out onto a rack to cool.

Cranberry-Cornmeal Bread

PREP: 10 MINUTES PLUS FERMENTING TIME /MAKES 1 LOAF/12 SLICE BREAD (1½ pounds)

Ingredients

1 cup plus 1 tablespoon water
3 tablespoons molasses or honey
2 tablespoons butter, softened
3 cups bread flour
⅓ cup cornmeal
1½ teaspoons salt
2 teaspoons bread machine yeast
½ cup sweetened dried cranberries

Directions

1. **Preparing the Ingredients.**

Measure carefully, placing all ingredients except cranberries in bread machine pan in the order recommended by the manufacturer. Add cranberries at the Raisin/Nut signal or 5 to 10 minutes before last kneading cycle ends.

2. **Select the Bake cycle**

Select Basic/White cycle. Use Medium or Light crust color. Do not use delay cycle. Remove baked bread from pan; cool on cooling rack.

Coconut Delight Bread

PREP: 10 MINUTES PLUS FERMENTING TIME /MAKES 1 LOAF/16 SLICE BREAD (2 pounds)

Ingredients
1⅓ cups lukewarm milk
1 egg, at room temperature
2 tablespoons unsalted butter, melted
2⅔ teaspoons pure coconut extract
3⅓ tablespoons sugar
1 teaspoon table salt
⅔ cup sweetened shredded coconut
4 cups white bread flour
2 teaspoons bread machine yeast

Directions
1. Preparing the Ingredients.

Choose the size of loaf you would like to make and measure your ingredients.

Add the ingredients to the bread pan in the order listed above.

Place the pan in the bread machine and close the lid.

2. Select the Bake cycle

Turn on the bread maker. Select the Sweet setting, then the loaf size, and finally the crust color. Start the cycle.

When the cycle is finished and the bread is baked, carefully remove the pan from the machine. Use a potholder as the handle will be very hot. Let rest for a few minutes.

Remove the bread from the pan and allow to cool down on a wire rack for at least 10 minutes or more before slicing.

Vanilla Almond Milk Bread

PREP: 10 MINUTES PLUS FERMENTING TIME /MAKES 1 LOAF/12 SLICE BREAD (1½ pounds)

Ingredients
½ cup plus 1 tablespoon milk, at 80°F to 90°F
3 tablespoons melted butter, cooled
3 tablespoons sugar
1 egg, at room temperature
1½ teaspoons pure vanilla extract
⅓ teaspoon almond extract
2½ cups white bread flour
1½ teaspoons bread machine or instant yeast

Directions
1. Preparing the Ingredients.

Place the ingredients in your bread machine as recommended by the manufacturer.

2. Select the Bake cycle

Program the machine for Basic/White bread, select light or medium crust, and press Start.

When the loaf is done, remove the bucket from the machine.

Let the loaf cool for 5 minutes.

Gently shake the bucket to remove the loaf, and turn it out onto a rack to cool.

Hot Cross Buns

PREP: 10 MINUTES PLUS FERMENTING TIME /MAKES 16 BOUNS

Ingredients

Dough

2 eggs plus enough water to equal 1⅓cups

½ cup butter, softened

4 cups bread flour

¾ teaspoon ground cinnamon

¼ teaspoon ground nutmeg

1½ teaspoons salt

2 tablespoons granulated sugar

1½ teaspoons bread machine or fast-acting dry yeast

½ cup raisins

½ cup golden raisins

1 egg

2 tablespoons cold water

Icing

1 cup powdered sugar

1 tablespoon milk or water

½ teaspoon vanilla

Directions

1. **Preparing the Ingredients.**

Measure carefully, placing all dough ingredients except raisins, 1 egg and the cold water in bread machine pan in the order recommended by the manufacturer. mAdd raisins at the Raisin/Nut signal.

2. **Select the Bake cycle**

Select Dough/Manual cycle. Do not use delay cycle. Remove dough from pan, using lightly floured hands. Cover and let rest 10 minutes on lightly floured surface. Grease cookie sheet or 2 (9-inch) round pans. Divide dough in half. Divide each half into 8 equal pieces. Shape each piece into a smooth ball. Place balls about 2 inches apart on cookie sheet or 1 inch apart in pans. Using scissors, snip a cross shape in top of each ball. Cover and let rise in warm place about 40 minutes or until doubled in size. Heat oven to 375°F. Beat egg and cold water slightly; brush on buns. Bake 18 to 20 minutes or until golden brown. Remove from cookie sheet to cooling rack. Cool slightly.

In small bowl, mix all icing ingredients until smooth and spreadable. Make a cross on top of each bun with icing.

Chocolate Chip Bread

PREP: 10 MINUTES PLUS FERMENTING TIME /MAKES 1 LOAF/12 SLICE BREAD (1½ pounds)

Ingredients

1 cup sour cream

2 eggs, at room temperature

1 cup sugar

½ cup unsalted butter, melted

¼ cup plain Greek yogurt

1¾ cups all-purpose flour

½ cup unsweetened cocoa powder

½ teaspoon baking powder

½ teaspoon table salt

1 cup milk chocolate chips

Directions

1. **Preparing the Ingredients.**

Choose the size of loaf you would like to make and measure your ingredients.

Add the ingredients to the bread pan in the order listed above. Place the pan in the bread machine and close the lid.

2. **Select the Bake cycle**

Turn on the bread maker. Select the Quick/Rapid setting, then the loaf size, and finally the crust color. Start the cycle.

When the cycle is finished and the bread is baked, carefully remove the pan from the machine. Use a potholder as the handle will be very hot. Let rest for a few minutes. Remove the bread from the pan and allow to cool down on a wire rack for at least 10 minutes or more before slicing.

Triple Chocolate Bread

PREP: 10 MINUTES PLUS FERMENTING TIME /MAKES 1 LOAF/8 SLICE BREAD (1pound)

Ingredients

⅔ cup milk, at 80°F to 90°F

1 egg, at room temperature

1½ tablespoons melted butter, cooled

1 teaspoon pure vanilla extract

2 tablespoons light brown sugar

1 tablespoon unsweetened cocoa powder

½ teaspoon salt

2 cups white bread flour

1 teaspoon bread machine or instant yeast

¼ cup semisweet chocolate chips

¼ cup white chocolate chips

Directions

1. Preparing the Ingredients.

Place the ingredients, except the chocolate chips, in your bread machine as recommended by the manufacturer.

2. Select the Bake cycle

Program the machine for Basic/White bread, select light or medium crust, and press Start.

When the machine signals, add the chocolate chips, or put them in the nut/raisin hopper and the machine will add them automatically.

When the loaf is done, remove the bucket from the machine.

Let the loaf cool for 5 minutes.

Gently shake the bucket to remove the loaf, and turn it out onto a rack to cool.

Crusty Mustard Focaccia

PREP: 10 MINUTES PLUS FERMENTING TIME /MAKES 8 SLICES

Ingredients

⅔ cup water

1 tablespoon olive or vegetable oil

2 tablespoons spicy mustard

2¼ cups bread flour

1 tablespoon sugar

1 teaspoon table salt

1½ teaspoons bread machine or fast-acting dry yeast

3 tablespoons olive or vegetable oil

Coarse (kosher or sea) salt, if desired

Directions

1. Preparing the Ingredients.

Measure carefully, placing all ingredients except 3 tablespoons oil and the coarse salt in bread machine pan in the order recommended by the manufacturer.

Select Dough/Manual cycle. Do not use delay cycle.

Remove dough from pan, using lightly floured hands. Knead 5 minutes on lightly floured surface (if necessary, knead in enough additional flour to make dough easy to handle). Cover and let rest 10 minutes.

2. Select the Bake cycle

Grease large cookie sheet. Roll or pat dough into 12-inch round on cookie sheet. Cover and let rise in warm place 10 minutes or until almost double.

Heat oven to 400°F. Prick dough with fork at 1-inch intervals or make deep depressions in dough with fingertips. Brush with 3 tablespoons oil. Sprinkle with coarse salt. Bake 15 to 18 minutes or until golden brown. Serve warm or cool.

Sweet Vanilla Bread

PREP: 10 MINUTES PLUS FERMENTING TIME /MAKES 1 LOAF/12 SLICE BREAD (1½ pounds)

Ingredients

½ cup + 1 tablespoon lukewarm milk

3 tablespoons unsalted butter, melted

3 tablespoons sugar

1 egg, at room temperature

1½ teaspoons pure vanilla extract

⅓ teaspoon almond extract

2½ cups white bread flour

1½ teaspoons bread machine yeast

Directions

1. Preparing the Ingredients.

Choose the size of loaf you would like to make and measure your ingredients.

Add the ingredients to the bread pan in the order listed above.

Place the pan in the bread machine and close the lid.

2. Select the Bake cycle

Turn on the bread maker. Select the White/Basic setting, then the loaf size, and finally the crust color. Start the cycle.

When the cycle is finished and the bread is baked, carefully remove the pan from the machine. Use a potholder as the handle will be very hot. Let rest for a few minutes.

Remove the bread from the pan and allow to cool on a wire rack for at least 10 minutes before slicing.

Chocolate Oatmeal Banana Bread

PREP: 10 MINUTES PLUS FERMENTING TIME /MAKES 1 LOAF/12 SLICE BREAD (1½ pounds)

Ingredients

3 bananas, mashed

2 eggs, at room temperature

¾ cup packed light brown sugar

½ cup (1 stick) butter, at room temperature

½ cup sour cream, at room temperature

¼ cup sugar

1½ teaspoons pure vanilla extract

1 cup all-purpose flour

½ cup quick oats

2 tablespoons unsweetened cocoa powder

1 teaspoon baking soda

Directions

1. Preparing the Ingredients.

Place the banana, eggs, brown sugar, butter, sour cream, sugar, and vanilla in your bread machine.

Program the machine for Quick/Rapid bread and press Start.

While the wet ingredients are mixing, stir together the flour, oats, cocoa powder, and baking soda in a small bowl.

2. Select the Bake cycle

After the first fast mixing is done and the machine signals, add the dry ingredients.

When the loaf is done, remove the bucket from the machine.

Let the loaf cool for 5 minutes.

Gently shake the bucket to remove the loaf, and turn it out onto a rack to cool.

SPECIALTY BREAD

Best-Ever Oatmeal-Flax Bread
PREP: 10 MINUTES /MAKES 1 LOAF/16 SLICE BREAD (2 pounds)

Ingredients
- 1¼ cups lukewarm water
- 2 tablespoons vegetable oil or olive oil
- ¼ cup honey or maple syrup
- 1½ teaspoons table salt
- 3½ cups whole wheat flour
- ¼ cup sesame, sunflower, or flax seeds (optional)
- 1½ teaspoons bread machine yeast

Directions

1. Preparing the Ingredients.
Choose the size of loaf you would like to make and measure your ingredients. Add the ingredients to the bread pan in the order listed above. Place the pan in the bread machine and close the lid..

2. Select the Bake cycle
Turn on the bread maker. Select the Whole Wheat/Wholegrain setting, then the loaf size, and finally the crust color. Start the cycle. When the cycle is finished, and the bread is baked, carefully remove the pan from the machine. Use a potholder as the handle will be very hot. Let rest for a few minutes. Remove the bread from the pan and allow to cool on a wire rack for at least 10 minutes before slicing.

Bread Machine
PREP: 10 MINUTES /MAKES 1 LOAF

Ingredients
- 1 cup all-purpose flour
- ⅔ cup packed dark brown sugar
- ½ cup old-fashioned oats
- ⅓ cup ground flaxseed or flaxseed meal
- 1 teaspoon baking soda
- 1 teaspoon salt
- 1⅔ cups buttermilk
- 1 tablespoon old-fashioned oats

Directions

1. Preparing the Ingredients.
Place the ingredients in your bread machine as recommended by the manufacturer.

2. Select the Bake cycle
Program the machine for Basic/White bread, select light or medium crust, and press Start.
When the loaf is done, remove the bucket from the machine.
Let the loaf cool for 5 minutes. Gently shake the bucket to remove the loaf, and turn it out onto a rack to cool.
Cool completely, about 2 hours, before slicing.

Panettone
PREP: 10 MINUTES /MAKES 1 LOAF

Ingredients
¾ cup warm water
6 Tbsp vegetable oil
1½ tsp salt
4 Tbsp sugar
2 eggs
3 cups bread flour
1 (¼ ounce) package Fleishman's yeast
½ cup candied fruit
⅓ cup chopped almonds
½ tsp almond extract

Directions

Preparing the Ingredients.
Add each ingredient to the bread machine in the order and at the temperature recommended by your bread machine manufacturer.

Select the Bake cycle
Close the lid, select the sweet loaf, low crust setting on your bread machine, and press start.
When the bread machine has finished baking, remove the bread and put it on a cooling rack.

Christmas Bread
PREP: 10 MINUTES /MAKES 8 SLICES

Ingredients
1¼ cups warm whole milk (70°F to 80°F)
½ tsp lemon juice
2 Tbsp butter, softened
2 Tbsp sugar
1½ tsp salt
3 cups bread flour
2 tsp active dry yeast
¾ cup golden raisins
¾ cup raisins
½ cup dried currants
1½ tsp grated lemon zest
Glaze:
½ cup powdered sugar
1½ tsp 2% milk
1 tsp melted butter
¼ tsp vanilla extract

Directions

1. **Preparing the Ingredients**
   Add each ingredient except the raisins, currants, and lemon zest to the bread machine in the order and at the temperature recommended by your bread machine manufacturer.

2. **Select the Bake cycle**
   Close the lid, select the sweet loaf, low crust setting on your bread machine, and press start.
   Just before the final kneading, add the raisins, currants and lemon zest.
   When the bread machine has finished baking, remove the bread and put it on a cooling rack.
   Combine the glaze ingredients in a bowl.
   Drizzle over the cooled bread.

Challah Bread
PREP: 10 MINUTES /MAKES 1 LOAF/16 SLICE BREAD (2 pounds)

Ingredients
1 cup +¾ teaspoon water, lukewarm between 80 and 90⁰F

2 ½ tablespoons unsalted butter, melted

2 small eggs, beaten

2 ½ tablespoons sugar

1 ¾ teaspoons salt

4 ½ cups white bread flour

2 teaspoons bread machine yeast or rapid rise yeast

Directions
1. Preparing the Ingredients.

Choose the size of loaf you would like to make and measure your ingredients. Add the ingredients to the bread pan in the order listed above. Place the pan in the bread machine and close the lid.

2. Select the Bake cycle

Turn on the bread maker. Select the Whole Wheat/Wholegrain setting, then the loaf size, and finally the crust color. Start the cycle. When the cycle is finished, and the bread is baked, carefully remove the pan from the machine. Use a potholder as the handle will be very hot. Let rest for a few minutes. Remove the bread from the pan and allow to cool on a wire rack for at least 10 minutes before slicing.

Golden Brown
PREP: 10 MINUTES /MAKES 1 LOAF/12 SLICE BREAD (1½ pounds)

Ingredients
¾ cup +1 tablespoon water, lukewarm between 80 and 90⁰F

2 tablespoons unsalted butter, melted

1 egg, beaten

2 tablespoons sugar

1 ½ teaspoons salt

3 ¼ cups white bread flour

1 ½ teaspoons bread machine yeast or rapid rise yeast

 For oven baking

1 egg yolk

2 tablespoons cold water

1 tablespoon poppy seed (optional)

Directions
1. Preparing the Ingredients.

Choose the size of loaf you would like to make and measure your ingredients.

Add the ingredients to the bread pan in the order listed above. Place the pan in the bread machine and close the lid.

2. Select the Bake cycle

Turn on the bread maker. Select the Dough setting, then the loaf size, and finally the crust color. Start the cycle.

Lightly flour a working surface and prepare a large baking sheet by greasing it with cooking spray or vegetable oil or line with parchment paper or a silicone mat. Preheat the oven to 375°F and place the oven rack in the middle position.

After the dough cycle is done, carefully remove the dough from the pan and place it on the working surface. Divide dough in three even parts. Roll each part into 13-inch-long cables for the 1 ½ pound Challah bread or 17-inch for the 2-pound loaf.

Arrange the dough cables side by side and start braiding from its middle part.

In order to make a seal, pinch ends and tuck the ends under the braid.

Arrange the loaf onto the baking sheet; cover the sheet with a clean kitchen towel. Let rise for 45-60 minutes or more until it doubles in size. In a mixing bowl, mix the egg yolk and cold water to make an egg wash. Gently brush the egg wash over the loaf. Sprinkle top with the poppy seed, if desired.

Bake for about 25-30 minutes or until loaf turns golden brown and is fully cooked.

Panettone Bread

PREP: 10 MINUTES /MAKES 1 LOAF/12 SLICE BREAD (1½ pounds)

Ingredients

¾ cup milk, at 80°F to 90°F
¼ cup melted butter, cooled
2 eggs, at room temperature
2 teaspoons pure vanilla extract
2 tablespoons sugar
1½ teaspoons salt
3¼ cups white bread flour
2 teaspoons bread machine or instant yeast
¼ cup candied lemon peel
¼ cup candied orange peel

Directions

1. Preparing the Ingredients.

Place the ingredients, except the candied fruit peel, in your bread machine as recommended by the manufacturer.

2. Select the Bake cycle

Program the machine for Sweet bread, select light or medium crust, and press Start.
When the machine signals, add the peel, or place in the nut/raisin hopper and let the machine add the peel automatically.
When the loaf is done, remove the bucket from the machine.
Let the loaf cool for 5 minutes. Gently shake the bucket to remove the loaf, and turn it out onto a rack to cool.

Irish Yogurt Bread

PREP: 10 MINUTES /MAKES 8 WEDGES

Ingredients

1¾ cups all-purpose flour
½ cup dried currants or raisins
1½ teaspoons baking powder
¼ teaspoon baking soda
¼ teaspoon salt
1 container (6 oz) lemon burst, orange crème
French vanilla yogurt 2 tablespoons vegetable oil

Directions

1. Preparing the Ingredients.

Place the ingredients in your bread machine as recommended by the manufacturer
Program the machine for Basic/White bread, select light or medium crust, and press Start.

2. Select the Bake cycle

When the loaf is done, remove the bucket from the machine. Let the loaf cool for 5 minutes.
Gently shake the bucket to remove the loaf, and turn it out onto a rack to cool

Dry Fruit Cinnamon Bread

PREP: 10 MINUTES /MAKES 1 LOAF/12 SLICE BREAD (1½ pounds)

Ingredients

1¼ cups lukewarm milk

¼ cup unsalted butter, melted

½ teaspoon pure vanilla extract

¼ teaspoon pure almond extract

3 tablespoons light brown sugar

1 teaspoon table salt

2 teaspoons ground cinnamon

3 cups white bread flour

1 teaspoon bread machine yeast

½ cup dried mixed fruit

½ cup golden raisins, chopped

Directions

1. Preparing the Ingredients.

Choose the size of loaf you would like to make and measure your ingredients. Add all of the ingredients except for the mixed fruit and raisins to the bread pan in the order listed above. Place the pan in the bread machine and close the lid.

2. Select the Bake cycle

Turn on the bread maker. Select the White/Basic or Fruit/Nut (if your machine has this setting) setting, then the loaf size, and finally the crust color. Start the cycle. When the machine signals to add ingredients, add the mixed fruit and raisins. (Some machines have a fruit/nut hopper where you can add the mixed fruit and raisins when you start the machine. The machine will automatically add them to the dough during the baking process.) When the cycle is finished and the bread is baked, carefully remove the pan from the machine. Use a potholder as the handle will be very hot. Let rest for a few minutes.

Remove the bread from the pan and allow to cool on a wire rack for at least 10 minutes before slicing.

White Chocolate Cranberry Bread

PREP: 10 MINUTES PLUS FERMENTING TIME /MAKES 1 LOAF/12 SLICE BREAD (1½ pounds)

Ingredients

¾ cup plus 2 tablespoons milk, at 80°F to 90°F

1 egg, at room temperature

1½ tablespoons melted butter, cooled

1 teaspoon pure vanilla extract

2 tablespoons sugar

¾ teaspoon salt

3 cups white bread flour

1 teaspoon bread machine or instant yeast

½ cup white chocolate chips

⅓ cup sweetened dried cranberries

Directions

1. Preparing the Ingredients.

Place the ingredients, except the chocolate chips and cranberries, in your bread machine as recommended by the manufacturer.

2. Select the Bake cycle

Program the machine for Basic/White bread, select light or medium crust, and press Start.

When the loaf is done, remove the bucket from the machine.

Add the white chocolate chips and cranberries when the machine signals or 5 minutes before the last knead cycle ends.

Let the loaf cool for 5 minutes.

Gently shake the bucket to remove the loaf, and turn it out onto a rack to cool.

Festive Raspberry Rolls

Ingredients

⅓cup milk

⅓cup water

3 tablespoons butter, softened

1 egg

2 cups bread flour

⅓cup sugar

½ teaspoon salt

1¾ teaspoons bread machine or fast-acting dry yeast

3 tablespoons raspberry preserves

Directions

1. Preparing the Ingredients.

Measure carefully, placing all ingredients except preserves in bread machine pan in the order recommended by the manufacturer.

2. Select the Bake cycle

Select Dough/Manual cycle. Do not use delay cycle.

Remove dough from pan, using lightly floured hands. Cover and let rest 10 minutes on lightly floured surface.

Grease 12 regular-size muffin cups. Roll or pat dough into 15×10-inch rectangle. Spread preserves over dough to within ¼ inch of edges. Starting with 15-inch side, roll up dough; pinch edge of dough into roll to seal. Stretch and shape roll to make even.

Cut roll into 12 equal slices. Place slices, cut side up, in muffin cups. Using kitchen scissors, snip through each slice twice, cutting into fourths. Gently spread dough pieces open. Cover and let rise in warm place about 25 minutes or until doubled in size. Dough is ready if indentation remains when touched. Heat oven to 375°F. Bake 15 to 20 minutes or until golden brown. Immediately remove from pan to cooling rack. Serve warm or cool.

Italian Easter Cake

Ingredients

1¾ cups wheat flour

2½ Tbsp quick-acting dry yeast

8 Tbsp sugar

½ tsp salt

3 chicken eggs

¾ cup milk

3 Tbsp butter

1 cup raisins

Directions

1. **Preparing the Ingredients**

    Add each ingredient except the raisins to the bread machine in the order and at the temperature recommended by your bread machine manufacturer.

2. **Select the Bake cycle**

    Close the lid, select the sweet loaf, low crust setting on your bread machine, and press start.

    When the dough is kneading, add the raisins.

    When the bread machine has finished baking, remove the bread and put it on a cooling rack.

Beer Pizza Dough

PREP: 10 MINUTES PLUS FERMENTING TIME /MAKES 1 LOAF/12 SLICE BREAD (1½ pounds)

Ingredients

1 cup beer, at room temperature

3 tablespoons olive oil

1 tablespoon sugar

1 teaspoon table salt

3 cups white bread flour or all-purpose flour

1½ teaspoons bread machine yeast

Directions

1. **Preparing the Ingredients.**

Choose the size of dough you would like to make and measure your ingredients.

Add the ingredients to the bread pan in the order listed above.

Place the pan in the bread machine and close the lid.

2. **Select the Bake cycle**

Turn on the bread maker. Select the Dough setting and then the dough size. Start the machine.

When the cycle is finished, carefully remove the dough from the pan.

Place the dough on a lightly floured surface and roll to make a pizza crust of your desired thickness. Set aside for 10–15 minutes. Top with your favorite pizza sauce, toppings, cheese, etc.

Bake in an oven at 400°F or 204°C for 15–20 minutes or until the edges turn lightly golden.

Eggnog Bread

PREP: 10 MINUTES PLUS FERMENTING TIME /MAKES 1 LOAF/8 SLICE BREAD (1 pound)

Ingredients

¾ cup eggnog, at 80°F to 90°F

¾ tablespoon melted butter, cooled

1 tablespoon sugar

⅔ teaspoon salt

¼ teaspoon ground cinnamon

¼ teaspoon ground nutmeg

2 cups white bread flour

¾ teaspoon bread machine or instant yeast

Directions

1. **Preparing the Ingredients.**

Place the ingredients in your bread machine as recommended by the manufacturer.

2. **Select the Bake cycle**

Program the machine for Basic/White bread, select light or medium crust, and press Start.

When the loaf is done, remove the bucket from the machine. Let the loaf cool for 5 minutes.

Gently shake the bucket to remove the loaf, and turn it out onto a rack to cool.

Basil Pizza Dough

Ingredients

1 cup lukewarm water
3 tablespoons olive oil
1 teaspoon table salt
1½ teaspoons sugar
1½ teaspoons basil, dried
3 cups white bread flour or all-purpose flour
1½ teaspoons bread machine yeast

Directions

1. Preparing the Ingredients.

Choose the size of dough you would like to make and measure your ingredients.

Add the ingredients to the bread pan in the order listed above.

Place the pan in the bread machine and close the lid.

2. Select the Bake cycle

Turn on the bread maker. Select the Dough setting and then the dough size. Start the machine.

When the cycle is finished, carefully remove the dough from the pan.

Place the dough on a lightly floured surface and roll to make a pizza crust of your desired thickness. Set aside for 10–15 minutes. Top with your favorite pizza sauce, toppings, cheese, etc.

Bake in an oven at 400°F or 204°C for 15–20 minutes or until the edges turn lightly golden.

Whole-Wheat Challah
PREP: 10 MINUTES PLUS FERMENTING TIME /MAKES 1 LOAF/12 SLICE BREAD (1½ pounds)

Ingredients

¾ cup water, at 80°F to 90°F
⅓ cup melted butter, cooled
2 eggs, at room temperature
1½ teaspoons salt
3 tablespoons sugar
1 cup whole-wheat flour
2 cups white bread flour
1⅔ teaspoons bread machine or instant yeast

Directions

1. Preparing the Ingredients.

Place the ingredients in your bread machine as recommended by the manufacturer.

2. Select the Bake cycle

Program the machine for Basic/White bread, select light or medium crust, and press Start.

When the loaf is done, remove the bucket from the machine.

Let the loaf cool for 5 minutes.

Gently shake the bucket to remove the loaf, and turn it out onto a rack to cool.

Classic Sourdough Bread

PREP: 10 MINUTES PLUS FERMENTING TIME /MAKES 1 LOAF/12 SLICE BREAD (1½ pounds)

Ingredients

2 tablespoons lukewarm water

2 cups sourdough starter

2 tablespoons unsalted butter, melted

2 teaspoons sugar

1½ teaspoons salt

2½ cups white bread flour

1½ teaspoons bread machine yeast

Sourdough Starter

2 cups lukewarm water

2 cups all-purpose flour

2½ teaspoons bread machine yeast

Directions

1. **Preparing the Ingredients.**

Add the water, flour, and yeast to a medium-size non-metallic bowl. Mix well until no lumps are visible.

Cover the bowl loosely and leave it in a warm area of your kitchen for 5–8 days. Do not place in a fridge or under direct sunlight.

Stir the mixture several times every day. Always put the cover back on the bowl afterward.

The starter is ready to use when it appears bubbly and has a sour smell.

2. **Select the Bake cycle**

Choose the size of loaf you would like to make and measure your ingredients.

Add the ingredients to the bread pan in the order listed above. Place the pan in the bread machine and close the lid.

Turn on the bread maker. Select the White/Basic setting, then the loaf size, and finally the crust color. Start the cycle.

When the cycle is finished and the bread is baked, carefully remove the pan from the machine. Use a potholder as the handle will be very hot. Let rest for a few minutes.

Remove the bread from the pan and allow to cool on a wire rack for at least 10 minutes before slicing.

Portuguese Sweet Bread

PREP: 10 MINUTES PLUS FERMENTING TIME /MAKES 1 LOAF/8 SLICE BREAD (1 pound)

Ingredients

⅔ cup milk, at 80°F to 90°F

1 egg, at room temperature

4 teaspoons butter, softened

⅓ cup sugar

⅔ teaspoon salt

2 cups white bread flour

1½ teaspoons bread machine or instant yeast

Directions

1. **Preparing the Ingredients.**

Place the ingredients in your bread machine as recommended by the manufacturer.

2. **Select the Bake cycle**

Program the machine for Sweet bread and press Start. When the loaf is done, remove the bucket from the machine.

Let the loaf cool for 5 minutes.

Gently shake the bucket to remove the loaf, and turn it out onto a rack to cool.

Milk Honey Sourdough Bread

PREP: 10 MINUTES PLUS FERMENTING TIME /MAKES 1 LOAF/16 SLICE BREAD (2 pounds)

Ingredients

½ cup lukewarm milk

2 cups sourdough starter

¼ cup olive oil

2 tablespoons honey

1⅓ teaspoons salt

4 cups white bread flour

1⅓ teaspoons bread machine yeast

Directions

1. **Preparing the Ingredients.**

Choose the size of loaf you would like to make and measure your ingredients.

Add the ingredients to the bread pan in the order listed above.

Place the pan in the bread machine and close the lid.

2. **Select the Bake cycle**

Turn on the bread maker. Select the White/Basic setting, then the loaf size, and finally the crust color. Start the cycle.

When the cycle is finished and the bread is baked, carefully remove the pan from the machine. Use a potholder as the handle will be very hot. Let rest for a few minutes.

Remove the bread from the pan and allow to cool on a wire rack for at least 10 minutes before slicing.

Pecan Maple Bread

PREP: 10 MINUTES PLUS FERMENTING TIME /MAKES 1 LOAF/16 SLICE BREAD (2 pounds)

Ingredients

1½ cups (3 sticks) butter, at room temperature

4 eggs, at room temperature

⅔ cup maple syrup

⅔ cup sugar

3 cups all-purpose flour

1 cup chopped pecans

2 teaspoons baking powder

½ teaspoon salt

Directions

1. **Preparing the Ingredients.**

Place the butter, eggs, maple syrup, and sugar in your bread machine.

2. **Select the Bake cycle**

Program the machine for Quick/Rapid bread and press Start. While the wet ingredients are mixing, stir together the flour, pecans, baking powder, and salt in a small bowl. After the first fast mixing is done and the machine signals, add the dry ingredients. When the loaf is done, remove the bucket from the machine.

Let the loaf cool for 5 minutes. Gently shake the bucket to remove the loaf, and turn it out onto a rack to cool.

Cherry Christmas Bread

PREP: 10 MINUTES PLUS FERMENTING TIME /MAKES 1 LOAF/16 SLICE BREAD (2 pounds)

Ingredients

1 cup + 1 tablespoon lukewarm milk
1 egg, at room temperature
2 tablespoons unsalted butter, melted
3 tablespoons light brown sugar
⅛ teaspoon ground cinnamon
4 cups white bread flour, divided
1½ teaspoons bread machine yeast
⅔ cup candied cherries
½ cup chopped almonds
½ cup raisins, chopped

Directions

1. Preparing the Ingredients.

Choose the size of loaf you would like to make and measure your ingredients.

Add all of the ingredients except for the cherries, raisins, and almonds to the bread pan in the order listed above.

Place the pan in the bread machine and close the lid.

Turn on the bread maker. Select the White/Basic or Fruit/Nut (if your machine has this setting) setting, then the loaf size, and finally the crust color. Start the cycle.

2. Select the Bake cycle

When the machine signals to add ingredients, add the cherries, raisins, and almonds. (Some machines have a fruit/nut hopper where you can add the cherries, raisins, and almonds when you start the machine. The machine will automatically add them to the dough during the baking process.)

When the cycle is finished and the bread is baked, carefully remove the pan from the machine. Use a potholder as the handle will be very hot. Let rest for a few minutes.

Remove the bread from the pan and allow to cool on a wire rack for at least 10 minutes before slicing.

Nana's Gingerbread

PREP: 10 MINUTES PLUS FERMENTING TIME /MAKES 1 LOAF/8 SLICE BREAD (1 pounds)

Ingredients

⅔ cup buttermilk, at 80°F to 90°F
1 egg, at room temperature
2⅔ tablespoons dark molasses
2 teaspoons melted butter, cooled
2 tablespoons sugar
1 teaspoon salt
1 teaspoon ground ginger
⅔ teaspoon ground cinnamon
⅓ teaspoon ground nutmeg
⅛ teaspoon ground cloves
2⅓ cups white bread flour
1⅓ teaspoons bread machine or active dry yeast

Directions

1. Preparing the Ingredients.

Place the ingredients in your bread machine as recommended by the manufacturer.

2. Select the Bake cycle

Program the machine for Sweet bread and press Start. When the loaf is done, remove the bucket from the machine.

Let the loaf cool for 5 minutes. Gently shake the bucket to remove the loaf, and turn it out onto a rack to cool.

Maple-Walnut Twists
PREP: 10 MINUTES PLUS FERMENTING TIME /MAKES 1 LOAF

Ingredients

Dough
1 cup water
¼ butter, softened
1 egg
3½ cups bread flour
⅓cup granulated sugar
1 teaspoon salt
1½ teaspoons bread machine or fast-acting dry yeast

Filling
¼ cup finely chopped walnuts
2 tablespoons maple-flavored syrup
2 tablespoons butter, softened
½ teaspoon ground cinnamon

Icing
1 cup powdered sugar
½ teaspoon maple extract
About 1 tablespoon milk

Directions

1. **Preparing the Ingredients.**

Measure carefully, placing all dough ingredients in bread machine pan in the order recommended by the manufacturer.

2. **Select the Bake cycle**

Select Dough/Manual cycle. Do not use delay cycle. Remove dough from pan, using lightly floured hands. Cover and let rest 10 minutes on lightly floured surface. In small bowl, mix all filling ingredients.Grease 13×9-inch pan. Roll or pat dough into 16×10-inch rectangle on lightly floured surface. Spread half of the filling lengthwise down center third of rectangle. Fold one outer third of dough over filling; spread remaining filling over folded dough. Fold remaining third of dough over filling; pinch edge to seal. Cut crosswise into sixteen 1-inch strips. Holding a strip at each end, twist in opposite directions. Place strips about 1 inch apart in pan, forming 2 rows of 8 strips each. Cover and let rise in warm place 50 to 60 minutes or until doubled in size. Dough is ready if indentation remains when touched.

Heat oven to 350°F. Bake 35 to 40 minutes or until golden brown. In small bowl, mix all icing ingredients until smooth and thin enough to drizzle. Drizzle icing over warm twists. Serve warm.

Coffee Caraway Seed Bread
PREP: 10 MINUTES PLUS FERMENTING TIME /MAKES 1 LOAF/12 SLICE BREAD (1½ pounds)

Ingredients
¾ cup lukewarm water
⅓ cup brewed coffee, lukewarm
1½ tablespoons balsamic vinegar
1½ tablespoons olive oil
1½ tablespoons dark molasses
¾ tablespoon light brown sugar
¾ teaspoon table salt
1½ teaspoons caraway seeds
3 tablespoons unsweetened cocoa powder
¾ cup dark rye flour
1¾ cups white bread flour
1½ teaspoons bread machine yeast

Directions

1. **Preparing the Ingredients.**

Choose the size of loaf you would like to make and measure your ingredients.

Add the ingredients to the bread pan in the order listed above.

Place the pan in the bread machine and close the lid.

2. **Select the Bake cycle**

Turn on the bread maker. Select the Whole Wheat/Wholegrain setting, then the loaf size, and finally the crust color. Start the cycle. When the cycle is finished and the bread is baked, carefully remove the pan from the machine. Use a potholder as the handle will be very hot. Let rest for a few minutes.

Remove the bread from the pan and allow to cool down on a wire rack for at least 10 minutes or more before slicing.

Bread Machine Brioche

PREP: 10 MINUTES PLUS FERMENTING TIME /MAKES 1 LOAF/12 SLICE BREAD (1½ pounds)

Ingredients

½ cup plus 1 tablespoon milk, at 80°F to 90°F

3 eggs, at room temperature

2 tablespoons sugar

¾ teaspoon salt

3 cups white bread flour

1½ teaspoons bread machine or instant yeast

½ cup (1 stick) butter, softened

Directions
1. Preparing the Ingredients.
Place the ingredients in your bread machine as recommended by the manufacturer.

Program the machine for Basic/White bread, select light crust, and press Start.

Cut the butter into tablespoon-sized pieces.

2. Select the Bake cycle
About 10 minutes before the end of your first kneading cycle, begin adding the butter, 1 tablespoon each minute.

When the loaf is done, remove the bucket from the machine.

Let the loaf cool for 5 minutes.

Gently shake the bucket to remove the loaf, and turn it out onto a rack to cool.

Sun-Dried Tomato Rolls

PREP: 10 MINUTES PLUS FERMENTING TIME /MAKES 12 ROLLS

Ingredients

¾ cup warm milk (105°F to 115°F)

2 cups bread flour

¼ cup chopped sun-dried tomatoes in oil, drained, 1 tablespoon oil reserved 1 tablespoon sugar

1 teaspoon salt

1½ teaspoons bread machine yeast

Directions
1. Preparing the Ingredients.
Measure carefully, placing all ingredients in bread machine pan in the order recommended by the manufacturer.

Select Dough/Manual cycle. Do not use delay cycle.

Remove dough from pan; place on lightly floured surface. Cover and let rest 10 minutes.
2. Select the Bake cycle
Lightly grease cookie sheet with shortening or spray with cooking spray.

Gently push fist into dough to deflate. Divide dough into 12 equal pieces. Shape each piece into a ball. Place balls about 2 inches apart on cookie sheet. Cover and let rise in warm place 30 to 45 minutes or until almost doubled in size.

Heat oven to 350°F. Bake 12 to 16 minutes or until golden brown. Remove from cookie sheet to cooling rack. Serve warm or cool.

Bagels

PREP: 10 MINUTES PLUS FERMENTING TIME /MAKES 1 BAGELS

Ingredients
1 cup plus 1 tablespoon water
1½ tablespoons honey
3 cups bread flour
1¼ teaspoons salt
1½ teaspoons bread machine or fast-acting dry yeast
Old-fashioned oats, instant minced onion, sesame seed or poppy seed, if desired

Directions
1. Preparing the Ingredients.
Measure carefully, placing all ingredients except oats in bread machine pan in the order recommended by the manufacturer.
2. Select the Bake cycle
Select Dough/Manual cycle. Do not use delay cycle. Stop cycle after 50 minutes; remove dough from pan, using lightly floured hands. Grease cookie sheet. Cut dough into 10 equal pieces. Shape each piece into 3-inch round; poke 1-inch hole in center, using thumb. Smooth into bagel shape, using fingers. Place on cookie sheet. Cover and let rise in warm place about 20 minutes or until almost doubled in size.

Heat oven to 450°F. In Dutch oven, heat 2 quarts water to boiling. Lower 3 or 4 bagels at a time into boiling water. Boil 30 seconds, turning once after 15 seconds. Remove with slotted spoon; drain on paper towels. Sprinkle with oats.

Place on cookie sheet. Bake 8 minutes or until light golden brown. Remove from cookie sheet to cooling rack; cool.

Cinnamon Beer Bread

PREP: 10 MINUTES PLUS FERMENTING TIME /MAKES 1 LOAF/16 SLICE BREAD (2 pounds)

Ingredients
2 cups beer, at room temperature
1 cup unsalted butter, melted
⅓ cup honey
4 cups all-purpose flour
1⅓ teaspoons table salt
⅓ teaspoon ground cinnamon
1⅓ tablespoons baking powder

Directions
1. Preparing the Ingredients.
Choose the size of loaf you would like to make and measure your ingredients.
Add the ingredients to the bread pan in the order listed above.
Place the pan in the bread machine and close the lid.
2. Select the Bake cycle
Turn on the bread maker. Select the Quick/Rapid setting, then the loaf size, and finally the crust color. Start the cycle.
When the cycle is finished and the bread is baked, carefully remove the pan from the machine. Use a potholder as the handle will be very hot. Let rest for a few minutes.
Remove the bread from the pan and allow to cool on a wire rack for at least 10 minutes before slicing.

Traditional Paska
PREP: 10 MINUTES PLUS FERMENTING TIME /MAKES 1 LOAF/12 SLICE BREAD (1½ pounds)

Ingredients
¾ cup milk, at 80°F to 90°F
2 eggs, at room temperature
2 tablespoons butter, melted and cooled
¼ cup sugar
1 teaspoon salt
2 teaspoons lemon zest
3 cups white bread flour
2 teaspoons bread machine or instant yeast

Directions
1. **Preparing the Ingredients.**
Place the ingredients in your bread machine as recommended by the manufacturer.
2. **Select the Bake cycle**
Program the machine for Basic/White bread, select light or medium crust, and press Start.
When the loaf is done, remove the bucket from the machine.
Let the loaf cool for 5 minutes. Gently shake the bucket to remove the loaf, and turn it out onto a rack to cool.

French Butter Bread
PREP: 10 MINUTES PLUS FERMENTING TIME /MAKES 1 LOAF/12 SLICE BREAD (1½ pounds)

Ingredients
½ cup + 1 tablespoon lukewarm milk
3 eggs, at room temperature
2 tablespoons sugar
¾ teaspoon table salt
½ cup unsalted butter, melted
3 cups white bread flour
1½ teaspoons bread machine yeast

Directions
1. **Preparing the Ingredients.**
Choose the size of loaf you would like to make and measure your ingredients.
Add the ingredients to the bread pan in the order listed above.
Place the pan in the bread machine and close the lid.
2. **Select the Bake cycle**
Turn on the bread maker. Select the White/Basic setting, then the loaf size, and finally the crust color. Start the cycle.
When the cycle is finished and the bread is baked, carefully remove the pan from the machine. Use a potholder as the handle will be very hot. Let rest for a few minutes.
Remove the bread from the pan and allow to cool on a wire rack for at least 10 minutes before slicing.

Raisin and Nut Paska

PREP: 10 MINUTES PLUS FERMENTING TIME /MAKES 1 LOAF/12 SLICE BREAD (1½ pounds)

Ingredients

¾ cup milk, at 80°F to 90°F

2 eggs, at room temperature

2 tablespoons butter, melted and cooled

¼ cup sugar

1 teaspoon salt

2 teaspoons lemon zest

3 cups white bread flour

2 teaspoons bread machine or instant yeast

⅓ cup slivered almonds

⅓ cup golden raisins

Directions

1. Preparing the Ingredients.

Place the ingredients, except the almonds and raisins, in your bread machine as recommended by the manufacturer.

2. Select the Bake cycle

Program the machine for Basic/White bread, select light or medium crust, and press Start.

When the loaf is done, remove the bucket from the machine.

Add the almonds and raisins when the machine signals or 5 minutes before the second kneading cycle is finished.

Let the loaf cool for 5 minutes.

Gently shake the bucket to remove the loaf, and turn it out onto a rack to cool.

Holiday Chocolate Bread

PREP: 10 MINUTES PLUS FERMENTING TIME /MAKES 1 LOAF/12 SLICE BREAD (1½ pounds)

Ingredients

⅞ cup lukewarm milk

1 egg, at room temperature

1½ tablespoons unsalted butter, melted

1 teaspoon pure vanilla extract

2 tablespoons sugar

¾ teaspoon table salt

3 cups white bread flour

1 teaspoon bread machine yeast

½ cup white chocolate chips

⅓ cup dried cranberries

Directions

1. Preparing the Ingredients.

Choose the size of loaf you would like to make and measure your ingredients.

Add all of the ingredients except for the chocolate chips and cranberries to the bread pan in the order listed above.

Place the pan in the bread machine and close the lid.

2. Select the Bake cycle

Turn on the bread maker. Select the White/Basic or Fruit/Nut (if your machine has this setting) setting, then the loaf size, and finally the crust color. Start the cycle. When the machine signals to add ingredients, add the chocolate chips and cranberries. (Some machines have a fruit/nut hopper where you can add the chocolate chips and cranberries when you start the machine. The machine will automatically add them to the dough during the baking process.) When the cycle is finished and the bread is baked, carefully remove the pan from the machine. Use a potholder as the handle will be very hot. Let rest for a few minutes. Remove the bread from the pan and allow to cool on a wire rack for at least 10 minutes before slicing.

Honey Cake

PREP: 10 MINUTES PLUS FERMENTING TIME /MAKES 1 LOAF/12 SLICE BREAD (1½ pounds)

Ingredients

⅓ cup brewed coffee, cooled to room temperature

½ cup (1 stick) butter, melted and cooled

½ cup honey

¾ cup sugar

¼ cup dark brown sugar

2 eggs, at room temperature

2 tablespoons whiskey

¼ cup freshly squeezed orange juice, at room temperature

1 teaspoon pure vanilla extract

2 cups all-purpose flour

½ tablespoon baking powder

½ tablespoon ground cinnamon

½ teaspoon baking soda

¼ teaspoon ground allspice

¼ teaspoon salt

¼ teaspoon ground cloves

Directions

1. Preparing the Ingredients.

Place the coffee, butter, honey, sugar, brown sugar, eggs, whiskey, orange juice, and vanilla in your bread machine.

2. Select the Bake cycle

Program the machine for Quick/Rapid bread and press Start. While the wet ingredients are mixing, stir together the flour, baking powder, cinnamon, baking soda, allspice, salt, and cloves in a small bowl. After the first fast mixing is done and the machine signals, add the dry ingredients. When the loaf is done, remove the bucket from the machine.

Let the loaf cool for 5 minutes. Gently shake the bucket to remove the loaf, and turn it out onto a rack to cool.

New Year Spiced Bread

PREP: 10 MINUTES PLUS FERMENTING TIME /MAKES 1 LOAF/12 SLICE BREAD (1½ pounds)

Ingredients

⅓ cup brewed coffee, cooled to room temperature

½ cup unsalted butter, melted

½ cup honey

¾ cup sugar

¼ cup dark brown sugar

2 eggs, at room temperature

2 tablespoons whiskey

¼ cup orange juice, at room temperature

1 teaspoon pure vanilla extract

2 cups all-purpose flour

½ tablespoon ground cinnamon

½ teaspoon baking soda

¼ teaspoon ground allspice

¼ teaspoon table salt

¼ teaspoon ground cloves

½ tablespoon baking powder

Directions

1. Preparing the Ingredients.

Choose the size of loaf you would like to make and measure your ingredients.

Add the ingredients to the bread pan in the order listed above. Place the pan in the bread machine and close the lid.

2. Select the Bake cycle

Turn on the bread maker. Select the Quick/Rapid setting, then the loaf size, and finally the crust color. Start the cycle.

When the cycle is finished and the bread is baked, carefully remove the pan from the machine. Use a potholder as the handle will be very hot. Let rest for a few minutes.

Remove the bread from the pan and allow to cool on a wire rack for at least 10 minutes before slicing.

Christmas Fruit Bread

PREP: 10 MINUTES PLUS FERMENTING TIME /MAKES 1 LOAF/8 SLICE BREAD (1 pound)

Ingredients

¾ cup plus 1 tablespoon milk, at 80°F to 90°F

2⅔ tablespoons melted butter, cooled

⅓ teaspoon pure vanilla extract

⅛ teaspoon pure almond extract

2 tablespoons light brown sugar

⅔ teaspoon salt

1 teaspoon ground cinnamon

2 cups white bread flour

⅔ teaspoon bread machine or instant yeast

⅓ cup dried mixed fruit

⅓ cup golden raisins

Directions

1. **Preparing the Ingredients.**

Place the ingredients, except the dried fruit and raisins, in your bread machine as recommended by the manufacturer.

2. **Select the Bake cycle**

Program the machine for Basic/White bread, select light or medium crust, and press Start.

Add the dried fruit and raisins when the machine signals or 5 minutes before the second kneading cycle is finished. When the loaf is done, remove the bucket from the machine. Let the loaf cool for 5 minutes.

Gently shake the bucket to remove the loaf, and turn it out onto a rack to cool.

Cocoa Holiday Bread

PREP: 10 MINUTES PLUS FERMENTING TIME /MAKES 1 LOAF/12 SLICE BREAD (1½ pounds)

Ingredients

¾ cup brewed coffee, lukewarm

⅓ cup evaporated milk, lukewarm

1½ tablespoons unsalted butter, melted

2¼ tablespoons honey

¾ tablespoon dark molasses

¾ tablespoon sugar

1 tablespoon unsweetened cocoa powder

¾ teaspoon table salt

1⅔ cups whole-wheat bread flour

1⅔ cups white bread flour

1⅔ teaspoons bread machine yeast

Directions

1. **Preparing the Ingredients.**

Choose the size of loaf you would like to make and measure your ingredients.

Add the ingredients to the bread pan in the order listed above.

Place the pan in the bread machine and close the lid.

2. **Select the Bake cycle**

Turn on the bread maker. Select the Sweet setting, then the loaf size, and finally the crust color. Start the cycle.

When the cycle is finished and the bread is baked, carefully remove the pan from the machine. Use a potholder as the handle will be very hot. Let rest for a few minutes.

Remove the bread from the pan and allow to cool on a wire rack for at least 10 minutes before slicing.

Stollen

PREP: 10 MINUTES PLUS FERMENTING TIME /MAKES 1 LOAF/12 SLICE BREAD (1½ pounds)

Ingredients
¾ cup milk, at 80°F to 90°F

1 egg, at room temperature

1½ tablespoons butter, melted and cooled

2¼ tablespoons light brown sugar

⅛ teaspoon ground cinnamon

3 cups white bread flour, divided

1⅛ teaspoons bread machine or instant yeast

½ cup red and green candied cherries

⅓ cup chopped almonds

⅓ cup raisins

Directions
1. Preparing the Ingredients.
Place the ingredients, except the candied fruit, nuts, raisins, and ¼ cup of the flour, in your bread machine as recommended by the manufacturer.

2. Select the Bake cycle
Program the machine for Basic/White bread, select light or medium crust, and press Start.

In a small bowl, stir together the candied cherries, almonds, raisins, and ¼ cup of flour.

Add the fruit and nut mixture when the machine signals or 5 minutes before the second kneading cycle is finished.

When the loaf is done, remove the bucket from the machine.

Let the loaf cool for 5 minutes.

Gently shake the bucket to remove the loaf, and turn it out onto a rack to cool.

Holiday Eggnog Bread

PREP: 10 MINUTES PLUS FERMENTING TIME /MAKES 1 LOAF/12 SLICE BREAD (1½ pounds)

Ingredients
1⅛ cups eggnog, at room temperature

1⅛ tablespoons unsalted butter, melted

1½ tablespoons sugar

1 teaspoon table salt

⅓ teaspoon ground cinnamon

⅓ teaspoon ground nutmeg

3 cups white bread flour

1⅓ teaspoons bread machine yeast

Directions
1. Preparing the Ingredients.
Choose the size of loaf you would like to make and measure your ingredients.

Add the ingredients to the bread pan in the order listed above.

Place the pan in the bread machine and close the lid.

2. Select the Bake cycle
Turn on the bread maker. Select the White/Basic setting, then the loaf size, and finally the crust color. Start the cycle.

When the cycle is finished and the bread is baked, carefully remove the pan from the machine. Use a potholder as the handle will be very hot. Let rest for a few minutes.

Remove the bread from the pan and allow to cool on a wire rack for at least 10 minutes before slicing.

Julekake

PREP: 10 MINUTES PLUS FERMENTING TIME /MAKES 1 LOAF/8 SLICE BREAD (1 pound)

Ingredients

⅔ cup milk, at 80°F to 90°F

1 egg, at room temperature

⅓ cup butter, melted and cooled

2⅔ tablespoons honey

⅓ teaspoon salt

⅓ teaspoon ground cardamom

¼ teaspoon ground cinnamon

2¼ cups white bread flour, plus 1 tablespoon

1½ teaspoons bread machine or instant yeast

⅓ cup golden raisins

⅓ cup candied citrus fruit

2⅔ tablespoons candied cherries

Directions

1. Preparing the Ingredients.

Place the ingredients, except the raisins, candied citrus fruit, and 1 tablespoon of flour, in your bread machine as recommended by the manufacturer.

2. Select the Bake cycle

Program the machine for Basic/White bread, select light or medium crust, and press Start.

Toss the raisins, candied citrus fruit, and 1 tablespoon of flour together in a small bowl.

Add the raisins, candied citrus fruit, and flour when the machine signals or 5 minutes before the second kneading cycle is finished. When the loaf is done, remove the bucket from the machine.

Let the loaf cool for 5 minutes. Gently shake the bucket to remove the loaf, and turn it out onto a rack to cool.

Easter Bread

PREP: 10 MINUTES PLUS FERMENTING TIME /MAKES 1 LOAF/16 SLICE BREAD (2 pounds)

Ingredients

1 cup lukewarm milk

2 eggs, at room temperature

2⅔ tablespoons unsalted butter, melted

⅓ cup sugar

1 teaspoon table salt

2⅓ teaspoons lemon zest

4 cups white bread flour

2¼ teaspoons bread machine yeast

Directions

1. Preparing the Ingredients.

Choose the size of loaf you would like to make and measure your ingredients.

Add the ingredients to the bread pan in the order listed above.

Place the pan in the bread machine and close the lid.

2. Select the Bake cycle

Turn on the bread maker. Select the White/Basic setting, then the loaf size, and finally the crust color. Start the cycle.

When the cycle is finished and the bread is baked, carefully remove the pan from the machine. Use a potholder as the handle will be very hot. Let rest for a few minutes.

Remove the bread from the pan and allow to cool on a wire rack for at least 10 minutes before slicing.

Spiked Eggnog Bread

PREP: 10 MINUTES PLUS FERMENTING TIME /MAKES 1 LOAF/12 SLICE BREAD (1½ pounds)

Ingredients

1 cup eggnog, at room temperature

1 cup sugar

2 eggs, at room temperature

½ cup (1 stick) butter, at room temperature

1 tablespoon dark rum

1½ teaspoons pure vanilla extract

½ teaspoon rum extract

2¼ cups all-purpose flour

2 teaspoons baking powder

¼ teaspoon ground cinnamon

½ teaspoon ground nutmeg

½ teaspoon salt

Directions

1. **Preparing the Ingredients.**

Place the eggnog, sugar, eggs, butter, rum, vanilla, and rum extract in your bread machine.

2. **Select the Bake cycle**

Program the machine for Quick/Rapid bread and press Start.

While the wet ingredients are mixing, stir together the flour, baking powder, cinnamon, nutmeg, and salt in a small bowl.

After the first fast mixing is done and the machine signals, add the dry ingredients.

When the loaf is done, remove the bucket from the machine.

Let the loaf cool for 5 minutes. Gently shake the bucket to remove the loaf, and turn it out onto a rack to cool.

Hot Buttered Rum Bread

PREP: 10 MINUTES PLUS FERMENTING TIME /MAKES 1 LOAF/12 SLICE BREAD (1½ pounds)

Ingredients

¾ cup water, at 80°F to 90°F

1 egg, at room temperature

3 tablespoons butter, melted and cooled

3 tablespoons sugar

1 tablespoon rum extract

1¼ teaspoons salt

1 teaspoon ground cinnamon

¼ teaspoon ground nutmeg

3 cups white bread flour

1 teaspoon bread machine or instant yeast

Directions

1. **Preparing the Ingredients.**

Place the ingredients in your bread machine as recommended by the manufacturer.

Program the machine for Sweet bread and press Start.

2. **Select the Bake cycle**

When the loaf is done, remove the bucket from the machine.

Let the loaf cool for 5 minutes.

Gently shake the bucket to remove the loaf, and turn it out onto a rack to cool.

Zucchini Pecan Bread

PREP: 10 MINUTES PLUS FERMENTING TIME /MAKES 1 LOAF/12 SLICE BREAD (1½ pounds)

Ingredients

2 eggs, at room temperature
½ cup melted butter, cooled
¾ cup shredded zucchini
½ cup packed light brown sugar
2 tablespoons sugar
1½ cups all-purpose flour
1 teaspoon ground cinnamon
½ teaspoon salt
½ teaspoon baking powder
½ teaspoon baking soda
¼ teaspoon ground allspice
½ cup chopped pecans

Directions

1. **Preparing the Ingredients.**

Place the ingredients in your bread machine as recommended by the manufacturer.

Program the machine for Quick/Rapid bread and press Start.

When the mixing is done, use a rubber spatula to scrape down the sides of the bucket, then stir.

2. **Select the Bake cycle**

When the loaf is done, remove the bucket from the machine.

Let the loaf cool for 5 minutes.

Gently shake the bucket to remove the loaf, and turn it out onto a rack to cool.

Wrap the loaf in plastic wrap after it is completely cooled and store it in the refrigerator.

Raisin Bran Bread

PREP: 10 MINUTES PLUS FERMENTING TIME /MAKES 1 LOAF/12 SLICE BREAD (1½ pounds)

Ingredients

1⅛ cup milk, at 80°F to 90°F
2¼ tablespoons melted butter, cooled
3 tablespoons sugar
1½ teaspoons salt
⅓ cup wheat bran
2⅔ cups white bread flour
1½ teaspoons bread machine or instant yeast
¾ cup raisins

Directions

1. **Preparing the Ingredients.**

Place the ingredients, except the raisins, in your bread machine as recommended by the manufacturer.

2. **Select the Bake cycle**

Program the machine for Basic/White bread, select light or medium crust, and press Start.

When the machine signals, add the raisins, or put them in the nut/raisin hopper and let your machine add them automatically.

When the loaf is done, remove the bucket from the machine.

Let the loaf cool for 5 minutes. Gently shake the bucket to remove the loaf, and turn it out onto a rack to cool.

Lemon Poppy Seed Bread

Ingredients
¾ cup water, at 80°F to 90°F

1 egg, at room temperature

¼ cup freshly squeezed lemon juice, at room temperature

3 tablespoons melted butter, cooled

3 tablespoons sugar

2 teaspoons lemon zest

1 teaspoon salt

3 cups white bread flour

2 tablespoons poppy seeds

1¼ teaspoons bread machine or instant yeast

Directions
1. **Preparing the Ingredients.**

Place the ingredients in your bread machine as recommended by the manufacturer.

Program the machine for Basic/White bread, select light or medium crust, and press Start.

2. **Select the Bake cycle**

When the loaf is done, remove the bucket from the machine.

Let the loaf cool for 5 minutes.

Gently shake the bucket to remove the loaf, and turn it out onto a rack to cool.

Mustard Rye Bread

Ingredients
1¼ cups water, at 80°F to 90°F

¼ cup Dijon mustard

1½ tablespoons melted butter, cooled

1 tablespoon sugar

¾ teaspoon salt

1½ cups rye flour

2 cups white bread flour

1 teaspoon bread machine or instant yeast

Directions
1. **Preparing the Ingredients.**

Place the ingredients in your bread machine as recommended by the manufacturer.

2. **Select the Bake cycle**

Program the machine for Basic/White bread, select light or medium crust, and press Start.

When the loaf is done, remove the bucket from the machine. Let the loaf cool for 5 minutes.

Gently shake the bucket to remove the loaf, and turn it out onto a rack to cool.

Ham and Cheese Bread

PREP: 10 MINUTES PLUS FERMENTING TIME /MAKES 1 LOAF/12 SLICE BREAD (1½ pounds)

Ingredients
1 cup plus 2 tablespoons water, at 80°F to 90°F
2 tablespoons sugar
1½ teaspoons salt
2 teaspoons dried oregano
½ cup (2 ounces) shredded Swiss cheese
3¼ cups white bread flour
1½ teaspoons bread machine or active dry yeast
⅔ cup diced smoked ham

Directions
1. Preparing the Ingredients.
Place the ingredients, except the ham, in your bread machine as recommended by the manufacturer.
Program the machine for Basic/White bread, select light or medium crust, and press Start.
2. Select the Bake cycle
Add the ham about 5 minutes before the second kneading cycle ends.
When the loaf is done, remove the bucket from the machine.
Let the loaf cool for 5 minutes.
Gently shake the bucket to remove the loaf, and turn it out onto a rack to cool.

Sausage Herb Bread

PREP: 10 MINUTES PLUS FERMENTING TIME /MAKES 1 LOAF/12 SLICE BREAD (1½ pounds)

Ingredients
1 cup water, at 80°F to 90°F
1½ tablespoons olive oil
1½ tablespoons sugar
1⅛ teaspoons salt
⅓ teaspoon dried basil
⅓ teaspoon dried oregano
½ cup cooked chopped Italian sausage
3 cups white bread flour
1½ teaspoons bread machine or instant yeast

Directions
1. Preparing the Ingredients.
Place the ingredients in your bread machine as recommended by the manufacturer.
Program the machine for Basic/White bread, select light or medium crust, and press Start.
2. Select the Bake cycle
When the loaf is done, remove the bucket from the machine.
Let the loaf cool for 5 minutes. Gently shake the bucket to remove the loaf, and turn it out onto a rack to cool.

Wild Rice Hazelnut Bread

PREP: 10 MINUTES PLUS FERMENTING TIME / MAKES 1 LOAF/8 SLICE BREAD (1 pound)

Ingredients

½ cup milk, at 80°F to 90°F
2 teaspoons melted butter, cooled
2 teaspoons honey
⅔ teaspoon salt
⅓ cup cooked wild rice, cooled
⅓ cup whole-wheat flour
⅔ teaspoon caraway seeds
1 cup plus 1 tablespoon white bread flour
1 teaspoon bread machine or instant yeast
⅓ cup chopped hazelnuts

Directions

1. **Preparing the Ingredients.**

Place the ingredients in your bread machine as recommended by the manufacturer.

2. **Select the Bake cycle**

Program the machine for Basic/White bread, select light crust, and press Start. When the loaf is done, remove the bucket from the machine. Let the loaf cool for 5 minutes.

Gently shake the bucket to remove the loaf, and turn it out onto a rack to cool.

Spinach Feta Bread

PREP: 10 MINUTES PLUS FERMENTING TIME / MAKES 1 LOAF/8 SLICE BREAD (1 pound)

Ingredients

⅓ cup cooked chopped spinach, well-drained, cooled
¼ cup water, at 80°F to 90°F
1 small egg, at room temperature
1½ tablespoons melted butter, cooled
¾ tablespoon sugar
¾ teaspoon salt
⅛ teaspoon freshly ground black pepper
2 tablespoons oat bran
1½ cups white bread flour
1⅛ teaspoons bread machine or instant yeast
¼ cup crumbled feta cheese

Directions

1. **Preparing the Ingredients.**

Place the ingredients, except the feta cheese, in your bread machine as recommended by the manufacturer.

2. **Select the Bake cycle**

Program the machine for Basic/White bread, select light or medium crust, and press Start.

Add the cheese when the machine signals or 5 minutes before the second kneading cycle is finished.

When the loaf is done, remove the bucket from the machine.

Let the loaf cool for 5 minutes. Gently shake the bucket to remove the loaf, and turn it out onto a rack to cool.

Rum Raisin Bread

PREP: 10 MINUTES PLUS FERMENTING TIME /MAKES 1 LOAF/8 SLICE BREAD (1 pound)

Ingredients
2 tablespoons dark rum
½ cup raisins
½ cup plus 2 tablespoons milk, at 80°F to 90°F
1 egg, at room temperature
1 tablespoon melted butter, cooled
2 teaspoons light brown sugar
1 teaspoon salt
½ teaspoon rum flavored extract
2 cups white bread flour
1½ teaspoons bread machine or instant yeast

Directions
1. Preparing the Ingredients.
In a small bowl, stir together the rum and raisins, and let the fruit soak for 30 minutes; drain the raisins.
Place the ingredients, except the soaked raisins, in your bread machine as recommended by the manufacturer.
2. Select the Bake cycle
Program the machine for Basic/White bread, select light or medium crust, and press Start.
Add the raisins when the machine signals or 5 minutes before the second kneading cycle is finished.
When the loaf is done, remove the bucket from the machine.
Let the loaf cool for 5 minutes. Gently shake the bucket to remove the loaf, and turn it out onto a rack to cool.

Bacon Corn Bread

PREP: 10 MINUTES PLUS FERMENTING TIME /MAKES 1 LOAF/12 SLICE BREAD (1½ pounds)

Ingredients
1 cup milk, at room temperature
2 eggs, at room temperature
¼ cup butter, at room temperature
1 cup sugar
2 cups all-purpose flour
1 cup cornmeal
1 tablespoon baking powder
1 teaspoon salt
1 cup cooked crumbled bacon

Directions
1. Preparing the Ingredients.
Place the milk, eggs, butter, and sugar in your bread machine.
2. Select the Bake cycle
Program the machine for Quick/Rapid bread and press Start.
While the wet ingredients are mixing, stir together the flour, cornmeal, baking powder, salt, and bacon in a small bowl.
After the first fast mixing is done and the machine signals, add the dry ingredients. When the loaf is done, remove the bucket from the machine. Let the loaf cool for 5 minutes. Gently shake the bucket to remove the loaf, and turn it out onto a rack to cool.

Oatmeal Coffee Bread

PREP: 10 MINUTES PLUS FERMENTING TIME /MAKES 1 LOAF/12 SLICE BREAD (1½ pounds)

Ingredients
1 cup water, at 80°F to 90°F
1½ tablespoons Kahlúa or other coffee liqueur
¼ cup honey
¾ teaspoon salt
¾ cup quick oats
2¼ cups white bread flour
1⅔ teaspoons bread machine or instant yeast

Directions
1. Preparing the Ingredients.
Place the ingredients in your bread machine as recommended by the bread machine manufacturer.
2. Select the Bake cycle
Program the machine for Basic/White bread, select light or medium crust, and press Start.
When the loaf is done, remove the bucket from the machine.
Let the loaf cool for 5 minutes.
Gently shake the bucket to remove the loaf, and turn it out onto a rack to cool.

Cherry Pistachio Bread

PREP: 10 MINUTES PLUS FERMENTING TIME /MAKES 1 LOAF/8 SLICE BREAD (1 pound)

Ingredients
½ cup water, at 80°F to 90°F
1 egg, at room temperature
2 tablespoons butter, softened
2 tablespoons packed dark brown sugar
¾ teaspoon salt
¼ teaspoon ground nutmeg
Dash allspice
1¾ cups plus 1 tablespoon white bread flour
1 teaspoon bread machine or active dry yeast
½ cup dried cherries
¼ cup chopped unsalted pistachios

Directions
1. Preparing the Ingredients.
Place the ingredients, except the cherries and pistachios, in your bread machine as recommended by the manufacturer.
2. Select the Bake cycle
Program the machine for Basic/White bread, select light or medium crust, and press Start. Just before the final kneading is over or when the machine signals, add the cherries and pistachios.
When the loaf is done, remove the bucket from the machine. Let the loaf cool for 5 minutes.
Gently shake the bucket to remove the loaf, and turn it out onto a rack to cool.

Banana Coconut Bread

PREP: 10 MINUTES PLUS FERMENTING TIME /MAKES 1 LOAF/12 SLICE BREAD (1½ pounds)

Ingredients
2 ripe bananas, mashed
⅔ cup milk, at 80°F to 90°F
⅓ cup melted butter, cooled
2 eggs, at room temperature
⅔ cup sugar
⅔ teaspoon pure vanilla extract
⅔ teaspoon pure almond extract
1⅔ cups all-purpose flour
⅔ cup shredded sweet coconut
1 teaspoon baking soda
1 teaspoon baking powder
⅓ teaspoon salt

Directions
1. Preparing the Ingredients.
Place the bananas, milk, butter, eggs, sugar, vanilla, and almond extract in your bread machine.
2. Select the Bake cycle
Program the machine for Quick/Rapid bread and press Start.
While the wet ingredients are mixing, stir together the flour, coconut, baking soda, baking powder, and salt in a small bowl
After the first fast mixing is done and the machine signals, add the dry ingredients.
When the loaf is done, remove the bucket from the machine. Let the loaf cool for 5 minutes. Gently shake the bucket to remove the loaf, and turn it out onto a rack to cool.

Easy Honey Beer Bread

PREP: 10 MINUTES PLUS FERMENTING TIME / MAKES 1 LOAF/12 SLICE BREAD (1½ pounds)

Ingredients
12 ounces beer, at room temperature
⅓ cup melted butter, cooled
¼ cup honey
3 cups all-purpose flour
1 tablespoon baking powder
1 teaspoon salt
¼ teaspoon ground cinnamon

Directions
1. Preparing the Ingredients.
Place the beer, butter, and honey in your bread machine.
2. Select the Bake cycle
Program the machine for Quick/Rapid bread and press Start. While the wet ingredients are mixing, stir together the flour, baking powder, salt, and cinnamon in a small bowl. After the first fast mixing is done and the machine signals, add the dry ingredients. When the loaf is done, remove the bucket from the machine.
Let the loaf cool for 5 minutes. Gently shake the bucket to remove the loaf, and turn it out onto a rack to cool.

Coffee Molasses Bread

PREP: 10 MINUTES PLUS FERMENTING TIME /MAKES 1 LOAF/8 SLICE BREAD (1 pound)

Ingredients

½ cup brewed coffee, at 80°F to 90°F
½ cup evaporated milk, at 80°F to 90°F
1 tablespoon melted butter, cooled
1½ tablespoons honey
½ tablespoon dark molasses
½ tablespoon sugar
2 teaspoons unsweetened cocoa powder
½ teaspoon salt
1⅛ cups whole-wheat bread flour
1⅛ cups white bread flour
1⅛ teaspoons bread machine or instant yeast

Directions

1. Preparing the Ingredients.

Place the ingredients in your bread machine as recommended by the manufacturer.

2. Select the Bake cycle

Program the machine for Sweet bread and press Start. When the loaf is done, remove the bucket from the machine. Let the loaf cool for 5 minutes.

Gently shake the bucket to remove the loaf, and turn it out onto a rack to cool.

Pear Sweet Potato Bread

PREP: 10 MINUTES PLUS FERMENTING TIME /MAKES 1 LOAF/8 SLICE BREAD (1 pound)

Ingredients

⅓ cup plus 1 tablespoon milk, at 80°F to 90°F
⅓ cup shredded peeled pear
⅓ cup mashed cooked sweet potato, cooled
1½ tablespoons melted butter, cooled
1½ tablespoons sugar
¾ teaspoon salt
¼ teaspoon ground cinnamon
¼ teaspoon ground nutmeg
⅛ teaspoon ground ginger
2 cups white bread flour
⅔ teaspoons bread machine or instant yeast

Directions

1. Preparing the Ingredients.

Place the ingredients in your bread machine as recommended by the manufacturer.

2. Select the Bake cycle

Program the machine for Sweet bread and press Start.

When the loaf is done, remove the bucket from the machine. Let the loaf cool for 5 minutes. Gently shake the bucket to remove the loaf, and turn it out onto a rack to cool.

About the Author

Amanda is a New York-based food writer, experienced chef. She loves sharing Easy, Delicious and Healthy Bread Machine recipes. Amanda is a passionate advocate for the Gluten Free lifestyle. When she's not cooking, Amanda enjoys spending time with her husband and her kids, gardening and traveling.

Made in the USA
Middletown, DE
10 November 2021